Transactions of the Royal Historical Society

SIXTH SERIES

XXV

Published by the Press Syndicate of the University of Cambridge
University Printing House, Shaftesbury Road, Cambridge CB2 8BS,
United Kingdom
32 Avenue of the Americas, New York, NY 10013-2473, USA
477 Williamstown Road, Port Melbourne, VIC 3207, Australia
C/Orense, 4, Planta 13, 28020 Madrid, Spain
Lower Ground Floor, Nautica Building, The Water Club,
Beach Road, Granger Bay, 8005 Cape Town, South Africa

First published 2015

A catalogue record for this book is available from the British Library

ISBN 9781107143388 hardback

SUBSCRIPTIONS. The serial publications of the Royal Historical Society, *Royal Historical Society Transactions* (ISSN 0080–4401) and Camden Fifth Series (ISSN 0960–1163) volumes, may be purchased together on annual subscription. The 2015 subscription price, which includes print and electronic access (but not VAT), is £168 (US $280 in the USA, Canada, and Mexico) and includes Camden Fifth Series, volumes 47 and 48 and Transactions Sixth Series, volume 25 (published in December). The electronic-only price available to institutional subscribers is £141 (US $235 in the USA, Canada, and Mexico). Japanese prices are available from Kinokuniya Company Ltd, P.O. Box 55, Chitose, Tokyo 156, Japan. EU subscribers (outside the UK) who are not registered for VAT should add VAT at their country's rate. VAT registered subscribers should provide their VAT registration number. Prices include delivery by air.

Subscription orders, which must be accompanied by payment, may be sent to a bookseller, subscription agent, or direct to the publisher: Cambridge University Press, University Printing House, Shaftesbury Road, Cambridge CB2 8BS, UK; or in the USA, Canada, and Mexico: Cambridge University Press, Journals Fulfillment Department, 100 Brook Hill Drive, West Nyack, New York, 10994–2133, USA.

SINGLE VOLUMES AND BACK VOLUMES. A list of Royal Historical Society volumes available from Cambridge University Press may be obtained from the Humanities Marketing Department at the address above.

Printed in the UK by Bell & Bain Ltd, Glasgow

CONTENTS

Transactions of the RHS 25 (2015), pp. 1–26 © Royal Historical Society 2015
doi:10.1017/S0080440115000079

TRANSACTIONS OF THE

ROYAL HISTORICAL SOCIETY

PRESIDENTIAL ADDRESS

By Peter Mandler

EDUCATING THE NATION: II. UNIVERSITIES*

READ 28 NOVEMBER 2014

ABSTRACT. This paper continues the argument made in 'Educating the Nation: I. Schools', that democratic demand for ever widening access to education was the principal driver for expansion in the second half of the twentieth century. Demand for higher education was not as universalistic or egalitarian as demand for secondary schooling; nevertheless, it was pressing, especially from the late 1950s, and ultimately irresistible, enshrined in the 'Robbins principle' that higher education should be available to all qualified by ability and attainment. The paper tracks the fortunes of the Robbins principle from an initial period of rapid growth, through a mysterious period of sagging demand in the 1970s and 1980s, to the resumption of very rapid growth from the late 1980s. It remains the guiding light of higher-education policy today, though in very altered circumstances where the price is paid ultimately more by beneficiaries than from the public purse.

In my first address I argued that democracy, not meritocracy, was the driving force behind the provision of universal secondary education in Britain in the second half of the twentieth century. Before the Second World War, when state secondary education was only on offer to a portion of the population, thus by definition selective, meritocracy (though not yet so-called) had a powerful appeal, as it promised fair access to selective schools. After the Second World War, however, when universal secondary education was promised, the terms of the debate changed radically. Education was now viewed within a universal welfare-state context, like health, and just as most people wanted the best health-care they also wanted the best education for all. By the end of the 1950s, a

* I owe many thanks to those specialists who have introduced me to the difficult technical issues involved in measuring and assessing educational participation, especially Jane Elliott and her (then) colleagues at the Institute of Education, Brian Dodgeon and Alice Sullivan, and Anna Vignoles in the Cambridge Faculty of Education. I owe further debts to Lord (Kenneth) Baker, Bahram Bekhradnia, Michael Jubb and Peter Syme for sharing their memories of the DES in the 1980s. For comments on earlier drafts of this paper, I am grateful to Deborah Cohen, John Davis, James Vernon and Anna Vignoles.

cross-party consensus was emerging for 'grammar schools for all', and in the 1960s this materialised as cross-party support for comprehensivisation. This democratic consensus on secondary education was not confined to the 'consensus' era; post-consensus politicians of the Thatcher stripe have maintained it to the present day, with the focus shifting away from selection for some towards raising standards for all.[1]

Not quite the same argument can be made for higher education. Unlike secondary education, higher education has never been offered as a universal service. Only some people are deemed eligible for it. The governing principle since the 1960s has been the Robbins principle – 'that courses of higher education should be available for all those who are qualified by ability and attainment to pursue them and who wish to do so' – clearly a meritocratic principle.[2] Nevertheless, here I will argue that Robbins embedded this principle in a democratic context that assumed that not only the numbers of those 'qualified by ability and attainment' but also the numbers of those 'who wish to do so' would and should increase consistently for the foreseeable future. This was at least in part because access to higher education was umbilically connected to rising aspirations and attainments in secondary education, and thus implicated in the democratic discourse that governed secondary education. As with secondary education, this quasi-democratic approach to higher education, while born in the classic 'consensus' period, can be shown to have persisted and indeed intensified in allegedly post-consensus circumstances; though unlike secondary education its course did not run smooth. This makes, I think, for a more textured and a more interesting narrative, which I will trace from the 1960s to the present day.

I

Higher education did not figure prominently in the consciousness either of the nation or even of politicians at the end of the Second World War. Less than 3 per cent of the age-group entered full-time higher education and even at elite levels participation was patchy; Stanley Baldwin was the sole interwar prime minister with a university education. The only point at which the universities came regularly into the national consciousness was the Boat Race, which involved only two universities that enrolled few students.[3] There was a widespread assumption that the potential constituency for university was limited by innate ability to perhaps 5 per

[1] 'Educating the Nation: I. Schools', *Transactions of the Royal Historical Society*, sixth series, 24 (2014), 5–28.

[2] Committee on Higher Education, *Report* (1963), 8 (hereafter *Robbins Report*).

[3] A. H. Halsey, *Twentieth-Century Social Trends* (Basingstoke, 2000), 226; John Carswell, *Government and the Universities in Britain: Programme and Performance 1960–1980* (Cambridge, 1985), 1–2.

cent of the population, and as late as 1956 only 5 per cent of working-class parents with primary school children expected them to go to university.[4] There was, however, a new strain of political discourse about higher education in the immediate post-war years that was neither meritocratic nor democratic, but technocratic. Higher education was increasingly turned to by politicians for help with economic growth; thus the Percy Report of 1945 which called for a quadrupling of trained engineers, the Barlow Report of 1946 which called for a doubling of trained scientists and the Scientific Manpower Committee Report of 1956 which called for a further doubling. The context was not so much education as 'manpower planning', and the emphasis was not on quantity but on quality – the right kind of graduates rather than the right numbers. 'The prizes will not go to the countries with the largest population', said Anthony Eden at a speech in Bradford in January 1956. 'Those with the best systems of education will win. Science and technical skills give a dozen men the power to do as much as thousands did fifty years ago.' This speech formed part of a Conservative campaign to beef up technical education, which included upgrading of technical colleges, the creation of new Colleges of Advanced Technology (the CATs) and gentle prods of the University Grants Committee (the UGC) to shift the balance of university students from arts to sciences (which was, gently, achieved: the proportion of arts students in universities fell from 45 per cent in 1939 to 43 per cent in 1956).[5]

However, by the late 1950s, the focus on quality began to be eclipsed by issues of quantity, as a newly democratic tone had begun to enter the public discussion of higher education.[6] Even scientific manpower planning had required an expansion of the system, as it proved easier to create new institutions such as the CATs than to get the universities to swing to the sciences. The real driver by the end of the 1950s, however, was not the supply-side concern for manpower planning but the growing evidence of unsatisfied demand for higher education, as a direct result of the advent of universal secondary education and growing aspiration for the 'best' education for all. As I argued in my first address, these aspirations

[4] Sir Frederick Ogilvie, *British Universities* (1948), 12, 14; Research Services Limited, 'A Pilot Enquiry into Some Aspects of Working-Class Life in London' (1957), 37: Mark Abrams Papers, Churchill Archives Centre, Box 85/1.

[5] Jean Bocock, Lewis Baston, Peter Scott and David Smith, 'American Influence on British Higher Education: Science, Technology, and the Problem of University Expansion, 1945–1963', *Minerva*, 41 (2003), 328–43; Brian Simon, *Education and the Social Order 1940–1990* (1991), 83–4, 92–5, 199–200; Michael Sanderson, 'Higher Education in the Post-War Years', *Contemporary Record*, 5 (1991), 417; University Grants Committee (hereafter UGC), *University Development 1952–1957*, Cmnd 534 (1958), 8.

[6] Some but not all of the 'declinist' polemics of the 1956–63 period emphasised both quality and quantity; see, e.g., Anthony Sampson, *Anatomy of Britain* (1962), 195–217.

were widely doubted or even stifled within the political elite until the early 1960s, but they were evident to local authorities and to MPs with their ears to the ground as early as the mid-1950s. The same can be said of the knock-on effects for higher education. Social research monitored the demand for higher education closely in this period, developing a set of measures of demand which became the benchmarks for policymaking for the rest of the century. The most basic measure was the age-participation rate – the proportion of the 18- and 19-year-old cohort that actually took up places in higher education. This was the measure that had stood at 3 per cent before the war and by 1957 had pushed up to 7 per cent, thanks to steady expansion of both the university and other higher-education sectors – teacher-training colleges, art colleges, technical colleges and the CATs. It continued to rise to about 8 per cent in 1959, but then stuck at that level for the next few years. However, participation in higher education is not itself a pure expression of demand; it reflects also supply, how many places are available. To assess *potential* demand, researchers also tracked other measures – the staying-on rate (what proportion of the age-cohort stayed on at school after the school-leaving age of 15), and the qualified leaver rate (what proportion of the age-cohort achieved two A-Levels, then the minimum qualification for entry to university). Here lay the evidence of *unsatisfied* demand, a political problem. Widening access to O-Levels and therefore to A-Levels and qualified-leaver status led to a sudden jump in the qualified leaver rate from 7.5 per cent to 15 per cent between 1955 and 1959.[7] This spurt in demand pressure could not be easily (and certainly not quickly) accommodated by university expansion, and while the UGC did lay plans for expansion – fifteen new universities were opened or planned before Robbins – politicians were keenly aware that both short- and long-term demand pressures were creating a new political problem for them, much as the clamour for 'grammar schools for all' was at secondary level.[8] Just as there were many 'frustrated' parents failing to get grammar school places for their children, so there were smaller but increasing (and influential) numbers of 18-year-olds failing to get university places; whereas nearly 80 per cent of qualified leavers

[7] Christopher A. Pissarides, 'From School to University: The Demand for Post-Compulsory Education in Britain', *Economic Journal*, 92 (1982), 656, 663. For contemporary awareness of this 'hump' in potential demand, see Maurice Kogan, Edward Boyle and Anthony Crosland, *The Politics of Education* (Harmondsworth, 1971), 93; Jean Floud's evidence, *Robbins Report*, Evidence – Part II, Documentary Evidence, Cmnd 2154-XII (1963), 53, and Harold Perkin's account in 'University Planning in Britain in the 1960s', *Higher Education*, 1 (1972), 113–16.

[8] Michael Shattock, *Making Policy in British Higher Education 1945–2011* (Maidenhead, 2012), 4, argues that the Robbins principle was already tacitly accepted by the universities from 1945, but cf. 17, accepting the relative sluggishness of the universities' initial response to demand. By 1962, with Robbins under way, the universities were positioning themselves for more rapid expansion.

gained university places in 1956, by 1962 fewer than 60 per cent got them.[9] Accordingly, just as Conservative education ministers looked to expert committees to help them pave the road to comprehensivisation (the Crowther and Newsom Committees, which reported in 1959 and 1963), so they appointed in 1961 an expert committee chaired by Lionel Robbins to pave the road to the expansion of higher education that all parties knew would inevitably ensue from widening access to O- and A-Levels in all-ability schools.[10]

The seriousness with which the Robbins Committee was taken by the politicians (and by itself) speaks volumes both about the growing political significance attached to demand for higher education and to the greater care then taken about what is now called 'evidence-based policy-making' (as if there were any other kind). Robbins sat for two years, accumulated twelve volumes of evidence (and many more unpublished submissions), undertook seven study visits abroad and commissioned six national social surveys on various aspects of supply and demand. With so much evidence accumulated, and a cannily written report, it has been possible for subsequent commentators to label Robbins technocratic, meritocratic *and* democratic, indeed, even aristocratic.[11] Here, I make the case that both its language and especially its legacy were primarily democratic.

The central principle enshrined in the Report – 'that courses of higher education should be available for all those who are qualified by ability and attainment to pursue them and who wish to do so' – was avowedly a meritocratic principle. But it was embedded in the same democratic premises as the contemporaneous reform of secondary education. Robbins embraced the same critique of the 'pool of ability' – the meritocratic idea that there was a fixed stock of ability from which educational institutions had to select – and he drew on the same sources,

[9] R. Layard and J. King, 'The Impact of Robbins' (1968), in *Economics and Education Policy: A Reader*, ed. Carolyn Baxter, P. J. O'Leary and Adam Westoby (1977), 20–2. Somewhat different measures were employed by Robbins, but marking a similar trend: *Robbins Report*, Appendix I: The Demand for Places in Higher Education, Cmnd 2154-I (1963), 119–22.

[10] On the connection between Crowther, Newsom and Robbins, see Kogan, Boyle and Crosland, *Politics of Education*, 91–3.

[11] For technocratic, see Desmond King and Victoria Nash, 'Continuity of Ideas and the Politics of Higher Education Expansion in Britain from Robbins to Dearing', *Twentieth Century British History*, 12 (2001), 185–6, 191–2; for meritocratic, see Robert Anderson, *British Universities Past and Present* (2006), 148–51; for democratic, see Claire Callender, 'Student Numbers and Funding: Does Robbins Add Up?', *Higher Education Quarterly*, 68 (2014), 164–70; for 'aristocratic', see A. H. Halsey, *Decline of Donnish Dominion: The British Academic Professions in the Twentieth Century* (Oxford, 1992), 11–14. And cf. the aristocratic diagnosis of Peter Scott, *Knowledge & Nation* (Edinburgh, 1990), 113, with his later more democratic account, no doubt rendered rosier by the contrasts he draws with the gloomy present, 'Robbins, the Binary Policy and Mass Higher Education', *Higher Education Quarterly*, 68 (2014), 149, 151.

notably the work of the sociologist Jean Floud.[12] 'It is highly misleading', his report asserted, 'to suppose that one can determine an upper limit to the number of people who could benefit from higher education, given favourable circumstances', and a free and democratic society should create the favourable circumstances in which 'ability' would be ever more widely distributed. 'If there is to be talk of a pool of ability', the report continued, 'it must be of a pool which surpasses the widow's cruse in the Old Testament, in that when more is taken for higher education in one generation more will tend to be available in the next.'[13] Here, Robbins took recent rapid increases in the staying-on and qualified-leaver rates and extrapolated them forward. Extrapolations were made to 2020 based on 'sober' calculations of steadily growing staying-on and qualified-leaver rates, plus a return to growth in the proportion of qualified leavers successfully finding higher-education places, as a result of the continuous process of university expansion that Robbins recommended. 'These figures involve what to many will seem a startling increase in numbers', the Report conceded, but indicated (correctly) that they were probably an underestimate, given the difficulty of projecting the effects of the new norm of progression, especially for women. There was no going back to mere 'manpower planning', based on the alleged needs of the economy – consumer *demand* was to be the prime mover of higher-education planning, and it was assumed that demand would grow steadily (or perhaps more than steadily) for at least twenty and probably sixty years. The Robbins escalator had begun to roll.[14]

Because the Robbins Committee had been appointed to justify a policy already more-or-less agreed on, the Conservative government accepted its recommendations immediately, and placed their democratic premises at centre stage. The Robbins principle was presented as the 'basic assumption' of the Report.[15] The Labour government that succeeded soon after went further. From 1965, it created an entirely new layer of

[12] *Robbins Report*, Appendix I: The Demand for Places in Higher Education, Cmnd 2154-I (1963), esp. 80–5; memoranda from Jean Floud, 11 Mar. 1962, and Prof. P. E. Vernon, 18 July 1961: *Robbins Report*, Evidence – Part II, Documentary Evidence, Cmnd 2154-XII (1963), 45–57, 170–4.

[13] *Robbins Report*, 8, 49, 54.

[14] *Ibid.*, 48, 63–71. On Robbins's preference for 'social demand' over manpower planning, see Layard and King, 'Impact of Robbins', 24; Kenneth Gannicott and Mark Blaug, 'Scientists and Engineers in Britain' (1973), in *Economics and Education Policy*, ed. Baxter, O'Leary and Westoby, 128.

[15] Press Notice, Government Statement on the Robbins Report. Some civil servants urged the prime minister to assert the Robbins principle as 'a moral and social duty' and even to describe higher education as a 'universal' service that had the potential to become 'the greatest solvent of class differences', but cooler heads prevailed. 'Suggested points on the Robbins Report for inclusion in the Prime Minister's speech on the Debate on the Address', n.d.: The National Archives (hereafter TNA), ED 188/12.

higher-education institutions – the polytechnics, assembled from existing technical, art and education colleges – in order to speed up the pace of expansion being led painstakingly by the UGC. Robbins had explicitly advised against this, on the grounds (similar to the critique of the bipartite system in secondary education) that a binary system would never achieve parity of esteem. But Labour had both technocratic and democratic reasons for doing so. On the technocratic side, the expansion of the so-called public-sector institutions – polytechnics and colleges, then under the control of local authorities and subject to much more direct patronage from central government than the autonomous universities – permitted Labour to smuggle manpower planning in through the back door. On the democratic side, the public-sector institutions gave Labour more tools to speed up the expansion of places. Polytechnics and colleges could be run up quickly and cheaply, situated in city centres near to the target population, affording easier access by means of part-time study and sandwich courses (combining work and study). And indeed the public sector did expand more quickly than the university sector, such that it was providing half of all higher-education places by the early 1970s.[16] The catchphrase that Labour used to justify its expansion policy – 'social demand' – was nicely ambiguous: was demand to be defined by the government's estimate of 'national needs', a technocratic response, or by the countless individual choices of the mass of the people, the democratic response that Robbins had intended?

However, it would be a mistake to confine the impact of Robbins to questions of government policy: its true impact lay in the encouragement it gave to social demand at the grassroots. Contemporaries were well aware of the 'euphoria' that Robbins unleashed.[17] The demand pressures that had been building up before 1963 were now relieved by improved supply, and this improved supply itself incited further demand, in a positive feedback loop. Aspirational parents could be confident that if their children were able to stay on after 15, they could reasonably expect a higher-education place; as the prime minister, Alec Douglas-Home, himself said in parliament, embracing the Robbins principle, 'every father and mother in the country should know that if they have in the family a child who wishes to pursue a course of higher education, there should be a place at technical college or university for that boy or girl to fill'.[18] Teenagers and their teachers could see the glittering new institutions all around them – not only the plateglass universities on green-field sites

[16] Simon, *Education and the Social Order*, 259, 263–4.
[17] Layard and King, 'Impact of Robbins', 27–8; G. L. Williams, 'The Events of 1973–1974 in a Long-Term Planning Perspective' (1974), in *Economics and Education Policy*, ed. Baxter, O'Leary and Westoby, 40–2.
[18] *Hansard*, fifth series, 684 (1963–4), 39–40 [12 Nov. 1963].

but colleges and polytechnics in their midst. The supply bottleneck was clearing.

At the same time, as the feedback loop closed, the growth of demand was accelerating. Pressures were now building up from earlier in the life-cycle. Comprehensive education was beginning to expose more children to O-Levels. A survey in 1968 found parents were paying considerably more attention to their children's progress through school than they had done in a survey just a few years earlier, in 1964. By 1968, two-thirds of all parents of primary children wished those children to stay in education not only past 15 but past 18, and, even more tellingly, three-quarters of parents of children in the last year of compulsory education wished for further education.[19] As a result of these aspirations, by 1967 the qualified-leaver rate had increased to a level 25 per cent higher than Robbins had predicted for that date.[20] And because the supply constraints had been relaxed, especially in the public sector, the actual participation rate for higher education surged as well: having been stagnant between 1959 and 1962 at around 8 per cent, it grew rapidly to about 12 per cent by 1967, having by then already reached Robbins's target for 1970.[21] Indeed, the doors to higher education had not only been opened, but a welcome sign had been posted on them, in the form of a new student-grant regime which had become virtually universal (for qualified entrants) by 1969.[22]

In this euphoric period of the late 1960s, higher education became something aspired to by larger and larger segments of the population, regardless of whether they had prior experience of it. Demand had become the driving force that government was now committed to meeting regardless of its own manpower-planning or other agendas. Awareness of this new grassroots political force was keenly registered by experts and in government. There were different but congruent

[19] J. M. Bynner, *Parents' Attitudes to Education* (1972), 13–18. Bynner's survey for the OPCS Social Survey Division, undertaken in 1968, offers some useful comparisons with the 1964 Government Social Survey work undertaken for the Plowden Committee, although not all measures allow a straightforward comparison.

[20] Richard Layard, John King and Claus Moser, *The Impact of Robbins* (Harmondsworth, 1969), 14–16, 22–5.

[21] It is unwise to try to be too precise even about APR, as slightly different statistical measures even of the same rate were employed by contemporaries. For Robbins's estimate of APR in 1961 (8.3 per cent) and its target for 1970 (12.8 per cent), see *Robbins Report*, Appendix I: The Demand for Places in Higher Education, Cmnd 2154-I (1963), 151. For Layard, King and Moser's estimate of APR in 1961 (8.3 per cent) and in 1967 (14.3 per cent), see *Impact of Robbins*, 24. But cf. Michael Shattock, 'Demography and Social Class: The Fluctuating Demand for Higher Education in Britain', *European Journal of Education*, 16 (1981), 384, with lower estimates of APR in 1962 (7.2 per cent) and 1967 (11.8 per cent), rising to a peak of 14.2 per cent in 1972: these are the figures used in the DES in the 1970s, for which see below pp. 10–11, 17. Some uncertainty arises from the fact that in the earlier period it was harder to define what was included in 'higher education' below degree level.

[22] Williams, 'Events of 1973–1974', 47.

economic and sociological versions of this new understanding of demand. Among the economists, human-capital arguments saw education as an 'investment good', which accrued value to both individuals and society from the benefits it conveyed in terms of lifetime income and GDP growth.[23] A more sociological argument considered that the loosening class structure of modern societies meant that higher education for personal development could now be a goal for more if not all families, not just those with a past track-record in higher education.[24] In between lay another economic argument, which viewed education as a 'consumption good', which was valued for itself and thus more sought after naturally with growing affluence, regardless of its future payoff. Higher education had become, in the words of the American expert Martin Trow, 'one of the decencies of life rather than an extraordinary privilege reserved for people of high status or extraordinary ability'.[25] All of these arguments shifted attention away from the technocratic towards the democratic case for widening participation. That case was further fortified by a series of reports from the Organisation for Economic Co-operation and Development (OECD) showing that growing demand for higher education was evident across the developed world.[26] As a result of this new valuation placed on the demand side, supply-side planning went into decline, on the Left as much as on the Right. Robbins – a liberal economist after all – had already deprecated manpower planning as imprecise and probably futile. The consumer was king. Even at the time of his report, for example, it was clear that the technocratic 'swing to science' had gone into reverse; the new demand for higher education was in the arts and especially in the social sciences (either as better for personal development or better for the modern labour market, or both).[27] Despite further efforts by the Labour government to reverse what was now recognised as the 'swing away from science', by the end of the 1960s 'social demand' no

[23] On the entry of human capital arguments into educational planning, see Michael Sanderson, *Educational Opportunity and Social Change in England* (1987), 94–5; Vera Morris, 'Investment in Higher Education in England and Wales: A Subject Analysis' (1973), in *Economics and Education Policy*, ed. Baxter, O'Leary and Westoby, 72–5; Maurice Peston, 'Higher Education Policy', in *Higher Education and the Labour Market*, ed. Robert Lindley (Guildford, 1981), 120–47.

[24] Bocock, Baston, Scott and Smith, 'American Influence', 343 (citing A. H. Halsey and Jean Floud).

[25] Martin Trow, 'Problems in the Transition from Elite to Mass Higher Education', in OECD Conference on Future Structures of Post-Secondary Education, *General Report: Policies for Higher Education* (Paris, 1974), 90.

[26] See, e.g., OECD, Directorate for Scientific Affairs, 'Development of Higher Education in OECD Member Countries: Quantitative Trends', 3 Apr. 1969, a copy in TNA, UGC 7/1245.

[27] *Robbins Report*, 48, 71–4; *ibid.*, Appendix II (A): Students and their Education, Cmnd 2154-II (1963), 30–1.

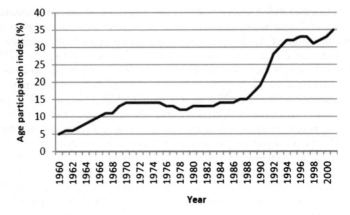

Figure 1 HE participation, 1960–2001.
Source: Reproduced from Walker and Zhu, 'Impact of University Degrees', 14.

longer meant what the Labour government demanded, but what millions of ordinary citizens demanded.[28] Bureaucratically, it was easier to use Robbins-style projections to plan for demand than highly suppositious manpower targets, and even the Treasury liked the predictability of public-expenditure targets that could be projected years ahead.[29] Thus, experts, bureaucrats and politicians alike had been nudged into accepting that the agenda for higher education was being set by teenagers and their parents. That agenda was a democratic one – higher education was achieving in ever widening circles the status of a new social norm. The Robbins escalator looked to be climbing a stairway to heaven.[30]

II

And then the Robbins escalator just stopped dead (Figure 1). Why exactly this happened has been one of the two great mysteries that I seek to

[28] I discuss the 'swing away from science' in 'The Two Cultures Revisited: The Humanities in British Universities since 1945', *Twentieth-Century British History*, forthcoming 2015. As contemporaries knew well, this was also an international trend: OECD, *Development of Higher Education 1950–1967* (Paris, 1971), 126, 129–36, 206–7, but cf. 227.

[29] Morris, 'Investment in Higher Education', 72–5; UGC, *University Development 1962–1967*, Cmnd 3820 (1968–9), 95–101.

[30] Carswell, *Government and the Universities*, 139–40, argues that right up until the 1972 White Paper governments of both parties had rejected the 'will o' the wisp' of manpower planning and embraced the ideal of higher education for 'personal development'. Carswell was the senior civil servant in the DES with responsibility for higher education. See also Perkin, 'University Planning', 119.

plumb in this address. (The other is why it started back up again, equally suddenly, almost two decades later.) There is no shortage of explanations – each academic constituency has its own: the economists think the labour market was overstocked with graduates; the sociologists cite the unchanging social order; the political scientists blame 'the cuts'; historians (on those few occasions when they deign to notice the deep freeze of higher education in the 1970s and 1980s) gesture vaguely at 'the end of consensus' or 'declining confidence in public institutions' or at best at a loose amalgam of all these explanations. I cannot pretend to improve greatly on the loose amalgam, but I can try at least to tighten it up chronologically and analytically, so that we can share to some extent in the series of confusions and discouragements that beset young people around school-leaving age in the 1970s and 1980s and that for such a long period put an effective damper on their 'social demand' for higher education.[31]

We should start with the economists, because they detect the change of weather earlier than anyone else – before any contemporaries were aware of it (and certainly before any policy shifts can be blamed) – and that change was a sudden slackening in the growth of the staying-on rate. After rapid growth in the 1960s, the growth rate at least among boys slowed to 1 per cent in 1969 and remained low for a decade.[32] Within a few years, this had knock-on effects on the qualified leaver rate – those leaving with two A-Levels – and on the all-important age participation rate, which peaked at 14.2 per cent in 1972 and did not reach that level again until 1986. The economists' explanation is that what we now call the 'graduate premium' – the salary advantage for graduates – dropped suddenly, in part due to the over-exuberant growth of the late 1960s (leading to an over-supply of graduates), though mostly due to the resurgence of demand for manual labour.[33] In the period 1969–74, 'the ratio of new-graduate earnings to juvenile earnings declined by over 30 per cent'.[34] Once they became aware of this flatlining in participation rates, contemporaries developed a variety of explanations for it that did not rely on young people's super-sensitivity to wage rates. Perhaps it was a temporary course-correction

---

[31] See Diego Gambetta, *Were They Pushed or Did They Jump? Individual Decision Mechanisms in Education* (Cambridge, 1987), a brilliant critique of the methodological fragmentation and an attempt to reassemble 'a dense combination of mechanisms' that might actually model the behaviour of real human beings – alas for present purposes, human beings in Italy, not Britain.

[32] Christopher A. Pissarides, 'Staying-on at School in England and Wales', *Economica*, 48 (1981), 346–7.

[33] *Ibid.*, 359.

[34] At the same time, the real value of the student grant began to fall as well. Christopher A. Pissarides, 'An Overview of the Demand for Post-Compulsory Education by British Men, 1955–77', in *Human Resources, Employment and Development*, III: *The Problems of Developed Countries and the International Economy*, ed. Burton Weisbrod and Helen Hughes (1983), 154–5.

after a burst of Robbins euphoria in the late 1960s, following the pattern of epidemic disease. Class barriers to educational mobility in Britain may have been higher than elsewhere, putting a lid on the feasible rate of expansion. There may even have been a hardening of class barriers at just this sensitive juncture, as aspirational working-class boys found too many middle-class girls ahead of them in the educational queue, and they turned against education altogether, embracing instead a lubricious, masculinist working-class 'counter-school culture' of hard play and hard manual labour.[35]

We must also consider the possibility of reinforcements to the 'counter-school culture' provided by the reorganisation of secondary education from the late 1960s, which might either have temporarily disrupted the progress of schooling and/or put a cap on attainment and ambition. There are two factors to consider: the raising of the school-leaving age to 16 in 1973, and the replacement of selection by comprehensive education in most local authorities over the course of the 1970s. Some contemporaries did think that raising the school-leaving age to 16, combined with the advent of a terminal school certificate (the CSE) which did *not* give access to higher education, may have encouraged school-leaving at 16.[36] But raising the school-leaving age to 16 also gave many more children access to O-Levels, the prerequisite for staying on to 18.[37] Much the same can be said of comprehensivisation. There may well have been temporary disruptions due to school reorganisation, and there is some evidence for the 1958 birth cohort (that is, 16-year-olds in 1974), that while lower-achieving children did better from reorganisation the highest-achieving did slightly worse. But once passed reorganisation

[35] Williams, 'Events of 1973–1974', 40–2; Guy R. Neave, 'Elite and Mass Higher Education in Britain: A Regressive Model?', *Comparative Education Review*, 29 (1985), 353–7; Paul Willis, *Learning to Labour: How Working Class Kids Get Working Class Jobs* (Aldershot, 1993; orig. publ. 1977), 2–3, 14–15, 36, 52, 94, 103–4, 127–8, based on ethnography done in 1972–5, but cf. Glenn Turner, 'Assessment in the Comprehensive School: What Criteria Count?', in *Selection, Certification and Control: Social Issues in Educational Assessment*, ed. Patricia Broadfoot (1984), 74–7. In a 1976 survey of leavers' motivations, 30 per cent gave labour-market reasons and 40 per cent counter-school reasons: Gareth Williams and Alan Gordon, '16 and 19 Year Olds: Attitudes to Education', *Higher Education Bulletin*, 4 (1975), 27.

[36] C. S. Rycroft to C. H. K. Williams, 25 Jan. 1983, citing Michael Rutter's *Changing Youth in a Changing Society* (1979): TNA, CAB 184/713.

[37] Nigel Wright, *Progress in Education: A Review of Schooling in England and Wales* (1977), 70–1, 100. The proportion of school-leavers attempting O-Levels rose from 41 per cent in 1969 to 49 per cent in 1975. DES, *Statistics of Education*, 1979, II: School Leavers, CSE and GCE, 4, gives historical statistics for CSE and O-Level candidatures across the 1970s which show rising participation rates in both exams across the decade, with CSE candidatures tapering off after 1974–5 but O- and A-Level candidatures continuing to grow.

again gave more rather than less access to O-Levels and A-Levels and thus potentially to higher education.[38]

Each of these explanations – declining economic incentives, a temporary correction to over-rapid growth, the development of a 'counter-school' culture, the immediate effect of reorganisation – has its merits, and they do seem to capture something about the peculiar brash philistinism of the early 1970s.[39] But even together they do not begin to explain the breadth and depth of the turn against higher education, which affected girls as much as boys, and middle-class girls especially (the group that Robbins had correctly identified as the prime new audience for higher education), and which long outlasted the temporary decline in the graduate premium.[40] In addition to factors encouraging early school-leaving, we must consider factors discouraging entry to higher education: that is, choices made at 18 as well as at 16. And here we must, I think, take into account a factor that the economists cannot see because they cannot measure it, which is the changing image of higher education among the general public. Precisely from around 1969, the presentation of universities in the mass media shifted sharply from golden places of uplift, aspiration and modernity to very tarnished places of conflict, rebellion and, above all, difference – a space apart from society rather than integrated into it. There is some evidence that 'student behaviour' came under more intense scrutiny in Britain than in other countries where student protest was actually more widespread and disruptive.[41] If I am allowed a personal anecdote, I remember being very surprised and indeed shocked when, coming from California to study as an undergraduate in this country in 1975, I found that the genus 'student' was portrayed even in the mainstream media as a class apart: scruffy, lazy, pampered and

[38] Judith Glaesser and Barry Cooper, 'Educational Achievement in Selective and Comprehensive Local Education Authorities: A Configurational Analysis', *British Journal of Sociology of Education*, 33 (2012), 236–40; Vikki Boliver and Adam Swift, 'Do Comprehensive Schools Reduce Social Mobility?', *British Journal of Sociology*, 62 (2011), 101–2; Alan Manning and Jörn-Steffen Pischke, 'Comprehensive versus Selective Schooling in England and Wales: What Do We Know?', Discussion Paper No. 2072, Apr. 2006, IZA Bonn, 17–18; and see previous note. In Scotland, there was a clear trend of rising attainment by the late 1970s: Peter Burnhill, Catherine Garner and Andrew McPherson, 'Social Change, School Attainment and Entry to Higher Education 1976–1986', in *Education and the Youth Labour Market: Schooling and Scheming*, ed. David Raffe (1988), 66–99.

[39] Thanks to my witty friend Andy Bell for memorably summing up this transition as 'from Status Quo to "Auf Wiedersehen, Pet"'.

[40] For a gender critique of Pissarides, see Keith Whitfield and R. A. Wilson, 'Staying on in Full-Time Education: The Educational Participation Rate of 16-Year-Olds', *Economica*, 58 (1991), 392–5.

[41] This at least was the diagnosis of Asa Briggs, 'Decade of Disenchantment', *Guardian*, 6 Feb. 1973, 15; and see Perkin, 'University Planning', 117; but cf. Peter Scott, 'British Universities 1968–1978', *Paedagogica Europaea*, 13 (1978), 29–43, which says more or less the opposite.

troublesome – a devastating combination. Though I cannot demonstrate this statistically, it seems highly likely that this repelling force was just as important in deterring the marginal entrant (especially a middle-class girl) from contemplating staying on at 16 to qualify for higher education as was the fluctuating graduate premium. Even amongst those who did stay on, those who achieved university entrance qualifications were now less likely to apply for or take up a university place.[42] And this repelling force applied to the public-sector institutions as well as the universities – the *cause célèbres* of the 1970s centred not only on places like Essex University (which as late as 1985 the *Sun* still hoped might crumble and fall into the North Sea) but also places like North-East London Polytechnic, alleged to have witnessed the 'rape of reason' in the student ructions of summer 1975.[43] This changing image of higher education was also an international phenomenon, which may help to explain declining uptake of higher education even in places where the graduate premium was not in decline, but where there was as in Britain an apparent mismatch (as the OECD put it) between 'the outlook and system of values in the teaching environment' on the one hand, and career aspirations, a search for income and security, and 'the pursuit of knowledge and the desire for self-fulfilment' amongst young people on the other.[44]

[42] 69 per cent of qualified leavers entered degree courses in 1967, but only 52 per cent in 1973; 87 per cent of leavers with CCC at A-Level entered in 1967, but only 80 per cent in 1973: Williams, 'Events of 1973–1974', 44–5. Participation rates of qualified leavers in higher education in general fell at least 10 per cent and possibly (by other measures) as much as 20 per cent over the course of the 1970s: *DES Statistical Bulletin* 12/80 (Sept. 1980). See further below n. 46.

[43] *Hansard*, sixth series, 80 (1984–5), 206 [4 June 1985]. We lack a systematic account of the representation of higher education in the media and public opinion across this period. Dominic Sandbrook, *Seasons in the Sun: The Battle for Britain, 1974–1979* (2012), 289–97, is probably right to see the mid-1970s as the apex of public disapprobation, but he misses entirely the context of stagnation across the decade (these were not 'surprisingly good years for Britain's universities' by any measure, still less was there an 'enormous boom'); a similar leap is made by the otherwise reliable Brian Harrison, *Finding a Role? The United Kingdom, 1970–1990* (Oxford, 2010), 391–4. It is striking that universities are not discussed at all in Sandbrook's predecessor volume, *State of Emergency: The Way We Were: Britain, 1970–1974* (2010), nor in any of the other specialist works on the 1970s that have appeared so far. See also, for acknowledgements of the changing student culture and its possible effects on public opinion, Carswell, *Government and the Universities*, 140–1; Maurice Kogan and Stephen Hanney, *Reforming Higher Education* (2000), 56–7.

[44] Eric Esnault and Jean Le Pas, 'New Relations between Post-Secondary Education and Employment', in OECD, *Towards Mass Higher Education: Issues and Dilemmas* (Paris, 1974), 156–8. Demand in France, the US, UK and Sweden all began to slacken from around 1968, and across the OECD from 1971: Jean-Pierre Pellegrin, 'Quantitative Trends in Post-Secondary Education', in OECD, *Towards Mass Higher Education*, 49–51; Ladislav Cerych, Dorotea Furth and George S. Papadopoulos, 'Overall Issues in the Development of Future Structures of Post-Secondary Education', in OECD Conference, *General Report*, 17–21.

In sum, a series of hammer-blows hit the image of higher education across the 1970s: an Indian Summer of industrial employment (this part unique to Britain), a crisis of confidence in the graduate labour market, reorganisation of secondary education and, perhaps above all, a crisis of confidence in the ability of higher education to deliver aspirations for either social mobility *or* self-fulfilment. As a number of OECD reports in this decade concluded, higher education across the Western world seemed stranded between the decline of industrial employment and uncertainty about a post-industrial future, which left it unclear whether higher education could deliver on material or personal aspirations.[45] On the other hand, there was not the same stagnation in general educational attainment during this period. As mentioned, secondary school reorganisation did not affect overall attainment levels. While it might have (in combination with the other factors cited) reduced aspiration to higher education, it increased attainment at 16, so that the relative number of CSE and O-Level passes continued to rise.[46] In other words, school attainment continued to improve, and since prior attainment is normally the best predictor of progress to higher education, the longer-term prospects for getting the Robbins escalator moving again were good, so long as faith in higher education itself could be restored.[47]

So far I have not mentioned 'the cuts'. This is not because they are unimportant, but I have wanted first to put them in proper context. They did not start to figure until 1974. As late as 1972 Thatcher's White Paper was repeating the established mantra – the Robbins principle was sacrosanct, higher education was not only for jobs but also for 'personal and social action' – and uprating Robbins's prediction of a 17 per cent age-participation rate by the end of the decade to 22 per cent, predicting 5 per cent per annum growth in higher-education expenditure

[45] OECD, *Employment Prospects for Higher Education Graduates* (Paris, 1981), 2, 6–7, 13–16, 25–9, 47; Esnault and Le Pas, 'New Relations', 133–5, 140; Cerych, Furth and Papadopoulos, 'Overall Issues', 23, 46–7.

[46] DES, *Education Statistics for the United Kingdom*, 1987, vi, shows stagnation at 1 A-Level but growth at 5 A–C O-Levels and 1–4 A–C O-Levels, and especially (thanks to the raising of the school-leaving age) a sharp drop in those with no qualifications, 1970–84; DES, *Report on Education*, 99 (Apr. 1983), shows a continuous though gentle rise in the qualified-leaver rate over the same period. In fact A-Level, O-Level and CSE candidatures all rise continuously across the 1970s, though there may of course be clumping of larger numbers of candidatures among fewer candidates, especially at A-Level. See n. 42, above, and Damon Clark, Gavan Conlon and Fernando Galindo-Rueda, 'Post-Compulsory Education and Qualification Attainment', in *What's the Good of Education? The Economics of Education in the UK*, ed. Stephen Machin and Anna Vignoles (Princeton, 2005), 75–86, on the concentration of attainment improvements in the lower levels.

[47] Indeed, in the DES it was held that the qualified-leaver rate was rising and the qualified-participation rate falling, and thus that attainment was rising at this higher level but willingness to proceed to higher education was not. Policy Group A, 'Higher Education into the 1990s', Sept. 1978, Annex B, Table 2: TNA, ED 181/497.

throughout the 1970s.[48] The financial crisis of 1974 then hit at the same time as the realisation that participation was in decline anyway.[49] This allowed the cash-strapped Labour government to slash the 1972 projections while defending the Robbins principle – cuts in supply were only responding to cuts in demand.[50] Thus, Labour accepted (though it did not necessarily trigger) stagnant participation rates throughout its 1974–9 term of government, upholding the Robbins principle at least in theory. There was one conspicuous exception to this rule. Even before Labour came to power in February 1974, the Conservative government was planning a huge cut in teacher training as a demographic downturn in the school-age population was imminent, seeking in its own way to turn declining demand to the service of public-expenditure cuts. Labour continued this policy, closing a third of all teacher-training colleges and merging most of the rest into the polytechnics.[51] Since teaching was still the ideal-type graduate profession for new entrants, these cuts made a further direct hit on participation rates, especially for women.[52] But otherwise, Labour relied successfully on naturally stagnant demand to

[48] *Robbins Report*, Appendix I: The Demand for Places in Higher Education, Cmnd 2154-I (1963), 152; *Education: A Framework for Expansion*, Cmnd 5174 (1972–3), 35–6. The White Paper's calculations took into account some of the slowdown since 1969; a straight projection from 1968 would have reached 24.5 per cent by 1980: Callender, 'Student Numbers and Funding', 171–2. Labour was arguing at the time for an even higher target, taking into account supposedly rising aspirations to follow from the raising of the school-leaving age and comprehensivisation: Roy Hattersley in *Hansard*, fifth series 81 (1972–3), 65–6 [19 Feb. 1973]. As late as Jan. 1974, when it was clear that the participation rate was not rising but falling, the DES was satisfied that the fall was 'entirely due to the reduction in the willingness of students to undertake higher education' rather than to any constraints on supply. Policy Steering Group, minutes, 11 Jan. 1974: TNA, ED181/273.

[49] Williams, 'Events of 1973–1974', 40–2, cites the impact of the 1972 staying-on statistics which did not come in until mid-1974. See the tentative debate over participation rates inside the DES in 1973–4, in which Williams himself participated, in TNA, ED181/273–4, which generated so much uncertainty about 'demand-based' projections that it was possible to develop separate 'policy-based' targets without explicitly departing from the Robbins principle.

[50] Shattock, *Making Policy*, 110–12, presents this simply as a matter of supply, but cf. 147 where demand is brought in. Howard Glennerster, 'Education: Reaping the Harvest?', in *The State of Welfare: The Economics of Public Spending*, ed. Howard Glennerster and John Hills (2nd edn, Oxford, 1998), 47, also presents as a matter of supply, acknowledging but not incorporating demand issues; and see further Anderson, *British Universities*, 158–60. For a devastating indictment of Labour's passive, demand-driven policy, from one of its own, see Lord Crowther-Hunt, 'Policy Making and Accountability in Higher Education', in *The Structure and Governance of Higher Education*, ed. Michael Shattock (Guildford, 1983), 46–67.

[51] David Hencke, *Colleges in Crisis: The Reorganization of Teacher Training 1971–7* (Harmondsworth, 1978).

[52] In the DES, they calculated that HE participation would have grown 'very slightly' without the teacher-training cuts. A. Thompson to secretary of state, 'Entry Prospects in Higher Education under Present and Possible Future Expenditure Plans', 2 July 1980: TNA, ED 181/385.

keep a lid on public expenditure and to maintain the fig-leaf of the Robbins principle.

It is striking nonetheless how vigorously even an enfeebled Labour government clung to the Robbins principle. Both in public and in private ministers and civil servants insisted they were still catering to demand. The government was now negotiating annually with both universities and the public-sector institutions on the number of places needed. There was deep concern inside the Department of Education and Science (DES) that keeping too tight a lid on student numbers would be seen as rationing, and thus a violation of the Robbins principle. Worse, there was a keen awareness that the control of student numbers was itself sending market signals – that demand and supply were intertwined. Civil servants began to speak not only of the staying-on rate or the age-participation rate but also of the 'opportunity/willingness' rate – that is, the effect that constricted *opportunity* to enter higher education might have on young people's *willingness* even to attempt it. Since Robbins, it had been unthinkable to posit any limitations on supply. To avoid this imputation, Shirley Williams as education secretary insisted that short-term projections incorporated a tiny annual uptick of the participation rate, in the hopes that this would keep the Robbins escalator moving upwards (at a crawl), until a demographic downturn in the 1980s might again permit more rapid expansion without paying the price in public spending.[53] But this was desperate stuff. After a decade of stagnant participation rates and five years of severe public-expenditure pressures, few people in government – or in higher education – had any real hopes that the expansionary days of Robbins would return.

Any lingering hopes of this type were then firmly dashed by the advent of a Conservative government that was determined on deep cuts in public expenditure *and* was willing (if at first only *sotto voce*) to question the Robbins principle itself. Higher education became a deliberate target for deep cuts in the first Thatcher government. Thatcher herself had bad memories of her time as education secretary and she did not feel that investment in higher education was a good use of public money; nor, with some justice, did she feel that her core lower-middle-class constituency (still poorly represented in higher education) was particularly attached to it. There was also an ideological element in her circle that was divided or agnostic about what the right level of participation was, but was determined to

[53] *The government's expenditure plans*, II, Cmnd 6721-II (1976–7), 70–1; Policy Group A, 'Higher Education into the 1990s', Sept. 1978, esp. Annex B; Gordon Oakes, 'Higher Education into the 1990s: Future Policy; Initial Reactions of the Minister of State', 18 Oct. 1978; Shirley Williams, 'Responses to Higher Education in the 1990s; Note by the Secretary of State', 27 Oct. 1978; note of meeting, 'Responses to "Higher Education into the 1990s": Future Policy for Higher Education', 20 Nov. 1978: TNA, ED 181/497.

apply more realistic market tests than the Robbins principle allowed, by shifting the cost burden towards the consumer and then seeing what happened to participation rates. This was the position of both Keith Joseph, her education secretary from 1980, who in his heart wanted lower participation rates, and also of his junior minister William Waldegrave, who wanted to boost the polytechnic sector and other low-cost forms of higher education that might attract greater participation and also prove good investments in human capital and economic growth.[54] The result was a two-pronged approach: an immediate cut in higher education (HE) provision, expected to induce a drop in the age-participation rate to 11 per cent, and market reforms (a new student loan scheme, offers of more places to polytechnics at cut-rate prices), expected to be neutral in their effects on demand. Although inside government the assumption was that ministers were quietly retracting from the Robbins principle, in public they still upheld it, relying in part (as had Labour) on declining demand and in part on cutting costs rather than places.[55]

But something odd was happening in the depths of the recession of the early 1980s – demand was increasing. This forms part of the second great mystery I have sought to plumb – why after a long period of stagnation in demand did it begin to recover during an economic downturn, precisely the conditions that the economists had used to explain the fall-off in demand in the first place? What was different about the conditions and the decision-making processes of young people in the 1970s versus the 1980s?

A number of unexpected things were happening in the recession of the early 1980s. First, in conditions of high unemployment, staying-on rates rose sharply to 32 per cent by 1983. Contemporaries were unsure why – this could have been what was called 'parking', staying in further education until the labour market recovered. Nevertheless, unlike in the 1970s, it indicated that parents (also being exposed to high unemployment) were willing to invest in their children's acquisition of more education.[56]

---

[54] For an insight into Thatcher and Joseph's positions, see J. R. Jameson to J. S. Street, 'Mid-Term Financial Options: Secretary of State's Meeting with Prime Minister and Others on 7 December', 1 Dec. 1982: TNA, ED 261/206; for Waldegrave's position, M. J. Elliott to HE Team, 7 Dec. 1982: TNA, CAB 184/712.

[55] For assumptions inside government, see A. Thompson to R. H. Bird, 20 June 1980; D. M. Forrester to J. R. Jameson, 2 July 1980; A. Thompson to secretary of state, 'Entry Prospects in Higher Education under Present and Possible Future Expenditure Plans', 2 July 1980: TNA, ED 181/385; Leon Brittan to Keith Joseph, 18 Mar. 1983: TNA, ED 261/206; Keith Joseph to prime minister, 'Long Term Public Expenditure', 25 Mar. 1983: TNA, T494/60. For public statements, see House of Commons, Committee of Public Accounts, Minutes of Evidence, 7 May 1980, 15; William Waldegrave in *Hansard*, sixth series, 20 (1981–2), 1347–8 [29 July 1982].

[56] As early as 1983 the Central Policy Review Staff detected the potential economic benefits to 'parking', but the effort to reconnect unemployed 16-year-olds with higher

Then, those already staying on past 16 were showing more interest in higher education: qualified leavers' participation grew from 83 to 88 per cent between 1979 and 1982. This might have been a form of parking, too, but it led to higher participation rates than the Conservative government had anticipated.[57] Most markedly, and encouraging to the more technocratic Tories like Waldegrave, these higher participation rates registered in the polytechnics, not the universities. New entrants after 1979 had little choice – the universities' numbers were being cut, but the polytechnics' were only cash-limited, so they could offer cut-rate places. What surprised everyone is that these new entrants, still mostly middle-class, seemed now willing to go to public-sector institutions when they might previously have held out for university.[58]

In short, although these new levels of demand might at first have indicated only temporary 'parking', they were transmuting – certainly transmutable – into more sustained demand, if only supply constraints could be lifted. As we move through the 1980s, we can certainly detect changing public attitudes to higher education, running ahead of government. High levels of blue-collar unemployment and a new glamour attaching to white-collar jobs, especially in financial services, reversed the values of the early 1970s, and made higher education for social mobility look more attractive. Graduate employment opportunities were more varied and despite later waves of expansion the graduate premium began to rise jerkily from 1980, practically to the present day.[59] The association of higher education with a separate class of student began to wear off and

education seemed at that point too onerous: M. J. Elliott, 'Higher Education: Draft Skeletal Report', 13 Jan. 1983: TNA, CAB 184/713.

[57] C. H. K. Williams to M. J. Elliott, 17 Jan. 1983, 'Higher Education: Demand to 2000': TNA, CAB 184/713; 'Future Demand for Higher Education in Great Britain', DES, *Report on Education*, 99 (Apr. 1983); Whitfield and Wilson, 'Staying on', 391–404; Gerry Makepeace, Peter Dolton, Laura Woods, Heather Joshi and Fernando Galinda-Rueda, 'From School to the Labour Market', in *Changing Britain, Changing Lives: Three Generations at the Turn of the Century*, ed. Elsa Ferri, John Bynner and Michael Wadsworth (2003), 35–6; Glennerster, 'Education: Reaping the Harvest?', 47.

[58] Leslie Wagner, 'National Policy and Institutional Development', in *Access and Institutional Change*, ed. Oliver Fulton (Milton Keynes, 1989), 150–2; Kogan and Hanney, *Reforming Higher Education*, 69–70, see this rather as a discouragement to expansion, alerting the Treasury to potentially rising demand.

[59] Helen Connor, 'Different Graduates, Different Labour Market: Is there a Mismatch in Supply-Demand?', in *Changing Relationships between Higher Education and the State*, ed. Mary Henkel and Brenda Little (1999), 91–7; Whitfield and Wilson, 'Staying on', 400–1; Arnaud Chevalier and Ian Walker, 'United Kingdom', in *Education and Earnings in Europe: A Cross Country Analysis of the Returns to Education*, ed. Colm Harmon, Ian Walker and Niels Westergaard-Nielsen (Cheltenham, 2001), 302–30; Anna Mountford-Zimdars, Steven Jones, Alice Sullivan and Anthony Heath, 'Framing Higher Education: Questions and Responses in the British Social Attitudes Survey, 1983–2010', *British Journal of Sociology of Education*, 34 (2013), 792–3, 797.

the psychic conditions, at least, were in place for the Robbins escalator to begin rolling again.

Although ministers were aware of all these tendencies, it was far from clear that they wanted to go with them. This is the latter part of the mystery of the 1980s – why did the government change its mind about contraction of the higher-education system? Soberingly, even one of the top civil servants in the DES, looking back just a few years later at this about-turn which he had witnessed as closely as anyone, concluded that 'I am not sure I can identify all the influences, let alone rate their relative importance . . . Regretfully, I must class the necessary analysis as "too difficult" and leave it to someone else.'[60] A challenge to the historian.

Although government was aware of growing demand, it did not show at first any immediate urgency to respond to it. Thatcher and Joseph had no attachment to the Robbins principle. Evidence of demand for low-cost higher education might have swayed some of the free-market ideologues away from contraction to expansion, but they had no influential champion in government. Joseph's 1985 Green Paper projected student numbers to 2000 assuming no increase at all in the participation rate, and still below 1972 levels. It explicitly applied a cost-benefit calculation to the Robbins principle, and for the first time in public admitted that it was revising it, adding 'the application to admissions of the criterion of "ability to benefit" from higher education, having regard to the intellectual competence, motivation and maturity of the candidate', undoubtedly a dig at the alleged immaturity displayed by so many students in the 1970s.[61] Tabloids still in full 1970s mode celebrated what the *Daily Express* called 'a crackdown on left-wing student bully boys'; this was the occasion when the *Sun* expressed the view that Essex might safely crumble into the North Sea, though it regretted the resultant risk of coastal pollution.[62]

However, by this point a fundamental change was already stirring in the heart of Conservative government, a few years behind public opinion. In part, this was due to the shift from austerity to growth, as unemployment rates began at last to come down, white-collar employment prospects improved and pressure on public expenditure eased. Even ministers who did not care about education might be willing to give it a piece of a slowly growing pie. But education benefited from an additional, demographic gift at just this time, as the 'hump' which had so bedevilled Labour at last fell away and the number of first 16-year-olds and then 18-year-olds began to drop from 1983. With this demographic slump, steadily

[60] Richard Bird, 'Reflections on the British Government and Higher Education', *Higher Education Quarterly*, 48 (1994), 75–6, 84.

[61] *The Development of Higher Education into the 1990s*, Cmnd 9524 (1984–5), 10–11, 41–2.

[62] See Giles Radice's review of the press reception in *Hansard*, sixth series, 80 (1984–5), 206 [4 Jun. 1985].

rising participation rates need not require more public expenditure. However, just as important, I would argue, was Keith Joseph's failure to pass his key market reforms and Thatcher's turn to a very different alternative in the person of Kenneth Baker. Joseph's bid to replace student grants with loans met with unexpectedly ferocious hostility from the Tory backbenches, and this gave the prime minister pause – perhaps her constituents did care about higher education after all?[63] As the cohort that had benefited from the Robbins-era boom now had children of post-compulsory education age, and as parental attainment is a good predictor of children's attainment, the truth was that parents in the mid-1980s *were* more likely to favour higher education, even without the changes in the labour market and popular attitudes already mentioned.[64]

Baker was a market reformer who believed in education, for personal *and* economic growth, and who was pragmatic about combining market reforms with a touch of technocracy if the combination would serve those ends.[65] Thatcher liked his ebullience and optimism, and she was probably a little shamed by his hints that she should have more confidence in the efficacy of her own government's efforts to raise standards in schools, which were always going to lift demand for higher education.[66] He was lucky, too, in inheriting one policy from his predecessors that could easily be turned to growth, the merging of the two school examination systems (CSE and GCE) into a single exam at 16, the GCSE. Although Joseph had meant the GCSE to reestablish a firm hierarchy of merit, criterion- rather than norm-referenced (that is, setting fixed standards of attainment), in fact, by vastly extending the number of 16-year-olds taking an exam that could facilitate staying on, the GCSE proved the *sine qua non* of rapid expansion in higher education.[67] Then all Baker had to do was to turn

[63] Kenneth Baker, *The Turbulent Years: My Life in Politics* (1993), 237–8; Andrew Denham and Mark Garnett, *Keith Joseph* (2001), 390–4.

[64] *Higher Education: Meeting the Challenge*, Cmnd 114 (1986–7), 5–6. This revelation followed an internal debate over new student-number projections in 1983–4, which not only registered the unexpected surge in participation during the economic downturn but also the likely impact of longer-term term social changes: 'Demand for Higher Education in Great Britain, 1984–2000', DES, *Report on Education*, 100 (July 1984).

[65] Michael Shattock, *The UGC and the Management of British Universities* (Buckingham, 1994), variously credits Baker's 'populism' and 'a radical switch to a market-driven approach', 134–5; Kogan and Hanney, *Reforming Higher Education*, 74–5, recognise Baker's personal stake in expansion but see it as fundamentally inertial and opportunistic. Baker had significant reinforcement in his junior minister, Robert Jackson, who pressed for explicit commitments to 'steadily increasing participation rates': see his input into the 1987 Ministerial Priorities Review in TNA, ED181/529.

[66] Shattock, *Making Policy*, 148–9; Baker, *Turbulent Years*, 170.

[67] Duncan McVicar and Patricia Rice, 'Participation in Further Education in England and Wales: An Analysis of Post-War Trends', *Oxford Economic Papers*, 53 (2001), 47–66; Steven McIntosh, 'The Demand for Post-Compulsory Education in Four European Countries', *Education Economics*, 9 (2001), 69–90.

on the supply tap of places in higher education. First, he adopted as a policy what Joseph had stumbled on by accident, expansion via low-cost polytechnic places. On this basis, he was already prepared in his 1987 White Paper to predict not further stagnation but steady growth in the participation rate – past the 14.2 per cent peak of 1972 to 18.5 per cent by 2000. Then he offered the universities the same deal he was offering the polytechnics: more places if they would accept lower prices. Seeing their market advantage slipping, the vice-chancellors snapped at the chance. By January 1989, Baker was ready to announce, in a famous speech at Lancaster University (actually not as famous as it should be), not just steady growth but a sudden transition to mass higher education. The goal was to reach for American levels of participation, as befitted a country aspiring to American levels of affluence. His new target for 2000 was 30 per cent. From 1989, therefore, the course was set for the revolution in higher-education participation that we experienced in the 1990s and the noughties.[68]

The after-effects of the Lancaster speech were much like the after-effects of Robbins, creating a kind of euphoria, compounded of pent-up demand, the entirely novel boost provided by GCSE, and the market signals sent by the unleashing of supply. The euphoria was in fact much greater amongst potential applicants than it was in the media, which on the whole remained sceptical about expansion on the grand scale, even in its leftish incarnations, because of the cuts in the unit of resource that made it possible. (If I may be allowed one more personal anecdote – I was hired by a polytechnic in 1991 to set up a new history degree in anticipation of rapid expansion in traditional 'university' subjects like history, and admitted dozens of students in the first few years who were frankly dazed to find themselves suddenly placed in higher education – though, and this is the point, also very keen to be there.) Baker fuelled this euphoria by sharply shifting government's own rhetoric away from utilitarian criteria. Thatcher and Joseph had been surprisingly attracted to 'manpower planning' of the 1960s variety, using higher education strictly to stoke economic growth. Baker instead spoke a new language of 'widening participation' – reaching out to under-represented groups, who deserved higher education for their own purposes – and in this he had some unlikely allies in high-tech industry, which disapproved of manpower planning. 'We must change our higher education system from one geared to a small minority to a more open system which brings many more people to a generally higher level of education than they attain

---

[68] *Times Higher Education Supplement*, 13 Jan. 1989, 7. It is noticeable that the educationalists asked by the *THES* to respond to Baker's speech expressed universal scepticism about the realism of these targets (which proved in the event to be under- rather than over-estimates).

now', insisted one key industry group in 1988, and the chairman of Shell chimed in, in quintessentially Robbins-esque terms,

> The wonders of classics and the mysteries of physics are as good a preparation for management as the disciplines of economics or the increasingly popular business studies. The enhancement and enrichment of the mind confer a perspective on the individual which will be called on in their future direction of human affairs.[69]

With these encouragements, the 30 per cent target was hit not in 2000 but as early as 1991 – in other words, the proportion of the cohort in higher education had more than doubled in a few years from its plateau level of 14 per cent held since the early 1970s. By then, the Treasury had begun to squeal loudly. The cuts in unit costs had been overwhelmed by the rise in numbers; over the whole period to 1997, unit costs fell 40 per cent but even so the higher-education budget increased in real terms by 45 per cent.[70] The Treasury sought – and thought it received – an agreement to hold participation rates at 30 per cent, but at this point New Labour began campaigning on education – 'education, education, education' was about HE as well as schools – and after 1997 the Treasury was bought off with the prospect of a growing student contribution, as recommended by the Dearing Review. Participation began to rise again, approaching 40 per cent by 2003. It was at this point that Labour set its notorious 50 per cent target, though at the same time changing the way it calculated participation rates, taking into account participation amongst older groups than 18- to 19-year-olds, which boosted the existing rate to 41 per cent. Though the 50 per cent target attracted much ridicule at the time, no party has been willing to move against it, and we have now nearly reached it. Only the huge tuition-fee hike of 2010 stands in the way. It was undoubtedly designed *not* to deter widening participation but early indications are that it may have done, at least temporarily freezing participation at 46 per cent.[71] It would take a bold historian to predict the course even of the immediate future – not me. Instead, let me move to some conclusions based on this last phase of rapid expansion we have experienced since the late 1980s.

While the name of Robbins has been on many lips recently in the 50th anniversary year of the famous report, there is a case to be made that the reforms of the late 1980s were vastly more important, not only

---

[69] Richard A. Brown with Patrick Coldstream, *A Successful Partnership* (Council for Industry and Higher Education, Nov. 2008), 6, 7. The CBI also took a determinedly demand-driven line in this period: see Kogan and Hanney, *Reforming Higher Education*, 61–4, 76–8.

[70] Kogan and Hanney, *Reforming Higher Education*, 13.

[71] The new measure, HEIPR, grew from 42 per cent to 46 per cent between 2006 and 2008. It then surged to 49 per cent in the final year before tuition fees, and slumped to 43 per cent the next year, averaging out at 46 per cent (51 per cent for women). See Parliamentary Briefing, 'Participation in Higher Education', SN/SG/2630, 1 Sept. 2014.

for the rate and extent of expansion, but for my main focus in these lectures, the democratic discourse of education. The Robbins principle, as I suggested at the beginning, was an explicitly meritocratic principle with a democratic promise. That promise was only gradually redeemed over the first twenty-five years, as participation grew rapidly, then stagnated, before it reached much beyond the upper-middle parts of the social spectrum. Only after GCSE put staying on within the reach of a majority of the population could substantial numbers from other groups have a reasonable expectation of achieving higher education. In the first ten years of GCSE, staying on increased among the lowest income group from 21 per cent to 61 per cent.[72] Although this did not yet put higher education immediately within the reach of this group, it undoubtedly established a platform and encouraged a new set of expectations.[73] The economists speak of a 'role-model effect', in which the breakthrough of some members of unrepresented groups has knock-on effects for others, particularly among women.[74] Perhaps the most thought-provoking statistic I have come across in this research addresses aspiration of young mothers in the lowest income group for their children. Even at the height of the Robbins euphoria of the 1960s perhaps only a quarter of parents in the lowest income group expressed a desire for higher education for their primary-age children.[75] But in a survey of the millennium birth-cohort in 2008, no fewer than 96 per cent of mothers in the lowest-qualification group wanted their 8-year-olds to go to university.[76]

Though only a portion of those children will realise their mothers' aspirations, the aspirations themselves clearly indicate that higher education is today a nearly universal social norm in a way it had not been in the late 1960s. Student life is no longer seen as a peculiar sub-culture but rather as a widely shared life-cycle experience. As the economists would point out, there are practical as well as cultural reasons for this. The old school-to-job transitions, based on fathers' contacts passed on to their

---

[72] Staying-on rates were, as we have noted, already rising in the early 1980s, but without necessarily leading to higher qualifications; inequality in attainment at 16 fell sharply after the advent of GCSE and the proportion achieving five 'good' (A–C) GCSEs, the normal threshold for proceeding to A-Levels, first reached 50 per cent in 1992. Gordon Stobart and Caroline Gipps, *Assessment: A Teacher's Guide to the Issues* (3rd edn, 1997), 44–5; Jo Blanden, Paul Gregg and Stephen Machin, 'Educational Inequality and Intergenerational Mobility', in *What's the Good of Education?*, ed. Machin and Vignoles, 101–2, 110–11; Stephen Machin and Anna Vignoles, 'Education Policy in the UK', Centre for the Economics of Education, Discussion Paper 57 (Mar. 2006), 4–7.

[73] Anthony Heath, Alice Sullivan, Vikki Boliver and Anna Zimdars, 'Education under New Labour, 1997–2010', *Oxford Review of Economic Policy*, 29 (2013), 238–40.

[74] McVicar and Rice, 'Participation in Further Education', 63.

[75] Bynner, *Parents' Attitudes to Education*, 16.

[76] 'Millennium mothers want university education for their children', 20 Oct. 2010, http://www.ioe.ac.uk/45855.html (accessed 1 Oct. 2014).

sons, have been disrupted by deindustrialisation and the feminisation of the labour market. There is now a huge, relatively undifferentiated white-collar labour market to which higher education provides the best access. This has helped to restore the graduate premium as employers use HE qualifications as gatekeepers to a wider range of jobs.[77] At the same time, higher education is now also again a consumption good; as Dolton and Vignoles have put it, 'people want to go to university because they enjoy the education process, irrespective of the financial return to a degree'.[78] It has become a normal part of the maturation process, bridging school and work. This is not to say that everyone can, should or will seek higher education. Even 50 per cent participation rates, which we have not yet reached, leave 50 per cent not participating. Indeed, a strong case is now made that the flight of so many people into higher education has left beached everyone else who mostly leave school at 16. In the OECD, Britain now has above-average rates of participation in higher education but also above-average rates of early school-leaving. This is why government has recently required that all young people must remain in education or job training to 18.

Nevertheless, it would be a mistake to underestimate the propulsive force of aspiration behind the Robbins escalator. It has been a central argument in my first two addresses that democratic aspirations to ever-higher levels of educational provision have been a driving force behind policy, even when they do not appear to be. There does not in fact need to be an organised education lobby to galvanise politicians, who are plenty aware of public opinion without it. In secondary education, councillors and MPs encountered the pressure of public opinion on every doorstep. In higher education, the establishment of a demand-led presumption by Robbins – itself a by-product of universal secondary education – set up a host of indicators (staying-on rates, qualified-leaver rates, age-participation rates and so on) as well as a climate of opinion which made it difficult for politicians, even when cash-strapped, and even when demand seemed to be flagging, to come out in public against limits. Thus, the touching insistence by Shirley Williams on a 0.1 per cent annual increase in participation even at a time when she was desperately reliant upon the stagnation of demand to keep public expenditure in check. The one government willing to retract from the Robbins principle – that is,

---

[77] Connor, 'Different Graduates', 93–7; and for a recent, authoritative analysis of the persistence of the graduate premium, see Ian Walker and Yu Zhu, 'The Impact of University Degrees on the Lifecycle of Earnings: Some Further Analysis', BIS Research Paper 112 (Aug. 2013).

[78] Peter J. Dolton and Anna Vignoles, 'Overeducation: Problem or Not?', in *Changing Relationships*, ed. Henkel and Little, 118–20.

Thatcher's of the early 1980s – found itself overtaken by a resurgence of demand and eventually became its willing servant.[79]

The worst forebodings of the education lobby proved unfounded. Throughout the period of stagnation, educationalists had argued that the 'natural' level of demand was too low and would have to be stimulated artificially by providing more sub-degree courses or shorter degree courses – anything to make staying on a little more attractive. If only, they mourned, they had more political clout.[80] But in fact they had political clout in demand that they never fully appreciated. As soon as all children were given a chance to take a staying-on exam, the GCSE, demand for university-level higher education soared again. Since then, there has been no more talk of abandoning the Robbins principle. The opportunity to qualify for and enter higher education is now widely seen not as a meritocratic opportunity but as a democratic right. Higher education now, like secondary education since the 1950s, benefits from a strong universalist presumption that all young people deserve an equal – that is, the best – start in life. Where the money comes from to achieve this goal bedevils us all, but the goal itself seems more consensual than it has ever been.

[79] Thatcher's revision of the Robbins principle to take account of 'intellectual competence, motivation and maturity' was quietly dropped by John Major; the last use of this phrase in any parliamentary proceeding was by Baroness Blatch, the government's education spokesperson in the Lords, on 10 Mar. 1994: *Hansard (Lords)*, fifth series, 552 (1993–4), 1668.

[80] See for example the volumes that came out of the Leverhulme-sponsored series of conferences on the future of higher education in the early 1980s, notably the tellingly-titled Gareth Williams and Tessa Blackstone, *Response to Adversity: Higher Education in a Harsh Climate* (Guildford, 1983).

Transactions of the RHS 25 (2015), pp. 27–52 © Royal Historical Society 2015
doi:10.1017/S0080440115000018

APOCALYPTIC AND ESCHATOLOGICAL THOUGHT IN ENGLAND AROUND THE YEAR 1000

By Catherine Cubitt

READ 7 FEBRUARY 2015

ABSTRACT. This article explores the ideas circulating in England *c.* 1000 about the fate of the soul after death, the afterlife and the Last Judgement. It looks at the discourse concerning these topics in the sermons of the Blickling Homilies, Vercelli Book and in sermons by Wulfstan and Ælfric, and argues for lively debate *c.* 1000 concerning the imminence of the End. It suggests that these texts, especially those by Wulfstan and Ælfric, should be seen in dialogue with one another, and argues that the recent revised dating of Wulfstan's apocalyptic sermons places them in relation to political and legal developments. It argues for a political dimension to this debate and highlights the responses of the king, Æthelred the Unready – demonstrated in diplomatic evidence – which suggests a heightened concern for his own salvation and for that of his family at this date. It places this royal anxiety not only in relation to ideas about the year 1000 and the End of the World but also in relation to the preaching in the homilies of Vercelli Book and of the Blickling collection concerning the fate of the soul and the higher standard of Christian conduct born by the wealthy and by those in responsibility. It concludes by emphasising the multiple and varied thinking about the Last Judgement in England *c.* 1000.

Now it must of necessity become very evil, because [Antichrist's] time is coming quickly, just as it is written and has long been prophesied: 'After a thousand years Satan will be unleashed.'. . . A thousand years and also more have now passed since Christ was among people in human form, and now Satan's bonds are very loose, and Antichrist's time is well at hand.[1]

With these words, Archbishop Wulfstan of York warned the English of the proximity of the advent of the Antichrist and of the terrors of the Last Days of the world. Wulfstan was responding not only to the passing of the millennium but to the devastating Viking attacks which were to cost his king, Æthelred, the kingdom. Dramatic words indeed, but how should a historian understand them. Are they merely the rousing rhetoric

---

[1] Translation by Joyce Lionarons at http://webpages.ursinus.edu/jlionarons/wulfstan/wulfstan.html 'Nu sceal hit nyde yfelian swyðe, forþam þe hit nealæcð georne his timan, ealswa hit awriten is 7 gefryn wæs gewitegod: *Post mille annos soluetur Satanas.* Þæt is on Englisc, æfter þusend gearum bið Satanas unbunden. Þusend geara 7 eac ma is nu agan syþþan Crist wæs mid mannum on menniscan hiwe, 7 nu syndon Satanases bendas swyðe toslopene, 7 Antecristes tima is wel gehende, 7 ðy is on worulde a swa leng swa wacre', *The Homilies of Wulfstan*, ed. Dorothy Bethurum (Oxford, 1957), sermon V, 134–41, at 136–7.

of a gifted preacher? Do we know what impact they had? Was Wulfstan's apocalyptic urgency and anticipation shared by others in the kingdom?

The year 1000 is a significant marker in Christian understandings of the end of time because of the amalgamation of a number of Scriptural traditions. Revelations 20:4–6 declared that Christ would reign for a thousand years, then Satan would be freed from his imprisonment in hell to cause havoc on earth before his final defeat. The Bible account of the six days of creation gave rise to the idea that world history could be divided into six ages, followed by a seventh age, a sabbatical rest. Since Scripture also reported that a thousand years was in God's sight a day, each of the six world ages could be reckoned to last a thousand years.[2] The sixth age had been initiated by Christ's incarnation – dated either from his birth or from his death. These calculations made it possible to foretell, therefore, the date of the Last Judgement although such a prediction contradicted Christ's own words in the New Testament, where he stated clearly that the time of the End was unknowable to all, including himself, and was only known to God.[3] Millenarian speculations were a source of disquiet and division within the early church. A turning point in defusing the Book of Revelation of its disturbing chronological implications was made by St Augustine who, while affirming a belief in the historical reality of the Last Days and Final Judgement, put forward an allegorical interpretation of Revelation which identified the predictions of the coming of the heavenly kingdom and to Christ's advent with the current church.[4] The final events had therefore already been accomplished.[5] Augustine defused the magic number, 1000, by arguing that it was a perfect number and its significance was not literal but allegorical. Although millennial predictions could not be so easily banished, nevertheless, Augustine's teaching was accepted by the church which emphasised the unknowability of the time of the End.

Apocalypticism, millenarianism and expectations of the Last Judgement are enduring themes of human history and continue to feed more political movements and religious groups.[6] Scholarship on apocalyptic thought in the early Middle Ages is a very widespread and diverse field and cannot be reviewed comprehensively here; instead, two historiographical strands will be emphasised.[7] First, there are those scholars who might be called Millennial Maximalists and who see

---

[2] Psalm 90:4, 2 Peter 3:8.

[3] Acts 1:7 and Mark 13:32.

[4] Paula Fredriksen, 'Apocalypse and Redemption in Early Christianity from John of Patmos to Augustine of Hippo', *Vigiliae Christianae*, 45 (1991), 151–83.

[5] *Ibid.*

[6] A useful survey is Eugen Weber, *Apocalypses Prophecies, Cults and Millennial Beliefs through the Ages* (2000).

[7] See, now, James Palmer, *The Apocalypse in the Early Middle Ages* (Cambridge, 2014).

individual texts and references as evidence of much more widespread fears and anxieties concerning the imminence of the End of the World. They interpret the silence of the sources about apocalyptic fears as a deliberate suppression by the ecclesiastical hierarchy of evidence of popular movements.[8] Foremost amongst these is Richard Landes who has argued for apocalyptic fears as a very significant spur to widespread public action in France, provoking, for example, the Peace of God movement.[9] Then there are the Cautious Sceptics who stress that anticipation of the Last Judgement was a commonplace in early medieval spirituality and who stress the tenuous nature of links between expressions of apocalypticism and fears concerning the year 1000.[10]

This debate highlights methodological issues – how far can we generalise from a minority of sources? Is it possible to detach specifically millennial anxieties from long-established traditions of eschatology? To what extent is apocalyptic imagery a rhetorical strategy harnessed for ideological purposes?[11] Debates over what has been called 'the apocalyptic year 1000' have stimulated a number of closely contextualised and nuanced studies such as that by Levi Roach on Otto III's deployment of apocalyptic imagery or that of Simon MacLean who has argued that the influential Frankish Letter on the Antichrist written by the monk Adso in the mid-tenth century was in part a rhetorical manifesto for monastic reform.[12]

Anglo-Saxonists have been mostly reluctant to see their forefathers as in the grip of millennial anxiety. While Malcolm Godden has described the 'imminence of the end of the world' as a 'framing concept... for Anglo-Saxon writers', he has argued that for both Ælfric and Wulfstan concerns about the End of the World wan in the course of their careers and became more muted.[13] Simon Keynes has argued that Viking invasion was

---

[8] See, for example, the collection of essays, *The Apocalyptic Year 1000: Religious Expectations and Social Change 950–1050*, ed. Richard Landes, Andrew Gow and David C. Van Meter (Oxford, 2003).

[9] Richard Landes, *Relics, Apocalypse, and the Deceits of History: Ademar of Chabannes, 989–1034* (Cambridge, MA, 1995); *idem*, 'Lest the Millennium be Fulfilled: Apocalyptic Expectations and the Pattern of Western Chronography 100–800 CE', in *The Use and Abuse of Eschatology in the Middle Ages*, ed. W. Verbeke, D. Verhulst and A. Welkenhuysen (Leuven, 1988), 137–211; *idem*, 'The Fear of an Apocalyptic Year 1000: Augustinian Historiography Medieval and Modern', *Speculum*, 75 (2000), 97–145.

[10] See the helpful review article by Simon MacLean, 'Apocalypse and Revolution: Europe around the Year 1000', *Early Medieval Europe*, 15 (2007), 86–106.

[11] *Ibid.*

[12] Levi Roach, 'Otto III and the End of Time', *Transactions of the Royal Historical Society*, sixth series, 23 (2013), 75–102; Simon MacLean, 'Reform, Queenship and the End of the World in Tenth-Century France: Adso's "Letter on the Origin and Time of the Antichrist Reconsidered"', *Revue belge de philologie et d'histoire*, 86 (2008), 645–75.

[13] Malcolm Godden, 'Apocalypse and Invasion in Late Anglo-Saxon England', in *From Anglo-Saxon to Early Middle English, Studies Presented to E. G. Stanley*, ed. Malcom Godden,

a greater preoccupation of the English than anticipation of the End.[14] By taking a fresh look at the homiletic texts and bringing some new evidence from the charters of King Æthelred, this article will argue that apocalyptic anxieties did intensify around the year 1000 and were a significant factor in courtly debate and in royal piety and policy.[15]

In a study of modern apocalyptic discourse, Stephen O'Leary argues that it serves to explain the problem of evil by placing it within a temporal framework.[16] In the early Middle Ages, the study of time was closely related to the debate over the End of the World as the work of Bede, for example, illustrates.[17] However, early medieval religious thinkers like Bede or Wulfstan were perhaps less concerned with the question of evil, but rather with that of sin – the unfailing propensity of man to disobey God and to be blind to the need to forgo worldly pleasures to win eternal joy. The prominence of Endtime anxiety in early medieval thinking derives from what Peter Brown has described as the 'peccatisation of the world' – the 'definitive reduction of all experience, of history, politics, and the social order quite as much as the destiny of individual souls, to two universal explanatory principles, sin and repentance'.[18] The suffusion of everyday living and of political action by a sense of the sinfulness of human life and thought, and of the implacable judgement of Christ at the end of time necessitated a profound urgency in reminding the Christian faithful of the need to repent and make amends before it was too late. The study of early medieval apocalypticism must be related to that of eschatology. The salvation of the individual sinner at death was inextricably bound up with their salvation or damnation at the Last Judgement. There could be no confession and repentance after death – those who died with major sins, such as murder or adultery, unconfessed would be damned at Doomsday. Lesser sins could be forgiven and washed away before the Final Assize by purgation and posthumous intercession. Since the time of our deaths is

Douglas Gray and Terry Hoad (Oxford, 1994), 130–62; and *idem*, 'The Millennium, Time, and History for the Anglo-Saxons', in *The Apocalyptic Year 1000*, ed. Landes, Gow and Van Meter, 155–80, quotation at 155.

[14] Simon Keynes, 'Apocalypse Then: England AD 1000', in *Europe around the Year 1000*, ed. Przemysław Urbańczyk (Warsaw, 2001), 247–70, esp. 267.

[15] But see now also Levi Roach, 'Apocalypse and Atonement in the Politics of Aethelredian England', *English Studies*, 95 (2014), 733–57, which appeared after the completion of this lecture.

[16] Stephen O'Leary, *Arguing the Apocalypse: A Theory of Millennial Rhetoric* (Oxford, 1998).

[17] Peter Darby, *Bede and the End of Time* (Farnham and Burlington, 2012).

[18] Peter Brown, 'The Decline of the Empire of God: Amnesty, Penace and the Afterlife from Late Antiquity to the Middle Ages', in *Last Things: Death and the Apocalypse in the Middle Ages*, ed. Caroline Walker Bynum and Paul Freedman (Philadelphia, 2000), 41–59, at 58; and *idem*, 'Vers la naissance du purgatoire: amnistie et pénitence dans le christianisme occidentale de l'antiquité tardive au Haut Moyen Âge', *Annales ESC*, 52.6 (1997), 1247–61.

unknown, Christians should live in a permanent state of readiness, both for death and for Judgement.[19]

The responses to the year 1000 in England were varied and complex. There was no one clear message, even for Wulfstan, who is the most explicit and outspoken in his preaching. England possessed a rich eschatological tradition in which Anglo-Saxon thinking about the imminence of the End was rooted.[20] Tensions existed between the need for urgency and for the assertion of unknowability, resulting from the orthodox hostility to predictions of the time of the End, and the necessity of impressing upon the faithful the vital importance of readiness for their own individual and collective end. The different methods of reading the Bible, literal in understanding the predicted portents of the Last Days as genuine future events and allegorical in seeking to understand the thousand years as a metaphor for perfection, created dissonances. It was understood that all those living after the incarnation of Christ were living in the sixth and last age, but there was no common understanding about how to interpret the signs of the End or whether they would take place in rapid succession or unfold over a long period. Moreover, individual understanding of the Last Days changed over time and in response to external circumstances, not just to natural disasters and to political and military catastrophes but also to texts and their interpretations. What did it mean to be living in the last age? Deliberations about the Last Judgement and the End of the World operated in different registers and in different contexts, with no single agreed meaning. But these different discourses intersect and were produced in dialogue with one another.

The passing of the millennial year was noted in England as a significant moment not just by Archbishop Wulfstan whose words opened this article but also by his learned Benedictine colleague, Byrhtferth, a monk at Ramsey who, writing a tract on time and the computus around the year 1011, commented on the prediction that Satan would be loosed after a thousand years, writing – 'The thousandth year has now been completed, according to the calculations of the human race, but remains to be determined in the presence of the Saviour. The number 1,000 is perfect: and he knows when it will come to completion, who created all

---

[19] For an excellent wide-ranging discussion, see Helen Foxhall Forbes, *Heaven and Earth in Anglo-Saxon England* (Farnham, 2013), 129–328.

[20] Milton McC. Gatch, 'Eschatology in the Anonymous Old English Homilies', *Traditio*, 21 (1965), 117–65; *idem, Preaching and Theology in Anglo-Saxon England: Ælfric and Wulfstan* (Toronto, 1977); Kathleen Greenfield, 'Changing Emphases in English Vernacular Homiletic Literature 990–1225', *Journal of Medieval History*, 7 (1981), 283–97; W. Prideaux-Collins, '"Satan's Bonds Are Extremely Loose": Apocalyptic Expectation in Anglo-Saxon England during the Millennial Era', in *The Apocalyptic Year 1000*, ed. Landes, Gow and Van Meter, 289–310.

things according to his command.'[21] Earlier, an anonymous Old English homilist writing in 971, in a discussion of Christ's teaching that the time of the End was unknown, warned that

> We learn that the time is so secret that no man in this world be he ever so holy... has ever known when our Lord shall decree this world's end on Doomsday... Nevertheless we know that it is not far off, because all the signs and foretokens that our Lord previously said would come before Doomsday, are all gone by, except one alone, that is, the accursed stranger, Antichrist, who, as yet, has not come hither upon earth. Yet the time is not far distant when that shall also come to pass; because this earth must of necessity come to an end in this age which is now present, for [five of the ages of the world] have come to pass in this age; wherefore this world must come to an end, and of this the greatest portion [already] has elapsed, even nine hundred and seventy-one years, in this (very) year. These [ages] were not alike long, but in these were three thousand years, in some less, in others more.[22]

These three authors all display not only an understanding that the millennium could be regarded as a possible mile post on the road to Armageddon but also a strong affirmation of the unknowability of the date of the End. These are not insignificant voices – Wulfstan and Byrhtferth were prominent figures and intellectuals – and their testimony shows that amongst the uppermost echelons of Anglo-Saxon society the significance of the millennium and its associated problems were well known.

Around the year 1000, England was in a crisis state. For over a decade, it had been under attack from Viking raids, which in the course of the first twenty years of the first millennium escalated to become campaigns

---

[21] *Byrhtferth's Enchiridion*, ed. Peter S. Baker and Michael Lapidge, Early English Text Society (EETS), SS 15 (Oxford, 1995), 236–7: 'Iam millenarius peractus numerus secundum numerum humani generis sed in presentia saluatoris est ipsum determinare. Millenarius perfectus est, cuius perfectionem ille nouit, qui cuncta suo nutu potenter creauit.'

[22] *The Blickling Homilies*, ed. R. Morris, EETS, OS 58, 63 and 73 (1874, 1876 and 1880, reprinted in 1 vol., 1967), XI, 116–19: 'we leorniaþ þæt seo tid sie toþæs digol þæt nære næfre nænig toþæs halig mon on þissum middangearde, ne furþum nænig on heofenum þe þæt æfre wiste, hwonne he ure Drihten þisse worlde ende gesettan wolde on domes dæge, buton him Drihtne anum; we witon þonne hweþre þæt hit nis no feor to þon; forþon þe ealle þa tacno & þa forebeacno þas þe her ure Drihten ær toweard sægde þæt ær domes dæge geweorþan sceoldan, ealle þa syndon agangen, buton þæm anum þæt se awerigda cuma Antecrist nuget hider on middangeard ne com. Nis þæt ðonne feor toþon þæt þæt eac geweorþan sceal; forþon þes middangeard nede on ðas eldo endian sceal ðe nu andweard is; forþon fife þara syndon agangen on þisse eldo. Þonne sceal þes middangeard endian & þisse is þonne se mæsta dæl agangen, efne nigon hund wintra & lxxi. on þys geare. Ne wæron þas ealle gelice lange, ac on þyssum wæs þreo þusend wintra, on sumre læsse, on sumere eft mare.' Translation from Morris, with a significant emendation of 117, line 36, of 'ages of the world' for 'fore-tokens'; see Charles D. Wright, 'The Apocalypse of Thomas: Some New Latin Texts and their Significance for the Old English Versions', in *Apocryphal Texts and Traditions in Anglo-Saxon England*, ed. Kathryn Powell and Donald Scragg (Cambridge, 2003), 27–83, at 48 n. 100; and see also Godden, 'The Millennium', 157. On the tradition of the six ages in Anglo-Saxon England, see Hildegard L. C. Tristram, *Sex aetates mundi. Die Weltzeitalter be den Angelsachsen und den Iren Untersuchungen und Texte*, Anglistische Forschungen 165 (Heidelberg, 1985).

of conquest under the Danish ruler Swein Forkbeard and his son, Cnut. In 1014, Æthelred was forced to flee and his restoration to the throne was only obtained when Swein died. Even then, it was shortlived as Æthelred himself died in 1016 and Swein's son, Cnut, was eventually able to take the throne.[23]

External Viking attack caused internal controversy and dissent. Following the shocking defeat of the Battle of Maldon in 991, when the ealdorman Byrhtnoth was killed, Æthelred was moved to a new penitential style of kingship.[24] At a council of Winchester held at Pentecost 993, the king and his leading men sought the cause of the divine wrath manifest in the misfortunes of the English. Our knowledge of this meeting derives from a charter in favour of Abingdon Abbey which describes how the king examined his conscience and found a cause for their troubles in his sale of the abbacy of the monastery, violating the community's right to free election.[25] The king made recompense for this sin, and in subsequent years made a series of restitutions of property to a number of churches which had suffered alienations permitted by Æthelred in the years before 993.

However, the king's attempts to restore divine favour to his kingdom by acts of conspicuous piety failed to prevent the relentless increase in Viking attacks.[26] From 996, the Anglo-Saxon Chronicle records annual raiding until 1005, when a great famine forced the Vikings to move to the continent. The Vikings became an unstoppable menace and the return of their forces in 1006 and then in 1009–12 left many of the English in despair. The famine of 1005 and the increased Viking attacks provoked more soul-searching on the part of the English led by Archbishop Wulfstan. In 1007–8, new measures were taken – the payment of tribute to the invaders, the building of a new fleet and greater provision of military equipment. These secular measures were matched by a spiritual campaign. At Pentecost 1008, the king held a council at Enham, Hampshire, which enacted a

[23] On Æthelred's reign, see Simon Keynes, *The Diplomas of Æthelred the Unready 978–1016: A Study in their Use as Historical Evidence* (Cambridge, 1980), esp. 154–231; Ann Williams, *Æthelred the Unready: The Ill-Counselled King* (2003); Ryan Lavelle, *AEthelred II King of the English 978–1016* (Stroud, 2004).

[24] Catherine Cubitt, 'The Politics of Remorse: Penance and Royal Piety', *Historical Research*, 85 (2012), 179–92; Levi Roach, 'Public Rites and Public Wrongs: Ritual Aspects of Diplomas in Tenth- and Eleventh-Century England', *Early Medieval Europe*, 19 (2011), 182–203.

[25] P. H. Sawyer, *Anglo-Saxon Charters: An Annotated List and Bibliography* (Royal Historical Society, 1968), no. 876 (hereafter S); *Charters of Abingdon Abbey*, ed. S. E. Kelly, Anglo-Saxon Charters VII (2 vols., Oxford, 2000), II, 477–83, no. 124, and see the discussion by Kelly at cxi–cxv; and Keynes, *Diplomas*, 98–101 and 176–86.

[26] Keynes, *Diplomas*, 209–28; Williams, *Æthelred*, 69–150; Simon Keynes, 'An Abbot, an Archbishop, and the Viking Raids of 1006–7 and 1009–12', *Anglo-Saxon England*, 36 (2007), 151–220.

comprehensive set of laws for the regulation of the Christian life.[27] These rulings were drafted by Archbishop Wulfstan whose hand also lay behind the decrees of the following year, 1009, which instituted a national penance of three days of fasting, almsgiving, expiatory processions and masses, and of confession.[28]

Æthelred's kingship illustrates the way that, by the tenth century, royal actions and authority could be shaped by expectations of royal piety and of the proper conduct for a Christian king.[29] The successes of an invading army, many of whom were pagans, were seen as a judgement upon the sins of the English by God.[30] The success of a kingdom depended on the right rule of its king and monarchs could be held to account. But – as the national penance of 1009 demonstrates – Viking conquest prompted wider introspection and many, including Wulfstan and the homilist Ælfric of Eynsham, pointed to the sins of the people as a whole. Both viewed the Viking raids as a sign of God's anger at the wickedness of the English.

It is this intersection between the tribulations of the reign of Æthelred and the advent of the millennium which makes England so interesting a place in which to explore the currency of ideas about the End of the World. The sources do not make precise predictions of the time of the Last Judgement but evince a heightened sense of its imminence which influences their responses to the contemporary crisis. Biblical, exegetical and other texts such as Adso's tract on the Antichrist offered a rich reservoir of ideas and images concerning the Last Days which lent themselves to adaptation and manipulation in response to the needs of the time and their user's perspectives and anxieties.

This article will now explore ideas about the Last Judgement and End of the World in four different sources – the anonymous vernacular homilies of the tenth and eleventh centuries, in charters issued by King Æthelred the Unready and in the preaching of Ælfric of Eynsham and of Wulfstan of York. These four sets of sources illustrate the diversity of eschatological traditions within England. It will emphasise the dialogue between these different discourses and argue for a living set of interactions taking place around the royal court.

---

[27] The Enham code is transmitted in three different vernacular texts, V and VI Æthelred and a Latin version, also designated VI Æthelred. All versions were printed by Felix Liebermann, *Die Gesetze der Angelsachsen* (3 vols., reprinted 1960), I, 236–59, and one text of V Æthelred and the Latin VI Æthelred by Dorothy Whitelock, in *Councils and Synods with Other Documents relating to the English Church I A. D. 871–1204*, ed. D. Whitelock, M. Brett and C. N. L. Brooke (2 vols., Oxford, 1981), I, 344–73, See below n. 93 for discussion.

[28] Printed in Liebermann, *Die Gesetze*, 260–2; and *Councils*, ed. Whitelock, Brett and Brooke, I, 373–82.

[29] Pauline Stafford, 'Political Ideas in Late Tenth-Century England: Charters as Evidence', in *Law, Laity and Solidarities: Essays in Honour of Susan Reynolds*, ed. Pauline Stafford, Janet L. Nelson and Jane Martindale (Manchester, 2001), 68–82.

[30] Keynes, 'An Abbot'.

Both Ælfric and Wulfstan are best known for their composition of vernacular sermons. Ælfric never held high office in the English church but penned his three great series of homilies from *c.* 990 to 998 while he was a monk at Cerne Abbas in Dorset. Later, in 1005, he became abbot of the monastery of Eynsham, Oxfordshire. He was a highly influential figure, dedicating his homilies to Archbishop Sigeric of Canterbury, corresponding with Archbishop Wulfstan, and enjoying the patronage of two of the most powerful nobles of the day, the ealdorman Æthelweard and his son Æthelmaer.[31]

While Ælfric was perhaps a backroom boy, politically influential behind the scenes, Archbishop Wulfstan of York was a major public and political figure. Promoted to the see of London in 996, he was archbishop of York until his death in 1023, holding also the bishopric of Worcester until 1016.[32] While details of his training and background are opaque, I have argued recently that it is most likely that he was a Benedictine monk, trained at Peterborough.[33] His life is best known through the survival of nearly fifty sermons authored by him, and by the lawcodes and other writings attributed to him on stylistic grounds. These evidence the influential role he played at court as a councillor of the king, drafting lawcodes for both Æthelred and for Cnut.

However, first the tradition of eschatological preaching found in the anonymous homilies needs to be discussed because this provides the backdrop to the discourses found in Æthelred's charters and to the sermons of Ælfric and Wulfstan, and gives an spiritual context in which to locate them.[34]

The eschatological tradition in Old English preaching before Ælfric and Wulfstan

The two oldest collections of vernacular sermons, the Vercelli Book and the Blickling Homilies, can both be dated by their manuscripts

---

[31] For Ælfric's biography and writings, see *A Companion to Ælfric*, ed. Hugh Magennis and Mary Swan (Brill, 2009), especially Joyce Hill, 'Ælfric: His Life and Works'; and Cubitt, 'Ælfric's Lay Patrons', 35–65 and 165–92.

[32] Dorothy Whitelock, 'Archbishop Wulfstan, Homilist and Statesman', *Transactions of the Royal Historical Society*, fourth series, 24 (1942), 42–60; Joyce Tally Lionarons, *The Homiletic Writings of Archbishop Wulfstan* (Woodbridge, 2010); and the essays edited by Matthew Townend, *Wulfstan Archbishop of York* (Turnhout, 2004), especially Patrick Wormald, 'Archbishop Wulfstan: Eleventh-Century State-Builder', 9–27.

[33] Catherine Cubitt, 'Personal Names, Identity and Family in Benedictine Reform England', in *Verwandschaft, Name und Soziale Ordnung (300–1000)*, ed. Steffen Patzold and Karl Ubl (Berlin, 2014), 223–42, at 230–7; and see Wormald, 'Archbishop Wulfstan', 12–13; and Joyce Hill, 'Archbishop Wulfstan: Reformer?', in *Wulfstan*, ed. Townend, 309–24, at 311–12.

[34] See the valuable survey by Gatch, 'Eschatology', 117–65.

to the late tenth century, but the homilies within them were collected from different sources and must have circulated independently before their transmission in these manuscripts.[35] These homilies are anonymous compositions, usually translations or vernacular adaptations of Latin texts and to some extent characterised by their reliance upon apocryphal and Irish writings.[36] They can be contrasted with the works of Ælfric and Wulfstan who both consciously eschewed many of these sources and rely instead upon the Fathers, especially the works of Augustine, Jerome, Gregory the Great and Bede, often mediated through Carolingian sermon collections.[37] However, these new and more polished sermons by Ælfric and Wulfstan did not displace the anonymous traditions which continued to circulate into the eleventh century and beyond.

The sermons in the Blickling Homilies and Vercelli Book are exhortatory and moralising.[38] A significant number dwell upon the terrible Day of Judgement as a stirring prompt to penance and conversion from sin. The five out of the twenty-three sermons in the Vercelli Book, for example,

---

[35] *Blickling Homilies*, ed. Morris; Princeton, Princeton University Library, W. H. Scheide Collection, MS 71. See also the edition of Richard J. Kelly, *The Blickling Homilies: Edition and Translation* (2003); and the review by Milton McC. Gatch in *Church History*, 73.4 (2004), 847–9. Neil Ker, *Catalogue of Manuscripts containing Anglo-Saxon* (Oxford, 1957), no. 382; Donald Scragg, 'The Homilies of the Blickling Manuscript', in *Learning and Literature in Anglo-Saxon England*, ed. Michael Lapidge and Helmut Gneuss (Cambridge, 1985), 299–316; Vercelli Book – Vercelli, Bibliotheca Capitolare, MS CXVII, edited by D. G. Scragg, *The Vercelli Homilies and Related Texts*, EETS OS 300 (Oxford, 1992), translations available in *The Vercelli Book Homilies: Translations from the Anglo-Saxon*, ed. Lewis E. Nicholson (Lanham, 1991); Ker, *Catalogue*, no. 394. For a recent account of the Vercelli homilies, see Samantha Zacher, *Preaching to the Converted. The Style and Rhetoric of the Vercelli Book Homilies* (Toronto, 2009).

[36] See, for example, on the Vercelli Homilies, Charles D. Wright, *The Irish Tradition in Old English Literature* (Cambridge, 1993).

[37] Charles Wright, 'Old English Homilies and Latin Sources', in *The Old English Homily: Precedent, Practice, and Appropriation*, ed. Aaron J. Kleist (Turnhout, 2007), 15–66. For further nuancing, see Zacher, *Preaching*, 46–51; and Joyce Hill, 'Reform and Resistance: Preaching Styles in Late Anglo-Saxon England', in *De l'homelie au sermon: histoire de la predication medievale, Actes du Colloque internationale de Louvain-la-Neuve*, ed. Jacqueline Hamesse and Xavier Hermand (Louvain-le-Neuve, 1993), 15–46. Ælfric did draw upon apocryphal accounts of the Apostles, but retained his critical sense, see Aideen O'Leary, 'An Orthodox Old English Homiliary?', *Neuphilologische Mitteilungen*, 100 (1999), 15–26; Frederick M. Biggs, 'Ælfric's Andrew and the Apocrypha', *Journal of the English Germanic Philology*, 104 (2005), 472–94; and see Scott De Gregorio, '*Þegenlic* or *Flæsclic*: The Old English Prose Legends of St Andrew', *Journal of the English Germanic Philology*, 103 (2003), 449–64, and 'Ælfric, *Gedwyld* and Vernacular Hagiography: Sanctity and Spirituality in the Old English Lives of SS Peter and Paul', in *Ælfric's Lives of Canonised Popes*, ed. Donald Scragg (Western Michigan, 2001), 75–98. A very valuable close study of the aims of one homilist can be found in Clare Lees, 'The Blickling Palm Sunday Homily and its Revised Version', *Leeds Studies in English*, 19 (1998), 1–23.

[38] See, for example, the discussion of Marcia A. Dalbey, 'Hortatory Tone in the Blickling Homilies. Two Adaptations of Caesarius', *Neuphilologische Mitteilungen*, 70 (1969), 641–58; Gatch, 'Eschatology', 134–6.

describe the Day of Judgement or dwell upon the events presaging the End of the World.[39] Fear of Judgement Day provides a menacing motivation for repentance and Christian reform in this life. The homilies frequently remind their audience that at the final reckoning, men and women will present themselves to the great Judge, shorn of their earthly wealth and prestige and dependent for their fate only upon their good or evil deeds. While the role of intercession for the dead is acknowledged and encouraged, the audience is admonished that this will be ineffective unless the sinner has repented and striven to lead a good life. But the sinner will face Judgement alone – the support of earthly wealth and of friends and family will avail him or her nothing at Doomsday.[40] The horror of the body's decay on death is presented as a constant reminder to men of the pressing need to repent.[41] The aging and decay of the body announces the end of this life and the imminence of Doomsday.[42] The things of the world are transient as the earth too decays and hastens to its end.

A number of sermons describe the final days and Last Judgement. One sermon in the Blickling Homilies, which immediately precedes the homily composed in 971 cited earlier, announces the approaching End of the World and that the signs predicted in the Gospels have taken place, giving an idiosyncratic list of signs – 'monstrous plagues and strange deaths', terrible wars prompted by evil, 'various diseases in many places of the world' and a flourishing of evil and a cooling of love towards God.[43] But the homilist is less concerned to identify the signs of the End with present disasters than to use them as a springboard for admonitions to lead a virtuous Christian life, to give alms, do good and keep peace. The liturgical season of Easter provided the occasion in the Blickling Homilies for a detailed description of the Last Judgement, prompted by the belief that Christ's second advent would take place at Eastertide. It gives a lovingly long description of the harrowing of hell and of Judgement Day with an elaborate account of the six days leading up to it, adapted from the apocryphal Gospel of Thomas.[44] It closes with a chilling call to repentance in this life:

---

[39] Gatch, 'Eschatology', 128–34, 151–60. See too Greenfield, 'Changing Emphases', esp. at 287–93; Prideaux-Collins, 'Satan's Bonds Are Very Loose'.

[40] Patrizia Lendinara, '"*Frater non redimit, redimit homo...*": A Homiletic Motif and its Variants in Old English', in *Early Medieval English Texts and Interpretations: Studies Presented to Donald G. Scragg*, ed. Elaine Treharne and Susan Rosser (Tempe, AZ, 2002), 67–80.

[41] *Blickling Homilies*, ed. Morris, VIII, 96–104.

[42] *Ibid.*, V, 54–64, at 56.

[43] *Ibid.*, X, 106–9.

[44] On the use of the apocryphal Apocalypse of Thomas, see Max Förster, 'A New Version of the Apocalypse of Thomas in Old English', *Anglia*, 73 (1955), 6–36; Milton McC. Gatch, 'Two Uses of the Apocrypha in Old English Homilies', *Church History*, 33 (1964), 379–91; Mary Swan, 'The Apocalypse of Thomas in Old English', *Leeds Studies in English*, NS 19 (1998), 333–46; Wright, 'The Apocalypse of Thomas'.

Wherefore we must now consider, the while we may and can, our soul's need, lest we lose this opportune time and desire to repent when we are no longer able ... For God himself shall then take no heed of any man's penitence, and no intercession shall avail us there; but he will then be more relentless and remorseless than any wild beast, or than any anger might ever be. And as much as man's might was greater and he was the richer in this world, so much the more then shall the supreme Judge require from him.[45]

Apocryphal texts and traditions were a significant element in Anglo-Saxon eschatology, particularly the *Visio Pauli* and other accounts of the afterlife. [46] One idiosyncratic tradition, probably derived from apocrypha concerning the Virgin Mary, recorded the belief that St Mary, St Peter and the Archangel Michael would successfully intercede for the forgiveness of sinners at Judgement Day itself.[47]

Despite their fondness for such ideas, the anonymous homilies maintain a careful silence over the exact time of the End. But their concern is not to warn the world of the time of its End, but rather to impress upon individual sinners their pressing need for action. This they do with great vitality and dramatic colour which lends these texts real urgency and impact.[48] Their teaching was a powerful force in Anglo-Saxon religious life in the late tenth and eleventh centuries as the wide manuscript circulation of such homilies attests.

King Æthelred the Unready and the Day of Judgement

The discourse of the anonymous Old English homilies and the learned Latin of Anglo-Saxon charter diplomatic are usually confined to different and separate scholarly boxes, with the homilies the preserve of literary specialists and the charters reserved for hard-core historians.[49] However,

---

[45] *Blickling Homilies*, ed. Morris, VII, 94–5: 'forþon we sceolon nu geþencean, þa hwile þe we magan & motan, ure saula þearfe, the læs we foryldon þas alyfdon tid, & þonne willon þone we ne magon. Uton beon eaþmode & mildheorte & ælmesgeorne, facen & leasunga & æfæste frin urum heortum adoon & afyrran, & beon rihtwise on urum mode wið oþre men; forþon þe God sylfa þonne ne gymeþ nænges mannes hreowe; ne þær nænige þingunga ne beoþ; ac biþ þonne reþra [&] þearlwisra þonne ænig wilde deor, oþþe æfre ænig mod gewurde. & swa myccle swa þæs mannes miht beo mare, & he biþ weligra on þisse worlde, swa him þonne se uplica Dema mare tosecþ'.

[46] Gatch, 'Eschatology', 127–8; Foxhall Forbes, *Heaven and Earth*, 116–18; and see, for example, the collection of texts in Oxford, Bodleian Library, Junius 85 + 86, Gneuss, no. 642, discussed by Jonathan Wilcox, 'The Use of Ælfric's Homilies: MSS Oxford Bodleian Library, Junius 85 and 86 in the Field', in *A Companion to Ælfric*, ed. Magennis and Swan, 345–68.

[47] *The Vercelli Homilies*, ed. Scragg, 259–60; see *Ælfric's Catholic Homilies: Introduction, Commentary and Glossary*, ed. Malcolm Godden, EETS SS 18 (Oxford, 2000), 660; and Mary Clayton, 'Delivering the Damned: A Motif in Old English Homiletic Prose', *Medium Aevum*, 55 (1986), 92–101.

[48] See the analyses of Dalbey, 'Hortatory Tone in the Blickling Homilies'; Zacher, *Preaching*.

[49] This separation is beginning to break down; see, for example, B. Snooks, *The Anglo-Saxon Chancery* (Woodbridge, 2015); Rolf Bremmer, 'The Final Countdown: Apocalyptic

the diplomatic formulae are suffused by eschatological motifs and ideas common to the anonymous homilies, and belonging to the same religious thought world. The proems in Anglo-Saxon charters are very often couched as a religious discourse, providing a motivation for the grant. Their sentiments often draw upon the same themes – the transience of earthly life, happiness and wealth and the need to exchange worldly riches for heavenly treasures and the decrepitude and final decay of the world.[50] In a charter of 994, for example, drafted by Archbishop Sigeric of Canterbury, the king is made to allude to his meditations on the transient earthly things and the eternal endurance of the spiritual. This follows a lengthy and elaboration preamble on the history of creation and of the Fall, which refers also to Christ's coming into the world after 5,000 years.[51]

The religiosity of Anglo-Saxon charter diplomatic seems often to fit ill with the overtly secular nature of the transactions themselves, such as sales of land or apparently entirely secular grants to the laity. But, after 993, the diplomatic of a number of Æthelred's charters becomes more discursive and at times their proems have a clear thematic unity with the grant itself. These charters issue from the royal chancery and can be linked, as Pauline Stafford has suggested, with royal policy.[52] Levi Roach has made a strong case too for a performative context for their issuance.[53]

Some charters place introspective sentiments in the mouth of the king, describing his motivation for the grant. These often include a desire for the expiation of the king's sins sometimes linked to a fear of divine judgement and to the need for the intercession of the saints. These charters are manifestations of the penitential style of Æthelred's kingship and these topoi are found in his charters restoring ecclesiastical lands. In a charter, returning property to Old Minster, Winchester, dated to 997, the king is made to say that his donation is motivated by the fear of the heavenly judge and of his provocation of the anger of Saints Peter and Paul, the patrons of

---

Expectations in Anglo-Saxon Charters', in *Time and Eternity: the Medieval Discourse*, ed. Gerhard Jaritz and Gerson Moreno-Riaño (Turnhout, 2003), 501–14; and D. Woodman, 'Æthelstan A and the Rhetoric of Rule', *Anglo-Saxon England*, 42 (2013), 217–48.

[50] The examples are numerous and predate the reign of Æthelred. See, for example, on the aging of the world and the approaching End, S 909 and S 912 dated to 1004 and 1005; on the uncertainty of leaving earthly inheritance to heirs, e.g. S 846, S 848 and S 904; on the admonitions of the wise or the Fathers on the need to gain heavenly riches, S 834, S 835. For the trope of the deterioration of the world at the end of time in literary texts, J. E. Cross, 'Aspects of Microcosm and Macrocosm in Old English Literature', in *Studies in Old English Literature in Honor of Arthur G. Brodeur*, ed. S. Greenfield (Eugene, 1963), 1–22; and see Godden, 'The Millennium', 156.

[51] S 880; J. M. Kemble, *Codex Diplomaticus Aevi Saxonici* (6 vols., 1839–48), no. 686. On the drafting of this charter, see Keynes, *Diplomas*, 110–11 and 124; and Catherine Cubitt, 'The Tenth-Century Benedictine Reform in England', *Early Medieval Europe*, 6.1 (1997), 92.

[52] Stafford, 'Political Ideas in Late Tenth-Century England'.

[53] Roach, 'Public Rites and Private Wrongs'.

the cathedral whose land had been despoiled with the connivance of the king. The charter proem cites a passage from Mark 13:19, concerning the tribulations which will precede the coming of the Kingdom.[54] Æthelred's need to appease the patron saint of the church which he had allowed to be robbed and to gain his suffrage is recorded again as a motive in a charter of the following year, 998, a restoration to Rochester Cathedral. Here, the king desires to win the favour of St Andrew who prayed for those who crucified him.[55]

Both these donations of 997 and 998 were made in the season of Easter, either just after the feast or at Easter itself. It is an interesting, if speculative, exercise to consider their penitential stance and expressed fears of judgement in the light of the sermon for Easter Day contained in the Blickling Homilies, with its pressing exhortations for Christians to consider the fates of their souls at the Final Assize and not to lose the opportunity to make reparations for their sins before it is too late. One might recall the closing words of the homily with their admonition to the rich and powerful that more is expected of them at the Last Judgement than of lesser men.[56] This may be conjectural but there is a clear link between the Rochester charter and the apocryphal texts so favoured by the anonymous homilists in the appeal which Æthelred is made to make to St Andrew referring to the saint's merciful stance at his crucifixion, which must be an allusion to an apocryphal passion of the saint.[57] It is worth noting that in allowing Old Minster, Winchester, and the Abbey of Abingdon to suffer at the hands of the laity, Æthelred might be thought to have offended against both St Peter and St Mary whom, as we have seen, were credited with a special role in saving sinners at Doomsday.

Explicit references to the Last Days are found sporadically, in a couple of charters in the late 990s, but what is more striking is the appearance of a distinctive set of diplomatic formulae around the year 1000 which culminates either in invocations of the Last Days or of the coming of the heavenly kingdom, and which coincides with donations made expressly

[54] S 891.

[55] S 893; *Charters of Rochester*, ed. A. Campbell, Anglo-Saxon Charters I (1973), no. 32, 42–4, at 43: 'credens me et gratiam inunenire in conspectu apostoli . qui in populo suo mitissimus apparuit . et pro crucifigentibus se exorauit'. And see also below n. 57.

[56] *Blickling Homilies*, ed. Morris, VII, 94–6.

[57] This allusion is obscure and I have not been able to trace this reference to Andrew's final intercession in the published editions. However, it may echo Christ's own intercession on the cross since Andrew's death echoes that of Christ. I hope to return to this problem in a later publication. See the passions published by in *Acta Apostolorum Apocrypha*, ed. R. A. Lipsius and M. Bonnet (3 vols., 1891–1903), II. 1, 1–37. For the transmission of the apocryphal passions to England, see Frederick M. Biggs, *The Apocrypha: Sources of Anglo-Saxon Culture* (Kalamazoo, 2007), 38–9 and 42; and Biggs, 'Ælfric's Andrew'.

for the salvation of Æthelred's family. [58] This is used in three grants of 1001, 1002 and 1004. Its last outing in 1004 took the form of the foundation charter for Burton Abbey, a Benedictine house. The grandiloquence and topicality of this style was probably why it was used for this solemn transaction.[59] However, the two donations of 1001 and 1002 are the most important in this discussion. These are grants to royal nunneries and Æthelred manifests in them a concern for the spiritual salvation of his family, a motivation also found in another charter from around the year 1000 concerning his father Edgar's bequests, but one which does not use this distinctive diplomatic.

The first of these donations (S 899) is a grant for Shaftesbury Abbey, a nunnery closely connected to the royal dynasty, to which the body of Edward the Martyr, Æthelred's murdered brother, had just been translated.[60] Æthelred made the gift of the church and estates at Bradford-on-Avon as a refuge against Viking attacks for the nuns and for the relics of his brother. This, the community's largest estate recorded in Doomsday Book, represented a very significant gift.[61] The proem culminates with the prediction of the signs of the End of the World from Luke 21:31–3 and the Gospel exhortation to give alms by selling one's goods. According to the charter, Æthelred's grant was prompted by frequent reminders on the part of his counsellors of these biblical exhortations. The grant is made not only for the expiation of his sins but also for those of his lineage, both past and future.[62]

The second donation drafted in this way was made in 1002 to another royal nunnery, Wherwell in Hampshire, a foundation patronised by Æthelred's mother, Ælfthryth.[63] Here, the proem culminates in John the Baptist's exhortation, 'Repent for the Kingdom of Heaven is at hand', followed by the biblical commandments to honour one's father and

---

[58] S 895; *Charters of Sherborne*, ed. M. A. O'Donovan, Anglo-Saxon Charters III (Oxford, 1988), no. 11, 39–44; and see Simon Keynes, 'King Æthelred's Charter for Sherborne Abbey, 998', and also his 'Wulfsige, Monk of Glastonbury, Abbot of Westminster (c. 990–3), and Bishop of Sherborne (c. 993–1002)', both in *St Wulfsige and Sherborne Essays to Celebrate the Millennium of the Benedictine Abbey 998–1998*, ed. Katherine Barker, David A. Hinton and Alan Hunt (Oxford, 2005), 10–14 and 53–94.

[59] *Charters of Burton Abbey*, ed. P. H. Sawyer, Anglo-Saxon Charters II (1979), no. 28, 48–53. On Benedictine foundation charters, see also Simon Keynes, 'King Æthelred's charter for Eynsham (1005)', in *Early Medieval Studies in Memory of Patrick Wormald*, ed. Stephen Baxter, Catherine Karkov, Janet L. Nelson and David Pelteret (Farnham, 2009), 451–73, esp. 456–9.

[60] *Charters of Shaftesbury Abbey*, ed. S. E. Kelly, Anglo-Saxon Charters V (Oxford, 1996), no. 29, 114–22. On Æthelred and the cult of Edward the Martyr, see Simon Keynes, 'The Cult of King Edward the Martyr during the Reign of Æthelred the Unready', in *Gender and Historiography Studies in the Earlier Middle Ages in Honour of Pauline Stafford*, ed. Janet L. Nelson, Susan Reynolds and Susan M. Johns (2012), 115–26.

[61] See Kelly's notes, *Charters of Shaftesbury*, 120–1.

[62] *Ibid.*, 115–16.

[63] S 904; Kemble, *Codex*, no. 707.

mother. These penitential urgings have a direct connection with the grant itself which was probably made shortly after the death of the dowager queen. Æthelred not only makes a grant of privileges to the community, but confirms their possession of 70 hides of land at Wherwell, and added land elsewhere at Æthelingadene in Sussex. These lands had been held by the queen and it would appear that Wherwell sought Æthelred's donation in order to confirm its possession of the lands and to avoid their alienation to the new queen.[64] Æthelred is said to make the gift prompted by his fear of the Last Judgement and the donation is made for the souls of his parents, Edgar and Ælfthryth. By this grant, the king was not only protecting the community from the possible loss of the property but also his mother from the consequences of failing to secure the lands for the nunnery.

The king's explicit concern for the salvation of his family is also found in another remarkable donation, probably made in 999.[65] This was an act of compensation to Abingdon Abbey for land bequeathed by King Edgar but confiscated by the counsellors of his son, King Edward the Martyr. The property had been reserved for the benefit of the *aethelings*, the heirs to the throne, so must have been enjoyed by Æthelred and his sons. The king is made to explain in the charter that he feared his father's curse for the failure to fulfil his wishes, and Æthelred hopes to win by this grant the intercession of the Virgin Mary, the house's patron, and benefits for the souls of himself, his family and of Edgar.

These three transactions make manifest a notable concern on the part of Æthelred for the salvation of his family. In the Abingdon and Wherwell grants, he takes measures to ensure that property formerly in the hands of his parents was held by the religious communities who claimed it. Through the grant to Shaftesbury, the king sought the prayers of the community for his living, dead and future family, emphasising too the importance of his martyred brother's intercession. The grants to Shaftesbury and Wherwell are said to have been prompted by the urgings of his leading men and by thoughts of the Last Days and of the Final Judgement. Did the preaching of the anonymous homilies concerning the lonely fate of the soul at judgement, alone without the assistance of family and friends, play a part?

Æthelred's penitential restitutions of ecclesiastical land evince both a personal and public response to teaching about the Last Judgement. His gifts were made for the benefit of the souls of himself and his family but this demonstrative piety was a public gesture, articulated before his council and recorded in royal diplomas. Does the use of eschatological references

---

[64] Pauline Stafford, *Queen Emma and Queen Edith: Queenship and Women's Power in Eleventh-Century England* (Oxford, 1997), 139–40, 153.
[65] S 937; *Charters of Abingdon*, ed. Kelly, no. 129, 503–7.

and language in their formal diplomatic reflect intensified anticipation of the Last Days around the millennium? One explanation for these references is to see them as the outworkings of pressure placed upon the king by a group of monastic reform advocates at court, both clerical and lay, who included Aelfric's patrons, Æthelweard and Æthelmaer. The appearance of these references, like that of the restitutions themselves, coincides with the prominence at court of these men from 993 to 1006 and, as we have seen, the charters refer to the urgings of the royal councillors.[66] But this explanation does not exclude the possibility of the exploitation of millennial fears. Indeed, the solemnity of the grants and the very necessity for the transactions themselves would have been increased by its deployment. It was precisely this strategy of invoking the imminence of the Apocalypse to reinforce calls for reform which was used so skillfully only a few years later by Wulfstan of York.

Ælfric and the Last Days

The pressure of living in the Endtime weighed heavily upon Ælfric.[67] In the preface to his very first publication, the first series of Catholic Homilies, probably completed between 991 × 994, Ælfric sets out at some length an account of the Last Days, the Day of Judgement and the coming of the Antichrist. He opens this by setting out why he has taken upon himself the task of composing this set of sermons

> because men have need of good instruction, especially at this time, which is the ending of the world, and there will be many calamities among mankind before the end comes, according to what our Lord in his Gospel said to his disciples, 'Then shall be such tribulations as have never been from the beginning of the world. Many false christs shall come in my name, saying "I am Christ"', and shall work many signs and wonders to deceive mankind . . . Everyone may the more easily understand the future temptation, through God's support, if he is strengthened by book learning, for they shall be preserved by faith to the end.'[68]

---

[66] Keynes, *Diplomas*, 186–93; Cubitt, 'Ælfric's Lay Patrons', 171–84.

[67] See Gatch, *Preaching and Theology*, 12–104; Godden, 'Apocalypse and Invasion', 131–42, and 'The Millennium', 158–67; and Joyce Hill, 'Ælfric and Wulfstan: Two Views of the Millennium', in *Essays on Anglo-Saxon and Related Themes in Memory of Lynne Grundy*, ed. Jane Roberts and Janet Nelson (2000), 231–5. Godden, 'The Millennium', 166–7, argues that Ælfric's apocalyptic urgency diminishes over his writing career.

[68] *Ælfric's Catholic Homilies: The First Series Text*, ed. Peter Clemoes, EETS SS 17 (Oxford, 1997) (hereafter *CH* I), 174–5: 'eac for ðam ðe menn behofiað godre lare swiðost on þisum timan þe is geendung þyssere worulde. 7 beoð fela frecednyssa on mancynne ær ðan þe se ende becume. swa swa ure drihten on his godspelle cwæð on his leorningcnihtum; þonne beoð swilce gedreccednyssa swilce næron næfre ær fram frymþe middangeardes; Manega lease cristas cumað on minum naman cweðende ic eom crist. 7 wyrcað fela tacna 7 wundra to bepæccenne mancynn . . . 7 butan se ælmihtiga god ða dagas gescyrte. eall mennisc forwurde ac for his gecorenum he gescyrte ða dagas; Gehwa mæg þe eaðelicor ða toweardan costnunge acuman ðurh godes fultum. gif he bið þurh boclice lare getrymmed,

Ælfric fears the deceptions and devilish seductions of the final age and seeks to arm the faithful against the wiles of the Antichrist by the provision of sound teaching. His writings show a frequent anxiety about erroneous teachings, which he labelled 'gedwyld', that is 'heresy'.[69] This concern was partly prompted by the anonymous homilies with their reliance upon apocryphal and heterodox texts. Ælfric's recurrent concern for heretical teachings is linked to his understanding of the Endtime and its lessons. Moreover, he possibly shared the belief, evidenced in other reformed Benedictine writings, that the virgin order of monks would join the holy virgins, in the account of Revelation, who judge with Christ at Doomsday.[70] Thus, Ælfric's sense of his own identity was shaped by the looming presence of the Last Days. The economy of salvation was underpinned by the Last Judgement and the place of the monastic order within that economy was interpreted by reference to the Last Judgement.

Ælfric saw himself and his audience as living in the times of tribulation predicted in the Gospels. In one sermon, he noted carefully how many of the predicted signs of the End had occurred, checking them off against the Gospel passage –

Nation shall rise up against Nation – tick
Occurrence of great earthquakes everywhere – tick
Pestilence – tick
Famine – tick

But when Ælfric comes to the portents in the sun, moon and stars, he provides a careful analysis, arguing that lunar and solar eclipses and comets are portents but they are not the harbingers of the End, because they are not the unprecedented and extraordinary occurrences to which Christ referred. These and the turmoil of the sea have not yet happened so the time of the Antichrist has not yet come. His sense of the Last Day is also a long one – the universal earthquakes which he notes have happened are said to have taken place in the reign of the Emperor Tiberius.[71] This rather cool and clear-eyed approach to the signs of the End meshes with his reluctance to identify contemporary tribulations and catastrophes with the Gospel signs of the Last Days. This sermon draws upon the writings

for ðan ðe ða beoð gehealdene þe oð ende on geleafan þurhwuniað'. Translation from *The Homilies of the Anglo-Saxon Church: The First Part containing The Sermones Catholici or Homilies of Aelfric*, ed. and trans. Benjamin Thorpe (2 vols., 1844–6), I, 3–5.

[69] Malcolm Godden, 'Ælfric and the Vernacular Prose Tradition', in *The Old English Homily and its Background*, ed. Paul E. Szarmach (Albany, 1978), 99–117, at 99–102.

[70] Dominique Iogna-Prat, 'Continence et virginité dans la conception clunisienne de l'ordre du monde autour de l'an mil', *Comptes-rendus de l'academie des Inscriptions et Belles Lettres* (1985), 127–46; MacLean, 'Reform, Queenship and the End of the World'.

[71] *CH* I, no. 40, 524–30, at 525–6; and see *Ælfric's Catholic Homilies: Introduction*, ed. Godden, 334–44.

of Gregory the Great and the Carolingian exegete, Haimo of Auxerre, but Ælfric suppresses their statements about how disasters in their own times fulfil the Scriptural prophecy.[72] His approach here is to discourage portent-spotting.[73]

But while Ælfric is reluctant to identify current catastrophes with the signs of the End, he sees the parlous state of society as a symptom of the Endtime. This is a period of great danger because the devil, furious that his time is now short, increases his attacks on mankind. Evils flourish as a presage of the greater evils to come, and society becomes more wicked. In his sermon, the Prayer of Moses, Ælfric identifies contemporary wickedness with the evil behaviour at the End of the World, in ideas and words drawn from the Bible. 'This time is the last time, and the end of the world, and men are made unjust amongst themselves, so that father contends with his own son, and one brother with another, to their own destruction.'[74]

Ælfric's reluctance to seek portents in his own age belongs to his deep sense of the unknowability of the time of the Last Days. His major eschatological sermon, on the Feastday of the Virgins, is partly devoted to the suppression of apocalyptic speculation.[75] He borrows from St Augustine to emphasise that signs of the End may appear to happen, but still Christ does not come.[76] This sermon impresses upon the believer the need for vigilance since death can come at any time. The sinner must repent and correct himself in this life to avoid eternal damnation. Christ's judgement on the Last Day is final and the damned are beyond help. Ælfric digresses explicitly to condemn the idea we have seen expressed in a homily in the Vercelli Book that the Virgin Mary would be able to save sinners at Judgement Day, describing this story as heretical.[77]

---

[72] See the discussion in Godden, 'The Millennium', 158–62, and in his *Ælfric's Catholic Homilies: Introduction*, ed. Goddard, 334–44.

[73] *CH* I, no. 40, 609–12.

[74] *Ælfric's Lives of Saints*, ed. Walter W. Skeat, EETS 76 and 82 (2 vols., 1881–5; repr. 1966), 304–5: 'þes tima is ende-next and ende þyssere worulde . and menn beoð geworhte wolice him betwynan . swa þaet se fæder wind wið his agenne sunu . and broðor wið operne to bealwe him sylfum'.

[75] *Ælfric's Catholic Homilies: The Second Series Text*, ed. Malcolm Godden, EETS SS 5 (Oxford, 1979) (hereafter *CH* II), no. 39: 'The Lord's day will come like a thief in the night. Men often say, Lo, now doomsday comes, because the prophecies are gone by, which were made concerning it. But war shall come upon war, tribulation upon tribulation, earthquake upon earthquake, famine upon famine, nation upon nation, and yet the bridegroom comes not. In like manner the six thousand years from Adam will be ended, and yet the bridegroom will tarry. How can we then know when he will come.' Translation from *Homilies*, ed. Thorpe, II, 569.

[76] *Ælfric's Catholic Homilies: Introduction*, ed. Godden, 654–6, 658.

[77] *CH* II, no. 39, 373: 'Some heretics said that the holy Mary, the mother of Christ, and some other saints, should after the doom, harrow the sinful from the devil', translation from *Homilies*, ed. Thorpe, II, 573. On this, see Godden, 'Ælfric and the Vernacular Prose

This sermon seems to have acted as a vehicle for Ælfric's desire to suppress heterodoxy concerning the Apocalypse. He returned to it in around the year 1005, adding a few lines to the effect that the Antichrist would not come until the Roman Empire had fallen. Here, his meaning must be to point to the continuation of the Empire under the Franks and Ottonians, a view probably derived from Adso.[78]

The imminence of the Last Judgement was as pressing for Ælfric as it was for his colleague Wulfstan, but his response to this pressure was rather different. With his concern for orthodoxy, Ælfric emphasised the unknowability of the time of the End. His concern for teaching on the Last Things did not diminish throughout his career, but manifested itself in renewed teaching in opposition to apocalyptic speculations.[79] And his audience for these admonitions is likely to have included the English religious and secular elite.

Wulfstan and the loosening of Satan's bonds

At the core of Ælfric's homilies lies a pastoral duty towards the individual Christian and his salvation. The preaching of Wulfstan, however, is rather concerned with the condition of society and calls for the spiritual reformation of the English people. It is he who preaches most urgently about the imminence of the Last Days and who clearly identifies the present with the signs preceding the coming of the Antichrist.[80]

Wulfstan composed five sermons in Old English on the Last Days.[81] These have been considered to be some of his earliest compositions and dated to around the year 1000. Dorothy Bethurum even surmised that Wulfstan owed his elevation to the see of York in 1002 to his prowess as a Doomsday preacher.[82] However, Malcolm Godden has recently pointed out on the basis of strong textual evidence (borrowings from the homilies of Ælfric) that the last of his five sermons must date to after 1006 and may have been composed as late as 1012, and that his fourth and penultimate

---

Tradition', 101–2; Clayton, 'Delivering the Damned'; Mary Clayton, *The Cult of the Virgin Mary in Anglo-Saxon England* (Cambridge, 1990), 253–7.

[78] *Homilies of Ælfric: A Supplementary Collection*, ed. John C. Pope, EETS 259 and 260 (2 vols., 1967–8), II, 783.

[79] Contra Godden, 'The Millennium', 166–7. I hope to return to Ælfric's continuing apocalyptic concerns in a separate article.

[80] *Homilies*, ed. Bethurum, 278–98; Gatch, *Preaching and Theology*, 105–16; Lionarons, *Homiletic Writings*, 43–74.

[81] These are nos. 1a (in Latin), 1b, 2–5, in *Homilies*, ed. Bethurum, 113–41. They are accessible in a translation by Joyce Lionarons at http://webpages.ursinus.edu/jlionarons/wulfstan/wulfstan.html, from which my translations are taken.

[82] *Homilies*, ed. Bethurum, 58.

homily very probably dates to after 1005.[83] While this revised chronology appears only a slight shift, it has significant consequences. For rather than Wulfstan's Doomsday sermons being an early period in his preaching career, a kind of apocalyptic phase (or even apoplectic) which he got over, rather they belong to the period of his archiepiscopacy and to the time when he was a major influence at Æthelred's court. Indeed, not only is at least one version of his famous sermon, the *Sermo Lupi ad Anglos*, preached probably in the years after 1012, heavily eschatological, but Joyce Lionarons has pointed out that a later sermon of Wulfstan's with significant apocalyptic content was perhaps preached at Cnut's court in 1018.[84]

Wulfstan's five eschatological sermons show him reacting and responding to the increasingly desperate times of the first decade of the millennium. The first of his sermons is a fairly straightforward paraphrase of Matthew's Gospel on the signs of the End. He warns of the terrible times to come but states confidently that the End will not happen until the Gospel has been preached around the world, a fact which he appears to forget in his later preaching.[85] His second sermon represents a very significant shift as the archbishop identifies the Viking attacks as the Gospel sign of the Last Days that 'Nation will rise up against nation.' This sermon continues, alluding obliquely to Isaiah 24, by explaining that the English are being punished for their sins by the infertility of the earth and by the dearth caused by storms.[86]

---

[83] Malcolm Godden, 'The Relations of Wulfstan and Ælfric: A Reassessment', in *Wulfstan*, ed. Townend, 353–74, at 370. And see the important review, cited by Godden: John C. Pope, review of Dorothy Bethurum, *The Homilies of Wulfstan*, in *Modern Language Notes*, 74 (1959), 338–9.

[84] *Wulfstan Sammlung der ihm zugeschriebenen Homilien nebst Untersuchungen über ihre Echtheit*, ed. Arthur Napier (Zurich, repr. Dublin, 1967). On the difficulties of dating the *Sermo Lupi*, see *Sermo Lupi ad Anglos*, ed. Dorothy Whitelock, rev. edn (1976), 1–5; *Homilies*, ed. Bethurum, 22–4; and Godden, 'Apocalypse and Invasion', 143–6; Stephanie Dien, '*Sermo Lupi ad Anglos*: The Order and Date of the Three Versions', *Neuphilologische Mitteilungen*, 76 (1975), 561–70; *eadem*, 'The Thematic Structure of the Sermo Lupi ad Anglos', *Anglo-Saxon England*, 6 (1977), 175–95; and Jonathan Wilcox, 'Wulfstan's *Sermo Lupi ad Anglos* as a Political Performance 16 February 1014 and Beyond', in *Wulfstan*, ed. Townend, 388–92, and valuable summary and insights by Keynes, 'An Abbot', 203–13, who notes on 209 the evidence for a version preached in 1012. See too Lionarons, *Homiletic Writings*, 147–63. Joyce Lionarons, 'Napier Homily L: Wulfstan's Eschatology at the Close of his Career', in *Wulfstan*, ed. Townend, 413–28.

[85] *Homilies*, ed. Bethurum, II, 119–22. For the relative dating of the eschatological sermons, see *Homilies*, ed. Bethurum, 282, who establishes the order, II, III, Ia and Ib, IV and V. And see Sara M. Pons Sanz, *Norse-Derived Vocabulary in Late Old English Texts Wulfstan's Works: A Case Study* (Odense, 2007), 25. Wulfstan's eschatological sermons are discussed by Godden, 'The Millennium', in their order of printing in Bethurum, rather than her chronological order.

[86] *Homilies*, ed. Bethurum, III, 123–7.

Like Ælfric, Wulfstan was influenced by Adso's tract on the Antichrist which provided the theme for his last three sermons. The first of these, in Latin and Old English, exploits the idea of the Antichrist to denounce false Christians, those who profess Christianity but do not practise it. In this sermon, the time of terror is less proximate – he states that many alive today will not live to see the Antichrist.[87]

But his mood shifts in his last two sermons. His fourth, perhaps written after 1005, displays great urgency: 'Now it will very quickly be Antichrist's time.' Wulfstan warns his audience that, because the Antichrist will come so soon, his persecution of the good will have to be very terrible to purge them of their sins before the Final Judgement: 'Those who have been dead for a hundred years or even longer may now be well cleansed. We may need to suffer more harshly, if we must be clean when judgement comes.'[88]

His final sermon contains the striking warning of the closeness of the End by its description of Satan's loosening bonds, quoted at the beginning of this article.[89] It begins by identifying the present wickedness of the English with St Paul's account in 2 Timothy of the intense evil of the Last Days when men's love of God cools: 'No one loves God as a person should. No one remains faithful to anything, but injustice rules far and wide, and loyalty among people is uncertain, and that is seen in many ways, let him know it who can.'[90]

The revised dating of these sermons allows us to see them in the longer context of the desperate times of the first decade or so of the first millennium, in the context of the great famine of 1005, the escalation of Viking raids after 1006 and set them alongside the lawcodes and penitential measures of 1008 and 1009. Indeed, there may be some direct correspondences between them and these events. Wulfstan's words explaining how storms and destitution of the earth represent God's punishment could refer to the dearth of 1005, which the Anglo-Saxon Chronicle described as 'such that no man had ever remembered one so cruel'.[91] Wulfstan's final sermon remarks how Antichrist will work many

---

[87] *Ibid.*, Ia and Ib – the Old English represents a modified version of the Latin.

[88] *Ibid.*, IV, 128–33, at 128: 'Nu bið swype rape Antecristes tima'; *ibid.*, 129: 'Ða ðe wæron forðferde for hund gearum oððon gyt firnor, wel þa magan beon nu geclænsode. We motan nyde þæt stiðre þolian, gyf we clæne beon sceolon þonne se dom cymð, nu we þæne fyrst nabbað þe þa hæfdon þe wiðforan is wæron.'

[89] *Ibid.*, V, 134–41.

[90] II Timothy 3:1–9; *Homilies*, ed. Bethurum, V, 134–41; *ibid.*, 136: 'Ne man God ne lufað swa swa man scolde, ne manna getrywða to ahte ne standað, ac unriht ricsað wide 7 side, 7 tealte getrywða syndon mid mannum, 7 þæt us gesyne on mænigfealde wisan, gecnawe se ðe cunne.'

[91] *The Anglo-Saxon Chronicle: A Collaborative Edition V, MS C*, ed. Katherine O'Brien O'Keeffe (Cambridge, 2001), 91, 'Her on þissum geare wæs se micla hungor geond Angelcyn swylce nan man ær ne gemunde swa grimne.'

illusions through sorcery, and an interpolation in his fourth sermon, which may well be authorial, warns specifically against the wicked actions of the devil in the past through sorcery.[92] These were a symptom of the Antichrist's deceit and hypocrisy. One version of Æthelred's lawcode promulgated at Enham in 1008 demands that sorcerors and magicians should be driven from the kingdom. Is this a coincidence? This Latin text was drafted by Wulfstan, and was perhaps specifically intended for the higher clergy.[93] It concludes with a statement that the king had decreed these measures to extirpate evil and injustice from the land so that truth and justice might prevail, and peace and plenty be restored to the kingdom.[94] This code was the first drafted for Æthelred by Wulfstan himself and it sets out his programme for the Christian renewal of the kingdom, and imposes upon the English obedience to God's commands. Its extensive regulation of the Christian life can be seen as a response to Wulfstan's cataloguing of contemporary sins in his eschatological sermons.[95] Patrick Wormald described this code – with his usual panache – as 'throbbing' with Wulfstan's 'millenarian expectations'.[96] He argued that Wulfstan took up authorship of Æthelred's lawcodes precisely because of his apocalyptic preaching and vision.[97]

As archbishop, Wulfstan was charged with the provision of moral leadership to the religious and secular orders. His response to the question

---

[92] *Homilies*, ed Bethurum, IV, lines 68–9, 138. The interpolation is present in the two earliest of the three MSS of this homily, but is omitted in Oxford, Bodleian Library, MS 343. See Lionarons, *Homiletic Writings*, 62–7, who argues with Jost and Pope, for its possible original inclusion in the sermon. Karl Jost, *Wulfstanstudien*, Schweizer Anglistische Arbeiten 23 (Bern, 1950), 191–2, and Pope, review, 338–9. For this interpolation, see http://webpages.ursinus.edu/jlionarons/wulfstan/IVframe.html, accessed 20 May 2015.

[93] *Councils*, ed. Whitelock, Brett and Brooke, c. 7, I, 366. The Enham code survives in one Latin (VI Æthelred) and two Old English texts (V and VI Æthelred). The vernacular VI Æthelred, printed by Liebermann, *Die Gesetze*, I, 246–9, c. 7; 248 also contains this prohibition. Wormald, *Making*, 332–5, argues that this text is a later revision by Wulfstan, closer in time to 1018. He raised the possibility that the Latin V Æthelred may also represent a later text. But for an alternative view, see *Councils*, ed. Whitelock, Brett and Brooke, I, 338–43; Jost, *Wulfstanstudien*, 35–43; and Kenneth Sisam, 'The Relationship of Æthelred's Codes V and VI', in his *Studies in the History of Old English Literature* (Oxford, 1953; repr. 1998), 278–87, and Keynes, 'An Abbot', 177–8.

[94] *Councils*, ed. Whitelock, Brett and Brooke, cc. 40 and 40.1, I, 373.

[95] On the close relation between Wulfstan's preaching and his lawcodes, see M. K. Lawson, 'Archbishop Wulfstan and the Homiletic Element in the Laws of Æthelred II', *English Historical Review*, 107 (1992), 565–86; and see Patrick Wormald, *The Making of English Law: King Alfred to the Twelfth Century* (Oxford, 1999), 451–4. Wormald suggests the Old English VI Æthelred may have been preliminary to Wulfstan's 1018 code and notes its similarities to the sermon, *Wulfstan Sammlung*, ed. Napier, no. L, an eschatological homily. See my discussion of the parallels between Wulfstan's eschatological preaching and his lawcodes forthcoming in the *Review of English Studies* (2016).

[96] Wormald, 'Archbishop Wulfstan', 244.

[97] Wormald, *Making*, 453.

of the Last Days attended to the condition of English society and it is no coincidence that it was he who was emboldened to identify present evils with signs of the End and to deploy explicitly the coming of the year 1000 to intensify the urgency of his preaching.

Conclusion

O'Leary has suggested that

> apocalypticism cannot be only understood as a series of movements with discrete and identifiable causes in historical events, but must also be seen as a tradition, a textually embodied community of discourse founded in the canon of Western sacred Scripture and occasionally augmented by the production of new revelations and interpretative strategies.[98]

His observation agrees with the Anglo-Saxon eschatological and apocalyptic evidence. The writings of Ælfric and Wulfstan are commentaries, informed by the exegesis of earlier Fathers, upon the Sacred Scripture. But these textual traditions are not static and unchanging but dynamic – Wulfstan interprets the teachings of Gospels to refer to the Viking attacks. Ælfric reuses the writings of Gregory the Great and Haimo of Auxerre but suppresses their identification of contemporary disasters with the Gospel signs of the End. But Ælfric writes in response to the apocryphal teachings of the anonymous homilies which, he fears, misled the faithful into complacency concerning the Final Judgement.[99] His own words in his preface on Antichrist were borrowed by Wulfstan for his fourth homily, which he then himself reshaped to create his fifth homily.

Adso's tract on the Antichrist provided a significant impetus to apocalyptic discourse. Both Wulfstan and Ælfric were advocates of monastic reform but their use of Adso was very different and, at one point, in conflict. Ælfric used the Antichrist in his preface to Catholic Homilies I to assert the need for his learning over the dangers of the deviant doctrine of others. Wulfstan exploited the potential of the terrors of the time of the Antichrist to ratchet up fears of the Last Days and to press for immediate reform. But Ælfric could use Adso's teaching to the opposite effect, to dampen down apocalyptic expectations by pointing out the Empire must fall before his coming.

These are not just textual interactions but must in some way represent and reflect living dialogues and personal encounters. Ælfric's correction of apocryphal stories about the Last Judgement was a response not just to texts in circulation but to current preaching. His addition c. 1005 concerning the Empire and the Antichrist looks like a response to

[98] O'Leary, *Arguing the Apocalypse*, 10.
[99] See above n. 37.

contemporary speculation fuelled by the dire situation of the English. Ælfric was reacting to live issues, perhaps even to the preaching of Wulfstan. Through the later dating of Wulfstan's five apocalyptic homilies, we can see too the evolution of Wulfstan's thought. His thinking was shaped by recent disasters and he in turn tried to influence current events by his appeal for social reformation. Wulfstan's apocalyptic sermons are more than the powerful rhetoric of an inspired preacher – the translation of his preaching into legislative action indicates his seriousness in this respect.

Wulfstan's 1008 code was issued at a royal council of religious and secular magnates, and promulgated by the king.[100] His eschatological ideas must have been discussed at court where they may have met with both acceptance and resistance. Certainly, the evidence for apocalyptic speculation in England around the year 1000 points to elite deliberation, not popular. The use of apocalyptic citations in Æthelred's charters may well reflect courtly concerns and a heightened awareness of the proximity of the Last Days. From his elevation to the see of London in 996, Wulfstan will have been a powerful figure in the royal council. The charters of Æthelred reveal the anxieties of a king who faced Judgement Day with a greater burden of responsibility than his people. The penitential discourse of the charters is a testimony to the intersection of royal policy and personal piety. Early medieval lay piety was heavily focused upon the family and the obligation of the kindred to obtain intercession for their dead. In the years around 1000, Æthelred took special measures to provide for the salvation of his family, showing special solicitude to rectify any omissions or failures with respect to the disposition of lands earmarked for the church. Did his anxiety reflect a feeling that Satan's bonds were indeed loosening and that the time for expurgation was running out? The right ordering of the family was an essential aspect of kingly conduct. It may have come into greater scrutiny at a time where the conflict of brother against brother and father against son was seen as a sign of the extreme evil of the Last Days.

Anglo-Saxon England in the late tenth and eleventh centuries was a place of many and often conflicting ideas about the Last Days and Final Judgement. These four examples exemplify different but interlocking and overlapping discourses. They each show anxiety about the Endtime but respond to it in different ways. Thinking about the Apocalypse was influenced not just by chronology. The unremitting

---

[100] The Latin VI Æthelred opens with a statement that Æthelred issued the rulings, prompted by the urgings of himself and Archbishop Ælfheah of Canterbury, and it concludes with a note stating that the leading men swore to observe them, see *Councils*, ed. Whitelock, Brett and Brooke, c. 40.2, I, 362 and 373.

Viking successes coupled with the terrible famine of 1005 provided a stimulus to apocalyptic thought. But then so too did traditional piety and the circulation of new texts, like the tract of Adso. While the responses of my three subjects, Æthelred, Ælfric and Wulfstan, reveal contrasting reactions to the imminence of the Last Judgement, for all of them it was a pressing concern and an essential element in their lives and conduct.

Transactions of the RHS 25 (2015), pp. 53–74 © Royal Historical Society 2015. This is an Open Access article, distributed under the terms of the Creative Commons Attribution licence (http://creativecommons.org/licenses/by/4.0/), which permits unrestricted re-use, distribution, and reproduction in any medium, provided the original work is properly cited.
doi:10.1017/S008044011500002X

MINDING THEIR OWN BUSINESS: MARRIED WOMEN AND CREDIT IN EARLY EIGHTEENTH-CENTURY LONDON*

By Alexandra Shepard

READ 21 OCTOBER 2014

ABSTRACT. Taking a micro-historical approach, this paper explores the business activities of Elizabeth Carter and Elizabeth Hatchett, two married women who operated together as pawnbrokers in London in the early decades of the eighteenth century. Based on a protracted inheritance dispute through which their extensive dealings come to light, the discussion assesses married women's lending and investment strategies in a burgeoning metropolitan economy; the networks through which women lenders operated; and the extent to which wives could sidestep the legal conventions of 'coverture' which restricted their ownership of moveable property. It is argued that the moneylending and asset management activities of women like Carter and Hatchett were an important part of married women's work that did not simply consolidate neighbourhood ties but that placed them at the heart of the early modern economy.

This paper takes a micro-historical approach to reflect on processes with macro-historical consequences, focusing on a case-study of women's lending activities during a period of rapid commercial development. The discussion centres on the enterprise of two married women – Elizabeth Carter and Elizabeth Hatchett – who operated together as pawnbrokers in London in the early decades of the eighteenth century. A protracted inheritance dispute over Carter and Hatchett's property, during which their extensive dealings were detailed by many witnesses, allows an unusual glimpse, first, of the networks through which female lenders operated, and, secondly, of the ways they sidestepped the legal conventions of coverture which (in theory) restricted married women's ownership of and contractual rights to moveable property. The paper concludes with some tentative suggestions of how we might, on the basis of this

* I am grateful to Karen Harvey, Amy Froide, Sarah Knott and Catriona MacLeod for their comments on earlier drafts of this paper, and to the participants at a workshop on 'Gender and the Urban Economy in Late Medieval and Early Modern Europe' at the Berkshire Conference of Women Historians, May 2014, who commented on my work in progress on this case in advance of its development into a public lecture for the RHS delivered at the University of Huddersfield in October 2014.

case, rethink married women's position in the early eighteenth-century economy.

In recent years there has been growing recognition among historians of the roles played by women's business activities in the expanding urban economies of eighteenth-century Britain, just as women's labour force participation has been identified by Maxine Berg as critical to the pace and character of industrialisation.[1] Jan de Vries has similarly cited women's 'industriousness' as a determinant of the growing demand that provided the stimulus for industrialisation, which, he claims, was linked to their aspirations for an expanding range and volume of consumer goods.[2] In this latter case, women's roles as consumers are arguably privileged above their contributions as producers. In addition, while social emulation has been effectively rejected as the driving force shaping women's consumption habits, there remains a historiographical tendency to construct women's consumption patterns in terms of taste, identity and desire, rather than as a form of economically driven investment.[3] My discussion here draws out the links between credit, consumption and investment, recasting consumption as a form of asset management in order to identify a further dimension of married women's work that formed a critical component of the eighteenth-century economy.

Not least because of the legal restrictions curtailing married women's property rights, wives' lending activities are extremely difficult to discern

---

[1] Elizabeth C. Sanderson, *Women and Work in Eighteenth-Century Edinburgh* (Basingstoke, 1996); Hannah Barker, *The Business of Women: Female Enterprise and Urban Development in Northern England 1760–1830* (Oxford, 2006); Nicola Phillips, *Women in Business 1700–1850* (Woodbridge, 2006); Christine Wiskin, 'Businesswomen and Financial Management: Three Eighteenth-Century Case Studies', *Accounting, Business and Financial History*, 16, 2 (2006), 143–61; Amy Louise Erickson, 'Married Women's Occupations in Eighteenth-Century London', *Continuity and Change*, 23 (2008), 267–307; Amy Louise Erickson, 'Eleanor Mosley and Other Milliners in the City of London Companies 1700–1750', *History Workshop Journal*, 71 (2011), 147–72; Deborah Simonton and Anne Montenach, eds., *Female Agency in the Urban Economy: Gender in European Towns, 1640–1830* (2013); Maxine Berg, 'What Difference Did Women's Work Make to the Industrial Revolution?', *History Workshop*, 35 (1993), 22–44.

[2] Jan de Vries, 'The Industrial Revolution and the Industrious Revolution', *Journal of Economic History*, 54, 2 (1994), 249–70; Jan de Vries, *The Industrious Revolution: Consumer Behaviour and the Household Economy, 1650 to the Present* (Cambridge, 2008).

[3] The classic statement linking eighteenth-century consumption to social emulation is Neil McKendrick, 'The Consumer Revolution of Eighteenth-Century England', in *The Birth of a Consumer Society: The Commercialization of Eighteenth-Century England*, ed. Neil McKendrick, John Brewer and J. H. Plumb (1982). For alternative explanation of novel consumption patterns, see especially Lorna Weatherill, *Consumer Behaviour and Material Culture in Britain 1660–1760* (1988); Carole Shammas, *The Pre-Industrial Consumer in England and America* (Oxford, 1990); Beverley Lemire, *Fashion's Favourite: The Cotton Trade and the Consumer in Britain 1660–1800* (Oxford, 1991); Maxine Berg, 'Women's Consumption and the Industrial Classes of Eighteenth-Century England', *Journal of Social History*, 30, 2 (1996), 415–34.

since they rarely generated any formal legal record.[4] By contrast, the credit extended by single and widowed women is becoming increasingly recognised by historians as a significant feature of the early modern English economy.[5] Amy Erickson has even argued that the cash supplied by single women provided the necessary capital investment underpinning England's distinctive trajectory of economic development, thereby attaching causal significance to single women's lending as a driver of change.[6] Married women's involvement in brokering credit, by contrast, is often represented not only as hedged by legal constraints but also as 'informal', and principally associated with networks of female solidarity. Small scale and short term, the lending and borrowing undertaken by married women might readily be cast as part of the support networks that enabled households to get by in the face of haphazard income streams and a limited cash flow.[7] Married women's credit relations therefore tend to be approached by historians (if acknowledged at all) as necessitated by a relatively primitive economy rather than possessing any other discernible rationale, suggesting a substantial disparity in women's economic agency on the basis of their marital status that was, moreover, in contradiction of the *social* authority ascribed to married women in relation to their single counterparts.[8]

This paper rejects any straightforward characterisation of married women's credit broking as relatively marginal or solely inspired by mutual reciprocity. Instead, it is argued here that married women's borrowing and lending activities stemmed from their responsibilities for asset management within their households, which were understood as a form of enterprise. In the early modern period, a good deal of most people's wealth was stored in household goods and literally vested in

[4] Craig Muldrew, '"A Mutual Assent of Her Mind"? Women, Debt Litigation and Contract in Early Modern England', *History Workshop Journal*, 55 (2003), 47–71.

[5] See especially B. A. Holderness, 'Credit in a Rural Community, 1660–1800: Some Neglected Aspects of Probate Inventories', *Midland History*, 3 (1975), 94–115; Amy Froide, *Never Married: Singlewomen in Early Modern England* (Oxford, 2005), 130–7; Judith Spicksley, '"Fly with a Duck in thy Mouth": Single Women as Sources of Credit in Seventeenth-Century England', *Social History*, 32 (2007), 187–207; Judith Spicksley, 'Usury Legislation, Cash and Credit: The Development of the Female Investor in the Late Tudor and Stuart Periods', *Economic History Review*, 61 (2008), 277–301.

[6] Amy Louise Erickson, 'Coverture and Capitalism', *History Workshop Journal*, 59 (2005), 1–16.

[7] Marjorie Keniston McIntosh, 'Women, Credit, and Family Relationships in England, 1300–1620', *Journal of Family History*, 30 (2005), 143–63. On the limited cash supply in the early modern economy, see Craig Muldrew, *The Economy of Obligation: The Culture of Credit and Social Relations in Early Modern England* (Basingstoke, 1998); Craig Muldrew, '"Hard Food for Midas": Cash and its Social Value in Early Modern England', *Past and Present*, 170 (2001), 78–120.

[8] On married women's authority, see especially Laura Gowing, *Common Bodies: Women, Touch and Power in Seventeeth-Century England* (New Haven and London, 2003).

clothes – those items over which women, and especially married women, tended to exercise responsibility. Anachronistic concepts of wealth, which prioritise money above other forms of moveable wealth, risk producing too narrow an approach to early modern consumption patterns. The consumption of goods represented investment strategies rather than simply 'spending', enmeshed within and enabling complex credit relations in which married women were crucial brokers. Just as historians have questioned expectations that rituals of childbirth in the early modern past were inspired by sisterhood, so we might also problematise assumptions that women lenders were more likely to privilege solidarity over self-interest.[9] Married women's responsibilities for saving and accounting for household goods placed them at the heart of the early modern economy – in terms of the daily workings of exchange – rather than at its margins. The case of Elizabeth Carter and Elizabeth Hatchett suggests that credit broking could establish some married women as important patrons within their neighbourhoods and beyond, and could also present them with significant business opportunities.

We might interpret the agency of women like Elizabeth Carter and Elizabeth Hatchett in terms of 'resistance' to patriarchal norms, not least since their business dealings involved adept negotiation of the legal constraints associated with coverture – that is, the common law expectation that assigned ownership of a woman's moveable property to her husband and that denied married women the right to enter in to contractual relations of debt and credit.[10] However, rather than exclusively constructing female economic agency in terms of resistance, there is also a case for questioning the extent to which such norms pervaded everyday life.[11] What we may, in fact, be glimpsing in this case is a set of routine expectations that married women held a major

---

[9] Linda Pollock, 'Childbearing and Female Bonding in Early Modern England', *Social History*, 22, 3 (1997), 286–30; Laura Gowing, 'Secret Births and Infanticide in Seventeenth-Century England', *Past and Present*, 156 (1997), 87–115; Laura Gowing, 'Ordering the Body: Illegitimacy and Female Authority in Seventeenth-Century England', in *Negotiating Power in Early Modern Society: Order, Hierarchy and Subordination in Britain and Ireland*, ed. Michael J. Braddick and John Walter (Cambridge, 2001).

[10] Tim Stretton, 'The Legal Identity of Married Women in England and Europe 1500–1700', in *Europa und seine Regionen: 2000 Jahre europäische Rechtsgeschichte*, ed. Andreas Bauer and Karl H. L. Welker (Cologne, 2006). On the complex implications of coverture, see Margot Finn, 'Women, Consumption and Coverture in England, c. 1760–1860', *Historical Journal*, 39 (1996), 703–22; Joanne Bailey, 'Favoured or Oppressed? Married Women, Property and "Coverture" in England, 1660–1800', *Continuity and Change*, 17 (2002), 351–72; Cordelia Beattie and Matthew Frank Stevens, eds., *Married Women and the Law in Premodern Northwest Europe* (Woodbridge, 2013); Tim Stretton and Krista J. Kesselring, eds., *Married Women and the Law: Coverture in England and in the Common Law World* (Montreal and Kingston, 2013).

[11] For the characterisation of women's agency principally in terms of resistance, see especially Bernard Capp, *When Gossips Meet: Women, Family, and Neighbourhood in Early Modern England* (Oxford, 2003).

and active stake in household enterprise, to which they might contribute independently as well as in partnership with a spouse.[12] The attraction of such an interpretation lies not least in the prospect it affords of an expanded approach to women's economic agency as *productive* of the economic landscape and not simply as *responsive* to its constraints.

Elizabeth Carter and Elizabeth Hatchett's activities were at the centre of a testamentary dispute heard in the bishop of London's Commissary Court between October 1723 and January 1726. The case concerned the estate of Elizabeth Carter, of St Stephen Coleman Street, who had died of a fever in 1722.[13] Described as a midwife, Carter had also been involved in moneylending and pawnbroking, letting rooms, leasing houses and selling tobacco. Carter was a widow when she died, having been predeceased about two years previously by her husband, Humphrey, who had been a baker. The litigation concerned Hatchett's claims to Carter's goods, which were in dispute following Hatchett's own death 'of Jaundice' in June 1723, a mere nine months after Carter's death.[14] The parties in dispute were a young singlewoman, Eleanor Jennings, who at the age of twenty-three was executrix and primary beneficiary of Hatchett's will, and Mary Lucas (wife of Samuel Lucas), who was Elizabeth Carter's sister. Eleanor Jennings was the eldest of three daughters belonging to a neighbouring couple of Elizabeth Carter and Elizabeth Hatchett. Mary Lucas sued Eleanor Jennings on the grounds that Elizabeth Hatchett had wrongfully bequeathed goods to Jennings that had belonged to Elizabeth Carter and to which Hatchett had no claim, and which therefore rightfully belonged to Lucas.[15]

The case revolved around the working relationship between Elizabeth Carter and Elizabeth Hatchett who had clearly had a long association for up to two decades before Carter's death. In dispute was whether they had been business partners, equally bound to each other by intimacy and friendship (on the one hand), or (on the other hand) whether they had been in each other's debt. Thirty-nine witnesses were produced to give evidence (twenty-three women and sixteen men), some of whom were called on more than once, in a case which lasted for more than two years. The case was unusually drawn out, and the number of witnesses well exceeded the average (which was between six and seven) established from

---

[12] On spousal cooperation, see the Special Issue of *Continuity and Change*, 23, 2 (2008); Ariadne Schmidt, 'The Profits of Unpaid Work. "Assisting Labour" of Women in the Early Modern Urban Dutch Economy', *History of the Family*, 19, 3 (2014), 301–22.

[13] London Metropolitan Archives (LMA), St Stephen Coleman Street, Rough Register of Deaths, 1711–23, P69/STE1/A/009/MS04455.

[14] LMA, P69/STE1/A/009/MS04455.

[15] For Elizabeth Hatchett's will, see The National Archives (TNA), PROB 11/591/465. There is no surviving copy of Elizabeth Carter's will, but Elizabeth Hatchett was named as executrix on 10 Oct. 1722, LMA, DL/C/B/001/MS 09168/034.

a sample of testamentary disputes heard by the same court between 1700 and 1728.[16] Since both Carter and Hatchett had died without any direct heirs (neither had any surviving children), at stake were the relative claims of Carter's sister and Hatchett's legatees to an indeterminate quantity of moveable property.[17] Items mentioned frequently in the witness testimony were a gold striking watch, a gold chain, a diamond brooch, leases to tenements, lottery tickets and varying amounts of cash and goods.

In support of Mary Lucas's case against Eleanor Jennings, Carter was represented by the majority of witnesses as an extremely wealthy and successful woman (both while a wife and as a widow), on whom Hatchett had depended as a servant, and whose extensive goods Hatchett had misappropriated during Carter's final sickness and after her death. The evidence in support of Eleanor Jennings's claims instead focused on the extent to which the women had worked in *partnership* with each other – with Hatchett as the senior partner – and stressed Carter's longer-term dependence on Hatchett for her basic maintenance and for her care in her final sickness. The dispute therefore produced divergent accounts of the women's relationship and the women's fortunes, which serve as a reminder that witness testimony was heavily shaped by the competing claims that on the one hand undoubtedly exaggerated Carter's wealth and success and that on the other hand stressed Hatchett's self-sufficiency and Carter's obligation to her. The details provided by witnesses in the case nonetheless testify to what was *imaginable* concerning these two women's dealings, even if we will never know which aspects of their relations were 'true'.[18]

---

[16] This sample is contained within the larger dataset, 'The "Worth" of Witnesses in the English Church Courts, 1550–1728', available from the UK Data Archive. The compilation of this dataset was funded by a research grant from the Economic and Social Research Council (RES-000–23–1111) and completed with the assistance of Dr Judith Spicksley, for which I am extremely grateful. For the character of litigation involving women, see David Lemmings, 'Women's Property, Popular Cultures, and the Consistory Court of London in the Eighteenth Century', in *Women, Property, and the Letters of the Law in Early Modern England*, ed. Nancy E. Wright, Margaret W. Ferguson and A. R. Buck (Toronto, 2004).

[17] Elizabeth Carter appears to have been childless. An 'Allexander', son of Alexander Hatchett, was buried on 21 May 1702 in St Giles Cripplegate and was most likely the son of Alexander and Elizabeth Hatchett, who had married in St Sepulchre on 13 Apr. 1699. LMA, P69/GIS/A/002/MS06419/012, P69/SEP/A/001/MS07219/002. One witness claimed that when Hatchett joined the Carter's household, Hatchett 'had a Child to keep', on account of which Carter 'tooke her in out of Charity'. LMA, DL/C/B/045/MS 09065A/012/001, fo. 469v.

[18] The judgment in the case awarded goods to the value of £30 to Mary Lucas, Carter's sister-in-law, and £30 towards her expenses. Lucas's account of her expenses amounted to £60 8s 2d, which meant that the judgment constituted a net loss for Lucas of 8s 2d: LMA, DL/C/A/002/MS 09065F/004, 4 Dec. 1725, DL/C/B/MS 09185/005, 13 Dec. 1725. For a critique of historians' attempts to discover truth in witness depositions, see Frances E. Dolan, *True Relations: Reading, Literature, and Evidence in Seventeenth-Century England* (Philadelphia, 2013).

The volume of testimony in this case (amounting to more than 100 folios of depositions alone) provides extraordinary insight into forms of work that married women routinely undertook, which involved asset management and credit broking.[19] This is evident not only from the details of Hatchett and Carter's dealings but also from the varied use of their services by a number of married women. The case also illustrates the extent to which married women were able to circumvent the legal constraints of coverture. The extensive, and often enterprising, initiatives pursued by Elizabeth Carter and Elizabeth Hatchett occurred during the best part of both women's married lives. Hatchett had joined the Carters' household in the early 1700s, not long in to her own marriage, affording up to twenty years for Carter and Hatchett to develop a working partnership. In fact, the case suggests that the relationship between these two married women was more significant than their conjugal ties for both women's material well-being and possibly also for their emotional well-being. The only occasion when either woman suffered the legal constraints of coverture was when their partnership broke down, a little over a year before Elizabeth Carter's death. It was acrimony between the two women (rather than any direct patriarchal intervention) that put an end to their successful negotiation of the opportunities offered by the fluidity between household and market; cash and goods; and the so-called 'formal' and 'informal' economy.

Women's lending networks

The incidental details of Carter and Hatchett's lending activities confirm the impressions pieced together by Beverly Lemire of women's responsibility for managing small-scale quotidian credit transactions on behalf of their households, as well as their wider role in facilitating the credit relations of others. Women were not only active borrowers in their own right, they also commonly acted as guarantors for others, overseeing the process of converting assets into credit and cash to facilitate a growing density of exchange.[20] Seven out of the eleven witnesses who detailed their own borrowing from Carter or Hatchett were women, all of whom, barring one widow, were married. The sums involved were relatively small, ranging from 20s ($£1$) to $£30$, and the majority of the loans actually specified by witnesses amounted to $£10$ or less. Some such instances were apparently one-off transactions. Carter's sister in law (married to

---

[19] LMA, DL/C/B/045/MS 09065A/012/001, fos. 379–501.

[20] Beverly Lemire, 'Petty Pawns and Informal Lending: Gender and the Transformation of Small-Scale Credit in England, *circa* 1600–1800', in *From Family Firms to Corporate Capitalism: Essays in Business and Industrial History in Honour of Peter Mathias*, ed. Kristine Bruland and Patrick O'Brien (Oxford, 1998); Beverly Lemire, *The Business of Everyday Life: Gender, Practice and Social Politics in England, c. 1600–1900* (Manchester, 2005).

a labourer) recounted borrowing 20s from Hatchett 'towards fitting out her son to be an Apprentice', offering a silver spoon and a silver salt as a pledge.[21] However, other witnesses detailed a longer history both of their own and of others' borrowing, so that although the individual sums involved were small, they multiplied through regular repetition. A butcher's wife, for example, who told the court that she got her living by taking in children to nurse and by selling fruit, recalled borrowing money frequently from Carter over a period of eighteen years, 'shee being recommended... as a person who lett out money either in greater or lesse sumes at usury'.[22]

There are various ways of contextualising the amounts of money that were reportedly lent by Carter and Hatchett. The most common sum cited by witnesses in the case was £5. While small compared with the larger and more formalised loans underwritten by well-to-do single women, or by London goldsmiths during the same period, £5 nonetheless amounted to between one and two years' wages for a domestic servant in London.[23] It was also relatively large compared with the sums detailed in cases of property crime reported in the *Proceedings of the Old Bailey* involving stolen goods that had been pawned. The twenty-three specific sums secured as loans by pawns that were detailed in the *Proceedings* in the five-year period between 1718 and 1722 ranged from 6 Guineas for a watch to 3s 6d for a drugget coat (a coat made of heavy wool).[24] The size of the loans extended by Carter and Hatchett routinely exceeded the sums recounted in Old Bailey trials, suggesting that they did not solely cater to the lower end of the pawnbroking market. The women who sought Carter and Hatchett's services testified to making their livings in a variety of ways, from washing clothes, cutting wool and taking children in to nurse, to retailing and keeping a public house. Their husbands' stated occupations included a labourer, butcher, porter, cloth-workers and a waterman, while the men who borrowed directly from Carter or Hatchett included shoemakers, a sexton, a gardener and a victualler.

The witnesses who explicitly identified themselves as borrowers were drawn from across and beyond the City of London, which also meant that Carter and Hatchett were not merely serving parochial or neighbourly

---

[21] LMA, DL/C/B/045/MS 09065A/012/001, fo. 391.

[22] LMA, DL/C/B/045/MS 09065A/012/001, fo. 369.

[23] It was alleged in this case that Hatchett had been paid 50s (£2 10s) annually to serve as the Carters' servant. On domestic servants' wages, see Peter Earle, *A City Full of People: Men and Women of London 1650–1750* (1994), 125. On goldsmith bankers, see D. M. Mitchell, '"Mr. Fowle Pray Pay the Washwoman": The Trade of a London Goldsmith Banker, 1660–1692', *Business and Economic History*, 23, 1 (1994), 27–38; D. M. Mitchell, ed., *Goldsmiths, Silversmiths and Bankers: Innovation and the Transfer of Skill, 1550–1750* (Stroud, 1995).

[24] *The Proceedings of the Old Bailey Online* (*OBO*), www.oldbaileyonline.org (last accessed July 2014).

needs. This was as true for their female as for their male debtors. None of their female clients lived in the same parish as Carter and Hatchett (St Stephen, Coleman Street). Three women debtors were from the neighbouring parish of St Giles Cripplegate (which was also the parish where Carter's husband, Humphrey, had been born).[25] The others were drawn from further afield, from both within and beyond the City, including one from St Sepulchre without Newgate and two from Christ Church, Southwark.[26] The male borrowers similarly hailed from parishes within and without the City, ranging from St Stephen Coleman Street to Battersea. The witnesses called to testify in the case also had widespread origins, including neighbours from Bell Alley (where Carter and Hatchett had lived), others drawn from a variety of parishes within the City of London and extending outwards to Shoreditch and St Anne Soho as well as to locations south of the River Thames including Stockwell and Newington. A further two witnesses were from Hayes, Middlesex, and one – the sister of a former lodger of Carter's, now married to a gentleman – had journeyed all the way from Bristol to provide evidence. Witnesses were connected to Carter and Hatchett through ties of kinship, friendship and neighbourhood, through Carter's midwifery practice (Carter had delivered the children of several deponents in the case), and through business links of various kinds, of which Carter and Hatchett's lending activities constituted a significant part.

While female-centred, the networks of credit that flowed from Carter and Hatchett were not female-specific. Two shoemakers, both of St James, Duke Place, admitted borrowing money from both women, along with a waterman from St Martin Orgar.[27] Richard Harris, a gardener from Battersea, first encountered Carter when standing surety for a loan of £5 which she extended to a carpenter who worked for Harris, after which point Harris also borrowed money from Carter 'as hee sometimes wanted it himselfe in his way of trade'.[28] Some of the men who borrowed from Carter and Hatchett were nonetheless linked to women borrowers who had secured the necessary introduction. The sexton of St Stephen Coleman Street, who was Carter and Hatchett's neighbour, recounted his mother borrowing £10 on several occasions from Hatchett, who a few years later was followed by his brother who regularly borrowed the smaller sum of 40s.[29]

---

[25] Humphrey Carter, son of a wire dresser, was baptised on 6 June 1669. LMA, P69/GIS/A/002/MS06419/007. I have been unable to find a record of Elizabeth and Humphrey Carter's marriage, or of Elizabeth Carter's birth (née Everett).

[26] Another female borrower was from St Martin, Canon Street. Several witnesses referred to other borrowers, whose residence was not detailed.

[27] LMA, DL/C/B/045/MS 09065A/012/001, fos. 465, 473, 487.

[28] LMA, DL/C/B/045/MS 09065A/012/001, fo. 418.

[29] LMA, DL/C/B/045/MS 09065A/012/001, fo. 397v.

The men as well as the women who had acquired cash from Carter and Hatchett spoke of their 'intimacy' with the two women, suggesting that their credit relations were woven into and generated broader networks of mixed sociability. Verifying his knowledge of Carter over a period of fifteen or sixteen years, a shoemaker claimed that through his frequent borrowing from her he contracted 'an intimate friendshipp & acquaintance' on account of which he had visited her once or twice a week.[30] Carter and Hatchett's lending activities *might* therefore be treated as an extension of the ties of reciprocity that secured the informal credit relations that were routinely brokered by women, and that in some circumstances represented mutual aid rather than enterprise. One witness even spoke of Carter herself seeking a loan when in straightened circumstances not long before her death. At this point, Carter reportedly approached Christiana James (the wife of one of Hatchett's former debtors), claiming that she had 'not a farthing to help herself', borrowing 5s from Christiana and 'begging' Christiana's husband to put his hand to a note for 40s, which loan Carter promised to pay off in weekly instalments.[31] However, extensions of 'friendship' also carried connotations of patronage and established webs of dependency.[32] When Carter and Hatchett 'let' their money out to use, they provided their 'friends' with a service which generated ties of obligation, and for which they also expected a good return.

While often flowing through channels of so-called 'friendship' and 'intimacy', Carter and Hatchett's business activities were clearly commercially driven. Their dealings do not fit the 'pattern of unassuming enterprise' that, according to Lemire, characterised women's lending, but were larger scale and more profit oriented.[33] According to one witness, Hatchett had borrowed £300 to set herself up in 'Employment' as a moneylender, and she was reputed to have grown rich from extending loans in return for pawns. Carter was described by several witnesses as directing a large-scale operation, with another of Carter's sisters claiming to have seen 'money lye by her in heaps in order to bee lent out'.[34] More often, and more importantly, witnesses described the many material markers of wealth and success on display in Carter's household and on her person in the form of fashionable clothes and jewellery. Carter's clothes were described in great detail by some witnesses, such as Elizabeth Perry,

---

[30] LMA, DL/C/B/045/MS 09065A/012/001, fo. 465. On the routine description of clients as 'friends' in the eighteenth century, see Barker, *Business of Women*, 82.

[31] LMA, DL/C/B/045/MS 09065A/012/001, fo. 393.

[32] On the multi-layered concept of friendship in early modern England, see Naomi Tadmor, *Family and Friends in Eighteenth-Century England: Household, Kinship, and Patronage* (Cambridge, 2001).

[33] Lemire, 'Petty Pawns and Informal Lending', 123.

[34] LMA, DL/C/B/045/MS 09065A/012/001, fo. 429v.

the wife of a clothworker, who remarked that she had gone about 'fine & toppingly drest in good & fashionable silkes & sattins & with very good lace in her head clothes'. A widow from Christchurch, Southwark, claimed that Carter 'went as fine & as richly drest as the best merchants wife in the Citty might doe'. Sara Carter, married to Elizabeth Carter's nephew Richard (a weaver), described her aunt as having been shortly before her death decked in 'a flower'd silke damask gowne & pettycoat, the ground whereof was yellow & the flower thereof white a very good laced suit of head clothes & ruffles & a scarlet Cloth Cloake trimmed with gold'. She also estimated that a 'crotchet' (or brooch) of diamonds, also worn by Carter, had been worth £50.[35] Others attempted to value a gold chain and a gold striking watch that had reportedly been in Carter's possession. These assessments attest to the importance of clothes not just as signifiers of status (in this case deemed 'as fine as any merchant's wife'), but also as repositories of wealth, and as a kind of 'alternative currency'.[36]

Witnesses also described with considerable precision the goods and furniture in Carter's possession, although those called on behalf of Eleanor Jennings stressed that it had not been Carter's own, but belonged to the lodgers to which Carter had rented rooms. Their appraisals attest to the ways in which domestic items other than clothes also functioned as repositories of wealth and a medium of exchange. Elizabeth Perry, married to a clothworker of the neighbouring parish, St Giles Cripplegate, recalled 'good & fashionable goods & furniture' including 'high back armed Chaires, red Curtaines[,] two Clockes, large looking glasses in the panel & in the Chimney & other such furniture as were fit & convenient for any Gentleman to lodge in'.[37] A former servant of Carter's itemised her household goods with remarkable detail and skill. She listed 'a great deale of plate' including 'two silver tankards, a silver pinte cup[,] a silver pinte mugg[,] two silver candlesticks[,] two silver coffee potts one for an ounce of Coffee & another for an ounce and a half[,] one silver porringer[,] salts, two silver salvers[,] a sett of Castors & several dozens of silver spoons'. She also estimated that, besides the

---

[35] LMA, DL/C/B/045/MS 09065A/012/001, fos. 427v, 434, 446.

[36] Beverly Lemire, 'Consumerism in Preindustrial and Early Industrial England: The Trade in Secondhand Clothes', *Journal of British Studies*, 27 (1988), 1–24; Beverly Lemire, 'Shifting Currency: The Culture and Economy of the Second Hand Trade in England, *c.* 1600–1850', in *Old Clothes, New Looks: Second Hand Fashion*, ed. Alexandra Palmer and Hazel Clark (2004). See also Sanderson, *Women and Work*, 150–7. Carter was also reported by one witness to have traded in second hand clothes, LMA, DL/C/B/045/MS 09065A/012/001, fo. 441v.

[37] LMA, DL/C/B/045/MS 09065A/012/001, fo. 427v. On the material markers of gentility, see H. R. French, *The Middle Sort of People in Provincial England 1600–1750* (Oxford, 2007), ch. 3.

furnishings in the rooms she let to tenants, Carter had possessed eight or nine beds made of cherry wood, 'laid one upon another' in one of the back garrets in her house. Among other items she also singled out 'foure handsome lookeing glasses, glasses, sconces three standing Clocks, a Scrutoire [escritoire] with a great deale of China, [and] Caine Chaires', all of which signified surroundings 'rather fitt for a Gentleman then a Tradesman to live in'.[38] Such knowledge was not just born of the intimacy afforded by domestic service. Several of Carter's friends, neighbours and acquaintances conjured similarly detailed descriptions of her material surroundings, with many (including her servant) assigning a cash value to particular items or to bundles of goods, using the same appraisal skills with which we are familiar from the processes undertaken to compile probate inventories.[39]

The female deponents in this case described Carter's possessions in much greater detail than their male counterparts, in ways which attested to the importance of moveable property in general as a form of investment (i.e. including, but not restricted to, clothes). This corresponds with women's use of a greater level of detail in wills to describe bequests of moveable property compared with men's, which might be attributed as much to their facility for evaluating investments as to the relative importance of women's affective ties.[40] Household goods (like clothes) not only signified status but functioned as a repository of wealth that could also serve as a cash equivalent. The skills involved in such assessments informed a wider culture of appraisal, in which judgments about the cash value of the goods in people's possession were central to assessments and assertions of credit. In a cash-scarce economy, the vast majority of transactions were conducted on trust. Craig Muldrew has argued that, as a consequence, credit relations were brokered in a moral economy and depended heavily on assessments of reputation in ethical terms. This process, according to Muldrew, was constituted by the social circulation of 'the self in terms of virtuous attributes'.[41] The ways in which witnesses enumerated the 'worth' of the goods in their own and others' possession are suggestive, however, of the material basis to assessments of credit and social standing. People monitored possessions as much as virtuous behaviour as the basis for decisions about the conditions of exchange. The 'selves' that consequently circulated were assigned a cash value. The

[38]LMA, DL/C/B/045/MS 09065A/012/001, fo. 446r–v.

[39]On probate inventories, see especially Weatherill, *Consumer Behaviour*; Tom Arkell, Nesta Evans and Nigel Goose, eds., *When Death Do Us Part: Understanding and Interpreting the Probate Records of Early Modern England* (Oxford, 2000), pt I.

[40]Berg, 'Women's Consumption'.

[41]Muldrew, *Economy of Obligation*, 156.

negotiation of trust in the early modern economy was therefore built on solid material foundations.[42]

Considerable skills of appraisal informed expectations that people in early modern England could routinely place a monetary value on their 'worth' (which was estimated with reference to their moveable property and the extent to which they were indebted). The routine assignment of a cash value to goods and to persons suffused daily life in the early modern period. Elizabeth Carter, for example, was reported by various witnesses as having attached values to her 'worth' ranging from £1,500 to £18,000 at various points during her life, which self-assessments were in turn judged with varying degrees of scepticism.[43] Especially in urban centres, where the bulk of people's worth was stored in clothes and household goods rather than in crops and livestock, intimate *knowledge* of each other's assets as well as one's own was crucial for establishing the relations of trust which underpinned the majority of exchange. This knowledge was gathered through the networks of sociability to which women were central, and it is clear that women developed considerable skills of appraisal that informed this process. The testimony of the married women in this case is further evidence of the considerable sense of entitlement they felt towards the moveable property that constituted their households (much of which they were charged with managing and protecting), as well as the skills they commanded in judging the value of the assets of others.[44] Women's consumption therefore constituted a form of investment, rather than simply a means of display and, when approached cannily, consumption formed part of the 'prudent economy' expected of wives rather than its antithesis.[45] Indeed, married women's responsibilities for saving and accounting for household resources comprised one of the few forms of women's work explicitly acknowledged by even the most conservative

[42] Alexandra Shepard and Judith Spicksley, 'Worth, Age and Social Status in Early Modern England', *Economic History Review*, 64 (2011), 493–530; Alexandra Shepard, *Accounting for Oneself: Worth, Status and the Social Order in Early Modern England* (Oxford, 2015).

[43] See, e.g., LMA, DL/C/B/045/MS 09065A/012/001, fos. 427v, 429v, 433v.

[44] Bailey, 'Favoured or Oppressed?'; Amy Louise Erickson, 'Possession – and the Other One-Tenth of the Law: Assessing Women's Ownership and Economic Roles in Early Modern England', *Women's History Review*, 16 (2007), 369–85; Alexandra Shepard, 'The Worth of Married Women in the English Church Courts, *c.* 1550–1730', in *Married Women*, ed. Beattie and Stevens.

[45] On women's consumption as a form of work, see Jane Whittle and Elizabeth Griffiths, *Consumption and Gender in the Early Seventeenth-Century Household: The World of Alice Le Strange* (Oxford, 2012). On the indistinct relationship between consumption and saving in the early modern period, see Shepard, *Accounting for Oneself*. On 'prudent economy', see Amanda Vickery, *The Gentleman's Daughter: Women's Lives in Georgian England* (New Haven, 1998), ch. 4. See also Alexandra Shepard, 'Crediting Women in the Early Modern English Economy', *History Workshop Journal*, 79 (2015), 1–24.

conduct writers concerned with delineating domestic duties.[46] Household management was a form of asset management.

Pawnbroking, of course, depended on – and honed – precisely these skills. The author of the *London Tradesman* opined that a seven-year apprenticeship to learn the business of a pawnbroker was 'rather too little' to 'become Judge of the almost infinite Number of Goods he is obliged to receive as Pledges'. This was because the trade required 'a great deal of Judgment and Acuteness to become thoroughly Master of it' (including being a 'Master of Figures').[47] However, the skills he identified were just those that informed women's quotidian social accounting whereby they assessed each other's credit and asserted their own. Judging from their ability to assign market value to goods (expressed in terms of a cash sum), the wives charged with their households' asset management, as well as single and widowed women, exercised 'mastery of figures' as well as expertise in the conditions of exchange. (This was evidently the case for the higher-ranking women who produced their own account books, but it was by no means dependent on literacy skills.)[48] It is therefore perhaps unsurprising that women were relatively well-represented among pawnbrokers as well as among those who facilitated the extension of their services by presenting goods on others' behalf.[49] A search of London and Middlesex Sessions papers, as well as the *Proceedings of the Old Bailey*, for the five-year period from 1718 to 1722, turned up ninety-seven references to pawnbrokers.[50] Of those whose gender was identified, 27 per cent were women. Women were also named as facilitators of exchange, acting as trusted intermediaries for others who wanted to realise the cash value of items in their possession.

Pawnbroking therefore represented the extension of skills which had long informed women's brokerage of credit and relations of trust, but

[46] E.g., *The Gentlewoman's Companion: or, A Guide to the Female Sex* (1675), attributed to Hannah Woolley, included careful money management as one of the principal duties of wives, and cautioned against 'being too lavish' in expenditure while remaining vigilant against servants spoiling household goods by their negligence, 107. While Woolley dismissed the 'employment' required to 'govern an House' as 'not difficult', she also advised that 'the active vigilance of a good and careful Wife is the ready way to enrich a bad Husband', 108.

[47] R. Campbell, *The London Tradesman* (1747), 296–7.

[48] For examples, see Judith Spicksley, ed., *The Business and Household Accounts of Joyce Jeffreys, Spinster of Hereford*, Records of Social and Economic History, New Series, 41 (Oxford, 2012); Whittle and Griffiths, *Consumption and Gender*. See also Keith Thomas, 'Numeracy in Early Modern England', *Transactions of the Royal Historical Society*, 37 (1987), 103–32; Rebecca Elisabeth Connor, *Women Accounting, and Narrative: Keeping Books in Eighteenth-Century England* (2004).

[49] Peter Earle, *The Making of the English Middle Class: Business, Society and Family Life in London, 1660–1730* (1989), 170; Margaret R. Hunt, *The Middling Sort: Commerce, Gender and the Family in England, 1680–1780* (Berkeley, 1996), 132–4.

[50] 'London Lives 1690 to 1800: Crime, Poverty and Social Policy in the Metropolis', www.londonlives.org (last accessed July 2014).

Table 1 *Value of loans raised on items pawned, detailed in the* Proceedings of the
Old Bailey, *1719–22*

Date	Item(s)	Value	Value of loan	Loan as % of value
1720	Pistols	£5	15s	15
1720	Coat and waistcoat	£1	3s 6d	17.5
1722	Watch	£5 5s	£1 1s	21
1720	Drugget coat	10s	2s 6d	25
1722	Coat and breeches	43s	13s	30
1722	Pair of bodices; petticoat	7s	2s 6d	36
1721	Silver watch	£4	30s	38
1720	Pair of linen sheets; silver spoon	19s	7s 6d	39
1719	Drugget coat	10s	4s	40
1721	2 silver spoons	14s	6s	43
1720	Silver cup	£9	£4 10s	50
1719	Pair of silk stockings	12s	6s	50
1722	Watch	£3	£1 15s	58

pawnbroking also contributed to the redefinition (and narrowing) of trust, with its demand for goods as securities. *Knowledge* of goods (which might be distrained in cases of default) in such circumstances did not suffice as the basis for a loan; credit was only forthcoming through transactions that appeared to have benefited the lender more than the debtor. When details of the value of stolen items can be compared with the amount they raised as pledges (derived from the *Proceedings of the Old Bailey*), it was unusual for the lender to lend as much as half the cash value of the goods concerned, and in the majority of cases it was a good deal less than 40 per cent (see Table 1).[51]

While pawnbroking may have overlapped with informal charity (when favourable terms were arranged, for example, or debts forgiven), it also represented a break from it by requiring securities from which brokers could protect themselves from loss and from which enterprising women such as Carter and Hatchett were well-placed to profit. Carter, for example, was quick to take advantage of a defaulting debtor (a porter) who had mortgaged his wife's house to Carter as security for a loan of £30.

[51] See also Peter Earle, *Making of the English Middle Class*, 50. For a contemporary assessment of the interest accrued on loans secured with pledges, as well as the relative value of loans to pledges, see *An Apology for the Business of Pawn-Broking* (1744).

Carter swiftly took possession of the property when the porter was unable to keep up his weekly payments. His wife, who subsequently was reduced to occupying her former house as a tenant (paying Carter between £4 and £5 per annum in rent), earning her living by washing clothes and running a chandler's shop, recounted how Carter had acquired this and other houses at a price well below their market value.[52]

Both Carter and Hatchett were represented as having a sharp eye for opportunities to turn a profit and to diversify their interests. Besides lending money and storing the associated returns in clothing and household goods, witnesses described a wider range of investment strategies pursued by Carter and to a lesser extent by Hatchett. Hatchett reportedly converted some of her profits into leases on tenements by 'purchasing estates'.[53] Both women appear to have invested in lottery orders, with one witness describing Carter as 'an adventurer in the state Lottery', and another recalling Hatchett collecting the interest due on lottery orders issued in her name.[54] Several witnesses also recounted Carter's attempts to diversify her interests (although they disagreed whether this was a sign of her wealth and enterprise or of her search for expedients in the face of poverty). In 1721, Carter had invested in a tobacco cutting engine and a hogshead of tobacco, which she intended to sell in customised papers that had been printed to bear the brand 'Carter's Best Virginia'. One of her nephews also testified that she had enquired about the costs required to set herself up in the business of 'Engine weaving'.[55]

Despite the fact that she was married for the bulk of the period which was being described, witnesses clearly assigned ownership of the goods they detailed to Carter, and credited her with considerable ability to generate income. Although part of Mary Lucas's strategy in attempting to secure any goods left by her deceased sister was to emphasise that Carter had been left a wealthy widow by Humphrey Carter (who reportedly had left off his trade as a baker having somewhat implausibly made a fortune sufficient to live like a gentleman), this was a relatively minor part of the stories told by Lucas's witnesses.[56] They instead predominantly

[52] LMA, DL/C/B/045/MS 09065A/012/001, fos. 453–4.

[53] LMA, DL/C/B/045/MS 09065A/012/001, fo. 390.

[54] LMA, DL/C/B/045/MS 09065A/012/001, fo. 448. On women's more formal investment practices in the eighteenth century, see Ann M. Carlos, Karen Maguire and Larry Neal, 'Women in the City: Financial Acumen during the South Sea Bubble'; Anne Laurence, 'Women, Banks and the Securities Market in Early Eighteenth-Century England'; Christine Wiskin, 'Accounting for Business: Financial Management in the Eighteenth Century', all in *Women and their Money 1700–1950*, ed. Anne Laurence, Josephine Maltby and Janette Rutterford (2009).

[55] LMA, DL/C/B/045/MS 09065A/012/001, fos. 461, 407.

[56] Humphrey Carter was assessed (on rent) at between £1 8s 0d and £3 4s in the Land Tax records between 1702 and 1720: LMA CLC/525/MS 11316/013–064. Carter also attended

ascribed Carter's wealth to her *own* enterprise and initiative. In part, they linked her riches to her proficiency as an 'eminent & experienced' midwife, enjoying a long career ministering to 'persons of good fashion & credit'.[57] Mostly, however, the descriptions of Carter's clothes, jewels and furniture were designed to signal her resourcefulness as a businesswoman and her consequent capacity for capital accumulation. Although sharing very different motivations, Jennings's witnesses also positioned Carter as the dominant partner in her marriage to Humphrey. Claiming that he had been forced to leave off his trade because he was unable to repay his accumulated debts, they implied that he had been dependent upon his wife for his maintenance. Carter had reportedly complained that her husband had 'run out many scores of pounds' and that had he continued to trade she would have had no bread to eat, not least since her gains would be entirely sunk in supporting his losses.[58] The retrospective accounting of Elizabeth Carter's goods, as well as Elizabeth Hatchett's right to them, represented both women as enterprising and active agents, exercising direct claims to the fruits of their own and each other's labour.

Married women, coverture and the early modern economy

Both women's husbands were represented as peripheral to their dealings. Hatchett lived apart from her husband, Alexander, for the best part of two decades. He constituted a shadowy figure in the case, described as a journeyman shoemaker in poor and miserable circumstances (albeit in response to a question that sought to establish that Hatchett had no means other than the wages paid to her by the Carters on which to live). One witness claimed that Alexander Hatchett had been reduced to poverty on account of his 'vicious life', which had rendered his one-time position as a master shoemaker unsustainable.[59] Several others confirmed that he had been confined in Wood Street Counter (a debtor's prison) for at least two years before Carter's death.

However, it appears that Alexander Hatchett's *name* was used in Hatchett's and possibly Carter's dealings in notes provided to secure their loans. One witness remarked that Carter and Hatchett 'let out money on Pawns in partnership in the Names of other People'.[60] In addition, when a shoemaker borrowed money from Elizabeth Carter he secured his loan by notes made payable to Alexander Hatchett (which

the vestry meetings of St Stephen Coleman Street between 1712 and 1718, and served as a questman in 1718, but he did not hold any other parish office. LMA P69/STE1/B/001/MS 04458/001/002.

[57] LMA, DL/C/B/045/MS 09065A/012/001, fos. 421v, 416.
[58] LMA, DL/C/B/045/MS 09065A/012/001, fo. 485v.
[59] LMA, DL/C/B/045/MS 09065A/012/001, fo. 485v.
[60] LMA, DL/C/B/045/MS 09065A/012/001, fo. 397v.

notes were subsequently in the possession of Eleanor Jennings, which she then destroyed in order to issue Hope a fresh note whereby she became his creditor).[61] Alexander Hatchett was also named in a trial heard at the Old Bailey as one of the victims of a theft involving the goods of Elizabeth Carter.[62] Whether Alexander Hatchett was aware of the use of his name to secure his wife's lending activities is unclear. Caesar Shuttleworth, a victualler in St Giles Cripplegate, and one of the witnesses who had been close to both Carter and Hatchett (named as a beneficiary in the latter's will), testified that he thought Alexander Hatchett had been imprisoned by a 'sham Action' at Elizabeth Hatchett's connivance.[63] Several witnesses deposed that Alexander Hatchett had been released from Wood Street Counter shortly after Carter's death, sporting a new suit of clothes. Shuttleworth, who went with Hatchett to release her husband, revealed that his freedom was granted by Hatchett on condition that Alexander 'executed a Deed whereby he barred himself from meddling with any of his Wifes effects upon Condition that she should give him a new Suit of Cloaths', which Shuttleworth valued at 23s.[64]

Alexander Hatchett's was not the only name used in the promissory notes in Carter's and Hatchett's possession. The leases to several tenements were purchased by Carter using her widowed mother's name, which she also used to secure loans in return for pawns. Carter's mother had also drawn up a letter of attorney to empower Hatchett to receive rents due to her from various tenants.[65] Elizabeth Carter and Elizabeth Hatchett's partnership broke down in 1719, when Hatchett faced two prosecutions in the Old Bailey for stealing Carter's goods – which charges the court deemed to have been maliciously instigated by Carter, without justification.[66] At this point, both women placed newspaper advertisements attempting to recover their debts and to ensure that funds out on loan did not end up in each other's hands. These advertisements also named a 'Mr Joseph Batt' as a party in Carter and Hatchett's dealings.[67]

Besides calling on the services of many proxies, it may well be that (when functional) Carter and Hatchett's partnership had also protected them

[62] The case was brought against four men for perverting the cause of justice, *OBO*, t17221205–43.
[63] LMA, DL/C/B/045/MS 09065A/012/001, fo. 496.
[64] LMA, DL/C/B/045/MS 09065A/012/001, fo. 496v.
[65] LMA, DL/C/B/045/MS 09065A/012/001, fo. 478r–v. This claim was denied by Mary Lucas in the second personal answer she supplied in the case, DL/C/B/047/MS 09065D, fo. 213.
[66] *OBO*, t17190408–8, t17191204–43. Hatchett was acquitted on both occasions.
[67] *Post Man and the Historical Account*, 7–10 and 10–12 Mar., 24–6 Mar., 14 Apr. 1719.

from some of the constraints of coverture they faced as married women. By remaining flexible about to whom debtors were legally obliged, they sidestepped the claims of their husbands to their earnings, but also (and perhaps more importantly) any claims of their husbands' *creditors*. Their negotiation of their legal position was not necessarily, therefore, craftily connived resistance to the patriarchal proscription of married women's property rights, but may have been a means of protecting their earnings from their husbands' liabilities. Both men were described as being heavily in debt. While it is clear that some married women used proxies and other devices to sidestep the constraints of marital property law to their sole advantage (without the knowledge of their husbands), such negotiations could also serve the mutual interest of couples. These kinds of devices were undoubtedly part of the culture of popular legalism that could be exploited by spouses working together as well as manipulated by women alone in attempts to reduce their legal disadvantage.

Both dynamics appear to have been at work in this case. Whether or not their business dealings were fully endorsed by their husbands, Carter and Hatchett clearly enjoyed considerable latitude in relation to their spouses. According to witnesses in the testamentary dispute, Carter and Hatchett's working partnership had – at its height – apparently taken precedence over their husbands' claims, in terms of the intimacy associated with it as well as any material obligations to their spouses. Supporting Eleanor Jennings's claims that Hatchett had rightfully inherited Carter's goods, a former lodger in Carter's house deposed that Hatchett and Carter had 'had a greater Love & kindness to & for each other than one Sister could have for another. And that they had solemnly protested before God that the longer Liver of them should have all that they were worth or to that effect.' Another witness (married to a gentleman), declared that she 'never saw more sincere Friendship & Affection between any two Persons then there appeared to be' between Carter and Hatchett, and also spoke of their agreement that 'the longer Liver of them should enjoy all that they had'. This agreement had been made while Humphrey Carter was still alive, with Elizabeth Carter promising her husband that Hatchett would 'take care to maintain him' should Elizabeth Carter die first.[68] The witnesses concerned appeared in no doubt about which was the more important bond.

The professed intimacy between these two women, and the mutual interests it served, did not last, however. Paradoxically, it was only when their partnership broke down that coverture explicitly came into play. The newspaper advertisements placed by Carter and Hatchett around the time of Hatchett's trial for theft at the Old Bailey suggest that Humphrey Carter was quick to protect his own interests by claiming his right to

---

[68]LMA, DL/C/B/045/MS 09065A/012/001, fos. 485, 491.

his wife's property and by denying Elizabeth Hatchett's rights to it. In March 1719, Carter placed a notice claiming that she had been robbed by Hatchett and requesting repayment of all the loans on notes she had in her possession.[69] Two weeks later, a correction was printed, declaring the contents of Carter's notice to be false, the prosecution malicious, and Hatchett was redescribed as 'no Servant but a Partner in Trade'.[70] (The record of the Old Bailey trial similarly reports that several witnesses 'made it appear very plain' that Carter and Hatchett were partners, sending out money 'in small Parcels' in return for pawns, adding that 'Mrs. Hatchet was the chief Manager'.[71]) This newspaper notice ended with the assertion that Elizabeth Carter was a *feme couvert*, adding that Humphrey Carter had issued a general release to Hatchett, and had since absconded. A further advertisement advised debtors not to pay any money to Elizabeth Carter but to apply themselves to Hatchett at the Oxford Bank in Forestreet, and Hatchett also offered a reward of 2 Guineas to anyone who could give notice of the whereabouts of Humphrey Carter so that a process at law could be served on him.[72] The balance between solidarity and strategy had clearly been tipped at this point. Any slipperiness about what belonged to whom no longer served any party's interests, in ways which invoked the blurred boundary between exchange and theft as well as the fuzzy distinction between possession and ownership that plagued marital property law.

There was a good deal more at work here, then, than coverture, which itself appears to have had a very selective, and not entirely debilitating, impact on Carter and Hatchett's enterprise. Concepts of coverture certainly did not prevent witnesses in this case from attributing skill, enterprise, resourcefulness and esteem to two married women working in partnership in the early eighteenth century, on the basis of which they amassed at the very least goods worth fighting an extensive legal battle over in court. The only point at which Carter and Hatchett appeared to have suffered coverture as a major hindrance was when their own relationship of trust broke down, at which point Humphrey Carter invoked his rights over his wife's property in order to protect himself, and possibly his wife, from the fall-out. It is likely that Elizabeth Carter's manipulation of the law of coverture was of benefit to her husband, whereas Elizabeth Hatchett apparently managed to distance herself successfully from any claims her husband might have had on her estate.[73] It is interesting that she chose a young single woman (Eleanor

[69] *Post Man and the Historical Account*, 10–12 Mar.

[70] *Ibid.*, 24–6 Mar.

[71] *OBO*, t17190408-8.

[72] *Post Man and the Historical Account*, 14 Apr. 1719.

[73] Alexander Hatchett appointed proctors to represent his claims to his late wife's estate in June 1723, but the case was shortlived and clearly unsuccessful, since it was Eleanor

Jennings) from among her neighbours as her executrix and the beneficiary of her will, clearly in the expectation that Jennings would continue her business after her death.[74] While some of these actions are indeed best interpreted as acts of female resistance, they also attest to the routine *centrality* of married women to the commercial lives of their communities, in terms of the roles they played in relations of exchange.

It is perhaps unsurprising that witnesses who described the intimacy between Hatchett and Carter in positive terms emphasised its sisterly quality, given that such an analogy placed Hatchett's claims to Carter's goods on a comparable footing with those of Carter's actual sister, Mary Lucas, the plaintiff in the cause. However, the appeal to sisterly bonds in this case, as well as the echo of conjugal obligation attributed to Carter and Hatchett's relationship, serves as a reminder that legally cemented partnerships between sisters, as well as between unrelated women, could rival and did indeed sometimes compete with the conventions established by marital property law.[75]

These women were not simply serving their neighbourhood by offering small-scale loans inspired by the pragmatics of mutual reciprocity. They sought to turn a profit and amass a fortune, responding deftly and strategically to the range of opportunities available in a rapidly expanding and diversifying metropolis. This is not to argue that they operated on a level playing field, either with their husbands or with other men. But they were clearly central players nonetheless, not incapable of out-manoeuvring male as well as female competitors and not unwilling to take advantage of others' misfortune. While this case is exceptional in its level of detail, and may have involved the activities of two exceptional women, it is also worth noting that not a single witness implied that Carter and Hatchett's enterprise was out of the ordinary. If Carter's own reported estimates of her fortune at the height of her achievements are even part-way credible, she may have enjoyed comparable success to Elizabeth Waltears, a London pawnbroker who insured her business for £1,000 with the Royal Exchange Insurance Company in 1734, and would have well-exceeded the business capacity of a Rotherhithe widow, Ann Tosler, who insured goods in pledge, her stock in trade and household wares to the value of £200 in 1740.[76]

Jennings who was the target of Mary Lucas's claims to Elizabeth Carter's goods. TNA, PROB 31/14/386. See also PROB 18/37/98, PROB 24/60, 4 July 1723.

[74] Her motives for favouring Eleanor Jennings perhaps also related to the support Hatchett may have received from Eleanor Jennings's mother in relation to Hatchett's attempts to secure Carter's goods.

[75] Phillips, *Women in Business*, 32–3, 169.

[76] Beverly Lemire, *Dress, Culture and Commerce: The English Clothing Trade before the Factory, 1660–1800* (Basingstoke, 1997), 108.

Yet the activities detailed in this case might also speak to the quotidian experiences of women in early modern England, especially in terms of the borrowing they undertook, and the associated management of household resources. Women's responsibilities for asset management, that began with singlewomen's investment of their portions, did not end at marriage but took on a new dimension as the assets in their possession were largely converted to the stock of goods that underpinned their households' ability to negotiate credit. Women's responsibility for their households' 'stuff' did not consign them to a domestic sphere, somehow detached from a commercial economy, but actually enabled that economy to function. We might liken them to bankers, and should not be surprised to discover that they sought to do as much as possible to maximise their investments.[77] Their consumption strategies served processes of saving and accumulation rather than simply fulfilled desires for comfort, emulation or display. The consequent asset management, which in an urban context like London some women were able to pursue on an extensive and commercially oriented scale, was, therefore, another form of married women's work which can be added to our growing appreciation of female enterprise as well as industriousness in a rapidly developing economy.

[77] Shepard, 'Crediting Women'.

Transactions of the RHS 25 (2015), pp. 75–93 © Royal Historical Society 2015
doi:10.1017/S0080440115000031

MAKING HISTORY ONLINE

The Colin Matthews Lecture for the Public Understanding of History

By Tim Hitchcock and Robert Shoemaker

READ 12 NOVEMBER 2014

ABSTRACT. This article considers the implications of recent innovations in digital history for the relationship between the academy and the public. It argues that while digitisation and the internet have attracted large new audiences, academic historians have been reluctant to engage with this new public. We suggest that recent innovations in academic digital history, such as the highly technocratic 'Culturomics' movement, have had the unintended effect of driving a wedge between higher education and the wider public. Similarly, academic history writing has been slow to embrace the possibilities of the internet as a means of dissemination and engagement; and academic publishing has moved even more reluctantly. Despite these issues, this article argues that the internet offers real opportunities for bridging the divide between the academy and a wider audience. Through non-traditional forms of publication such as blogging; through Open Access policies; and through new forms of visualisation of complex data, the digital and online allow us to present complex history to a wider audience. We conclude that historians need to embrace the 'affordances' and 'disruptions' posed by the internet to render the discipline more open and democratically accessible.

In the last twenty years the way in which we do historical research has been transformed by digitisation and the internet. With JSTOR, which has provided online access to a vast archive of periodical articles since 1995, Early English Books and Eighteenth-Century Collections Online (EEBO and ECCO, from 1998), Google Books (2004) and numerous other online resources, the traditional journey into the library and the archive and back out again has been reshaped.[1] We might call this the creation of the Western print archive – second edition.

Through this vast array of electronic resources, emerging from the private sector, museums and archives and higher education, British history in particular has been made newly available at the click of a mouse to anyone with an internet connection. Of course, there are limitations – issues of coverage and what is left undigitised, of access and paywalls, and of OCR quality and copyright – but in less than a generation, the British

---

[1] See www.jstor.org; www.eebo.chadwyck.com; www.gale.cengage.co.uk/product-highlights/history/eighteenth-century-collections-online.aspx; http://books.google.com.

past, particularly prior to the twentieth century when copyright restricts access, has become the most digitised where and when in the world.

We have been hugely privileged to have been able to contribute to this phenomenon, through our involvement in the creation of the Old Bailey Online, launched in 2003, London Lives and Locating London's Past in 2010, Connected Histories in 2011 and the ongoing Digital Panopticon project.[2] This experience has given us a strong sense both of the possibilities of digital history and its risks. A fundamental feature of digital history is the way it opens up history to the public, but the very publicity of the internet has proved problematic for academic historians. In this paper, we consider how recent innovations in the online provision of resources, and in the crowdsourcing and co-creation of research materials, have the potential to reconfigure the relationship between the academy and the public; and argue that for this to happen, academic historians need to embrace these new opportunities.

Digital resources on the internet have let historians do remarkable things. Just by way of a simple example, take the Londoner Sarah Durrant, one of almost 125,000 defendants convicted at the Old Bailey in the nineteenth century. Her experience was by no means unique, but quite suddenly that experience is available to us in a new way. Sarah claimed to have found two bank notes on the floor of the coffee house she ran in the London Road in 1871, at which point she pocketed them. In fact they had been stolen from the briefcase of Sydney Tomlin, at the Birkbeck Bank, Chancery Lane, a few days earlier. From her prison records, we can learn about her widowed status and physical description, including the existence of two moles on her face – one on her nose and the other on her chin (Figure 1). We can see her scared and resentful eyes staring at us from a mug shot. We also have the words recorded at her trial, from which we know that Sarah was convicted of receiving stolen goods; and that she had been turned in by a Mrs Seyfert – a drunk, to whom Durrant had refused a hand-out (Figure 2). On 11 January, she was found guilty of receiving stolen goods and sentenced to two years of imprisonment. And we can read the newspaper report of the same trial (Figure 3).

Later that year, while she was in Wandsworth Gaol, she was recorded in the census, along with all her fellow prisoners (Figure 4). From her trial, we know where Durrant had been living when the crime took place: in Southwark, at No. 1 London Road. We know that she was a little uncertain about her age from the different answers she provided to different clerks, and from the census we can find out both who she shared prison life with following her conviction, and who lived up one flight of stairs, and down

[2] See   www.oldbaileyonline.org;   www.londonlives.org;   www.locatinglondon.org; www.connectedhistories.org; www.digitalpanopticon.org.

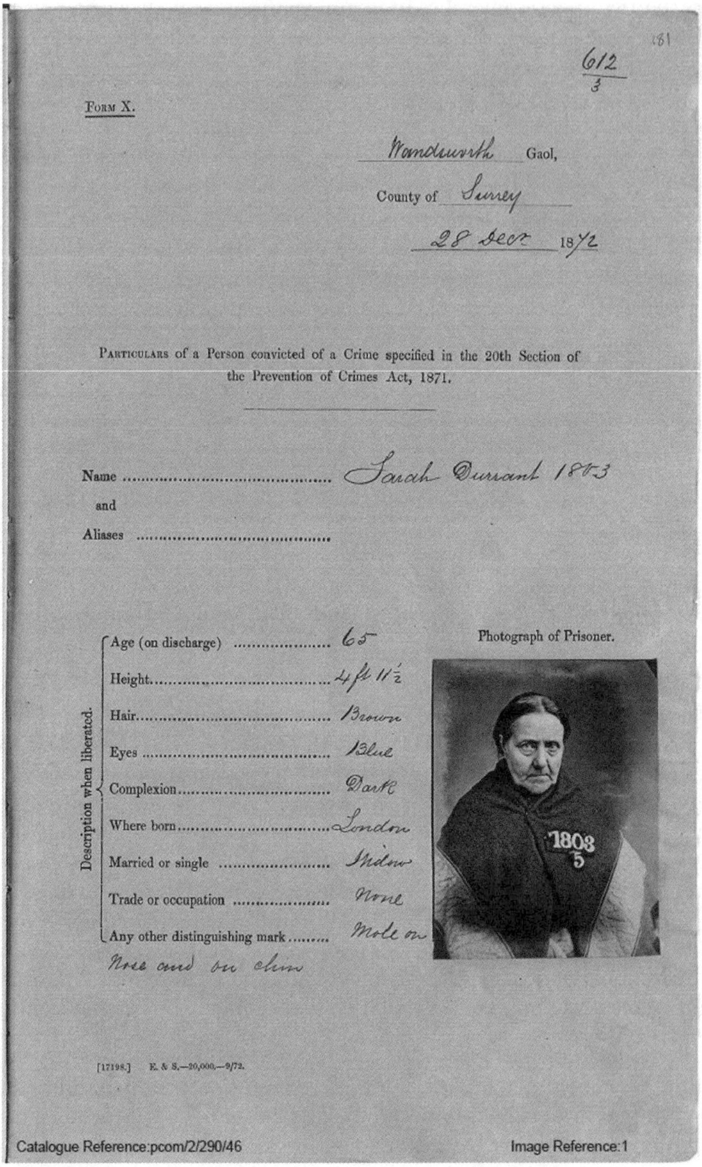

FORM X.

Wandsworth Gaol,

County of Surrey

28 Decr 1872

PARTICULARS of a Person convicted of a Crime specified in the 20th Section of the Prevention of Crimes Act, 1871.

Name .... Sarah Durrant 1803
and
Aliases ....

Age (on discharge) 65

Height............................... 4 ft 11½

Hair.................................... Brown

Eyes .... Blue

Complexion................................ Dark

Where born.............................. London

Married or single .... Widow

Trade or occupation .... None

Any other distinguishing mark .... Mole on

Nose and on chin

Description when liberated.

Photograph of Prisoner.

[17198.] E. & S.—20,000.—9/72.

Catalogue Reference:pcom/2/290/46   Image Reference:1

Figure 1 The National Archives: 'Prisoners Photograph Album', Sarah Durrant, 28 December 1872, PCOM2/290/46 (http://discovery. nationalarchives.gov.uk/details/r/C9072200, 28 Apr. 2015).

Figure 2 (Colour online) *Old Bailey Proceedings Online* (www.oldbaileyonline.org, version 7.2, 28 Apr. 2015), January 1871, trial of Sarah Durrant (t18710109–137).

another in her previous home in Southwark. From here, it is a small step on the web to go to the Charles Booth Online Archive posted by the London School of Economics in 2001 (a digitised version of Booth's *Life and Labour of the People in London*, 1889–1903), which in turn lets us know a bit more about the street and its residents (Figure 5). According to a policeman's notebook and Booth's map, the street was 'a busy shopping street', with the social class of the residents declining sharply to the west, where it comprised 'some comfortable [households], others poor'.[3]

In half an hour's search we can put together a life, an experience and an emotional and empathetic contact with one of the more than three million mostly anonymous (to us) men and women who lived in London in 1871.

In the process of making this kind of research possible, digitisation and the internet have helped spirit into being new audiences for history, new practitioners of history writing and new forms of historical practice. That there was an enormous appetite for resources like this was made strikingly

---

[3] *Charles Booth Online Archive*: Police Notebooks, 'District 31: Lambeth and St Saviour's Southwark', B363, pp. 16–17 (http://booth.lse.ac.uk/static/b/districts.html, 28 Apr. 2015).

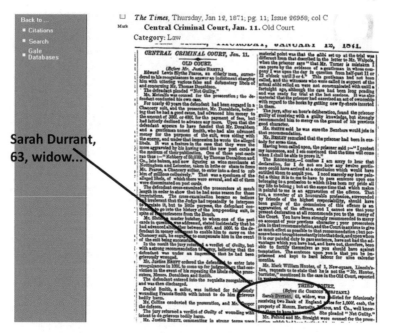

Figure 3 (Colour online) *The Times*, Thursday, 12 January 1871, 11; issue 26958 (http://gale.cengage.co.uk/times.aspx/, 28 Apr. 2015).

apparent in January 2002, when the first British census was made available online – and immediately crashed through overwhelming demand.[4] Over the past fifteen years, following the creation of dozens of similar resources, it has become clear that a new cohort of historians has come into being. Despite the fact some online resources depend on institutionally based subscription models which effectively exclude independent scholars, a vast amount of material online is readily accessible to everyone. The public sector, which posted all the sources of information about Sarah Durrant cited above except the newspaper article, typically provides free online access. While privately run resources such as Ancestry and Findmypast charge their users, most have developed business models based on affordable subscriptions, while others, such as Google Books, are free. As a result, the non-academic historian with internet access has at their fingertips more real data than can be found in any single archive or hard-copy library.

[4] *BBC News*, 'Census website a crashing success', 2 Jan. 2002 (http://news.bbc.co.uk/1/hi/uk/1737861.stm, 28 Apr. 2015).

RYAN, Mary	Prisoner	F	60	1811	Ireland	VIEW
DAVIDSON, Louisa	Prisoner	F	30	1841	Isle of Wight	VIEW
GROVENOR, Ellen	Prisoner	F	19	1852	Nottinghamshire	VIEW
DUKES, Mary Ann	Prisoner	F	15	1856	Sussex	VIEW
GRIFFITHS, Ann	Prisoner	F	17	1854	Surrey	VIEW
PHILLIPS, Rebecca	Prisoner	F	48	1823	Oxfordshire	VIEW
PRITCHARD, Mary Ann	Prisoner	F	60	1811	Middlesex	VIEW
COOKSEY, Ellen	Prisoner	F	18	1853	Essex	VIEW
WOOD, Annie	Prisoner	F	29	1842	County Durham	VIEW
EVANS, Sarah	Prisoner	F	35	1836	Hampshire	VIEW
DURRANT, Sarah	Prisoner	F	63	1808	Middlesex	VIEW
HUNTER, Elizabeth	Prisoner	F	17	1854	Surrey	VIEW
DAVIS, Anne	Prisoner	F	40	1831	Middlesex	VIEW
SHELBY, Charlotte	Prisoner	F	26	1845	Middlesex	VIEW
WELSH, Elizabeth	Prisoner	F	16	1855	Kent	VIEW
WEEKS, Emma	Prisoner	F	28	1843	Surrey	VIEW
BENNETT, Elizabeth	Prisoner	F	19	1852	Surrey	VIEW
LEWIS, Elizabeth	Prisoner	F	19	1852	Norfolk	VIEW
HOUGH, James	Prisoner	M	21	1850	Surrey	VIEW
BAILEY, William	Prisoner	M	37	1834	Middlesex	VIEW
SCOTT, Samuel	Prisoner	M	21	1850	London	VIEW
SIMMONS, Charles	Prisoner	M	30	1841	Hampshire	VIEW
CLARK, William	Prisoner	M	28	1843	Lancashire	VIEW
GRIFFIN, John	Prisoner	M	52	1819	Surrey	VIEW
EAGER, Thomas	Prisoner	M	21	1850	Sussex	VIEW

Figure 4 (Colour online) 1871 Census, Ancestry (http://home.ancestry.co.uk/, 28 Apr. 2015).

In an average week, the Old Bailey Online attracts around 15,000 visits from dozens of countries around the world, and the vast majority are from private individuals accessing the site from outside of higher education. The first academic URL to appear in our lists normally comes in around thirty places from the top.[5] And it is not just usage of the internet that has changed historical practice. The four million plus people who watched episodes of the television series *Garrow's Law* over three seasons, the six million who tune in to each episode of *Who Do You Think You Are?* and the three million who sought out the first screenings of *Secrets from the Workhouse* are evidence of a vastly expanded audience for history, both online and

[5] See Sharon Howard, Tim Hitchcock and Robert Shoemaker, 'Crime in the Community Impact Report' (2010) (www.webarchive.org.uk/wayback/archive/20140614185215/http://www.jisc.ac.uk/media/documents/programmes/digitisation/analysis_cic.pdf).

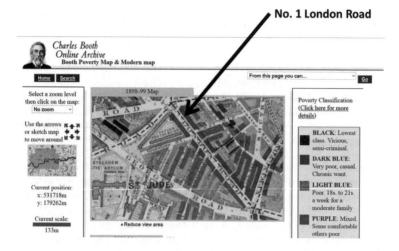

Figure 5 (Colour online) *Charles Booth Online Archive*: Booth poverty map and modern map (http://booth.lse.ac.uk/cgi-bin/do.pl?sub=view_booth_and_barth&args=531000,180400,6,large,5, 28 Apr. 2015).

on TV.[6] And many of these 'viewers' are not just passively consuming history. They are doing their own research and writing.

Perhaps the best example of the involvement of a wider public in research and, via crowdsourcing, in the creation of new historical materials, is *Trove*. A resource which may be unfamiliar to many academic historians, *Trove* is the most successful historical crowdsourcing project in the world. It gives direct public access, and input, to around 400 million items held in the libraries of Australia, most notably the newspapers published up until the 1950s. On an average day, users of Trove make around 100,000 corrections to the newspaper archive – combining good citizenship with research of their own. In the process, *Trove* has built a community of historically interested users that significantly contributes to Australian public culture.[7]

Less dramatically, the same could be said of the online resources in the UK created by The National Archives and British Library, and to a lesser extent *Connected Histories*. The British Library's 'Million Images'

---

[6] For viewing figures, see 'Garrow's Law', *Wikipedia* (http://en.wikipedia.org/wiki/Garrow's_Law, 1 May 2015); 'Who Do You Think You Are? (UK TV Series), *Wikipedia* (http://en.wikipedia.org/wiki/Who_Do_You_Think_You_Are%3F_(UK_TV_series, 1 May 2015); and '"Secrets from the Workhouse" opens to over 3 million on ITV', *Digital Spy* (www.digitalspy.co.uk/tv/news/a493302/pbqJcUMHG6Nnr3, 1 May 2015).

[7] National Library of Australia, *Trove* (http://trove.nla.gov.au/, 28 Apr. 2015).

project has attracted a global community of active users.[8] A new audience of consumers and producers of history has evolved – many of them co-creating the sources of historical research, in the process of undertaking their own investigations.

The digital revolution has been a fantastic development for history, but it is not without its problems. The new resources threaten to deracinate the leavings of the past, and allow them to be used with little sense of context or meaning – all flashy quotes, located using keyword searches. But in our estimation, there has not been such a vibrant audience for history writing since the heydays of Macaulay and Gibbon.

Academic historians are obvious beneficiaries of this sea of change, but, with some exceptions, they have been rather reluctant to embrace and work with this new public of practising historians. Even when they have been willing, they have discovered that digital public engagement demands skills they do not have and resources they did not plan for. As with *Trove*, crowdsourcing has been used by a few academic projects. But in contrast to *Trove* – a project run by the National Library of Australia, an institution with public engagement embedded in its mission – academic projects have had some difficulty recruiting the help of a wider audience.

One of the most successful examples to date is *Transcribe Bentham*, which has invited public volunteers to transcribe the voluminous and often difficult to read papers of the utilitarian philosopher Jeremy Bentham, with the specific aim of breaking down traditional barriers between the public and academic research.[9] In five years, some 13,000 manuscripts have been transcribed or partially transcribed by volunteers, or 29 per cent of the 45,000 manuscripts which remained untranscribed at the start of the project. This is a tremendous achievement, but it has been a long and difficult journey. At this pace, the project will need another twelve years or so to complete the task. And although many people have participated, most have only worked on a few pages, while the vast majority of the pages have been transcribed by a small number of volunteers. The 'crowd' turns out to be rather small, and, given the fact all the transcriptions still needed editorial work, it is questionable whether this methodology has actually saved the project any money.[10] Indeed, saving money – as opposed to

[8] The British Library on flickr (https://www.flickr.com/photos/britishlibrary, 28 Apr. 2015). See also 'British Library uploads more than a million public domain images to Flickr', *Wired.co.uk*, 15 Dec. 2013 (http://www.wired.co.uk/news/archive/2013–12/15/british-library, 28 Apr. 2015).

[9] *Transcribe Bentham: A Participatory Initiative* (http://blogs.ucl.ac.uk/transcribe-bentham/, 28 Apr. 2015).

[10] T. Causer, J. Tonra and V. Wallace, 'Transcription Maximized; Expense Minimized? Crowdsourcing and Editing The Collected Works of Jeremy Bentham', *Literary and Linguistic Computing*, 27.2 (2012) (e-journal).

deepening public engagement – may be the wrong motivation for using this methodology.[11]

Our own experience with crowdsourcing has been even less successful – when we invited people to contribute content to the *Old Bailey Online* through specially created wiki pages, the response was underwhelming, and eventually the wiki was discontinued.[12] We have had more success with very specific tasks, which take advantage of the way users are already interacting with the resource. When we added a simple correction feature to the Old Bailey site users responded with a variety of helpful comments on a wider range of topics than we expected. A similar approach was used with our parallel project, *London Lives*. The site provides access to over 240,000 manuscripts about poverty and crime in eighteenth-century London, and includes over three million separate name instances. We enabled registered users to link records together which they think concern the same individual, and so far some 3,000 of these 'sets' have been created.

The point is that crowdsourcing and public engagement are difficult, and require considerable skill, time and effort.[13] Academics cannot just assume that the 'public' will do what we ask them to do. In part, people are making their own histories, and do not necessarily want to be led by the academy. As both *London Lives* and the *Transcribe Bentham* projects have discovered, there needs to be a substantive dialogue between project staff and volunteers. A community of people working on the project needs to be created – so that both feel that they are getting something out of it, and the resulting resource is truly co-created. Unfortunately, current structures for funding projects, and allocating academic workloads, do not normally make the level of human resource necessary for this work available.

It is not just that academics have had limited success in creating a dialogue with family, local and public historians; there are also moves from within academic digital history which have had the effect of driving a wedge between historians working in higher education and a wider public. One of the virtues of digital history is that it has attracted scholars from different disciplines, with different skills, to look afresh at the evidence now that it has been transformed from mere words and objects into data. But the results of these interdisciplinary collaborations can be problematic.

[11] Trevor Owens, 'Crowdsourcing Cultural Heritage: The Objectives Are Upside Down' (2012), www.trevorowens.org/2012/03/crowdsourcing-cultural-heritage-the-objectives-are-upside-down/.

[12] Howard, Hitchcock, and Shoemaker, 'Crime in the Community Impact Report'.

[13] Sharon Howard, 'Bloody Code: Reflecting on a Decade of the Old Bailey Online and the Digital Futures of our Criminal Past', *Law, Crime and History*, 5.1 (2015), 21–4 (www.pbs.plymouth.ac.uk/solon/journal/vol.5%20issue1%202015/Howard%20Bloody%20Code.pdf, 28 Apr. 2015).

Perhaps the best-known example is the Culturomics movement, emerging from the Cultural Observatory at Harvard, using Google's Ngram viewer to analyse word frequencies in Google Books. The Ngram viewer allows users to chart the relative frequency of words and phrases, year by year, in the full body of Google Books from 1800 to 2000. At its best, this forms a powerful way of exploring the content of what is now some 14 million volumes digitised by Google. But while the Ngram viewer is available to all, and easy to use and comprehend, some of the academic history that is being written on the basis of this tool can seem both divorced from context and increasingly arcane. The viewer has been used by its creators, Jean-Baptiste Michel and Erez Lieberman Aiden, to generate what they consider to be a newly 'scientific' reading of the past, that privileges varieties of history that are highly technocratic. Their most powerful claim to date is that the Ngram viewer demonstrates that irregular verbs in English have declined steadily over the last 400 years.[14] This is a potentially significant (if contentious) finding that implies language change is not subject to human agency. But whatever it is, it is not the stuff of popular history. Not only does the evidence produced ignore the limitations of the source collection (Google Books), but the mathematical methodology used and its results are too complex to be understood by most academic historians, let alone the wider public.

At its best, this sort of work can be deeply illuminating. Ben Schmidt's 'Prochronism' projects, for example, take the individual words in modern cinema and television scripts that purport to represent past events and compare them to every word published in the year they are meant to represent. In the process, he illustrates all the anachronism in *Downton Abbey*, and, more impressively, the subtle changes in the presentation of masculinity, decade by decade, in the evolving world of *Mad Men*.[15]

But this type of history moves the focus resolutely away from people like Sarah Durrant, and towards a variety of cliometrics – a 'scientific' approach to history that has little relevance for the new audience for history evidenced in popular culture. We are guilty of this too. One of our own projects, *Data Mining with Criminal Intent*, took us in precisely this direction.[16] In collaboration with Bill Turkel, at Western University (Ontario), we started to treat the Old Bailey text not as a collection of individual dramas, but as a 'massive text object'. Figure 6, for instance,

---

[14] Jean-Baptiste Michel *et al.*, 'Quantitative Analysis of Culture Using Millions of Digitized Books', *Science*, 331 (14 Jan. 2011), 177–8.

[15] Ben Schmidt, 'Prochronisms or: Downton Crabbey. Using TV anachronisms to learn about change in language' (http://www.prochronism.com/, 28 Apr. 2015).

[16] *With Criminal Intent* (http://criminalintent.org/, 28 Apr. 2015).

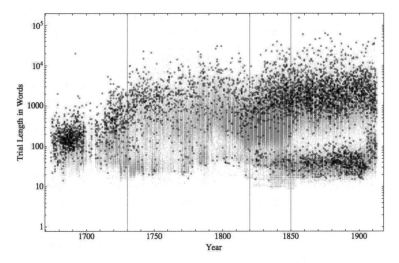

Figure 6 Distribution of trial lengths in words. Cases categorised as 'killing' displayed as black circles; all other trials as grey dots. 'Killing' includes all trials tagged for the offences of 'infanticide', 'murder', 'petty treason', 'manslaughter' and 'killing: other', by the Old Bailey Online (http://criminalintent.org/, 28 Apr. 2015).

represents all 200,000 trials in the Old Bailey Online, divided between those for forms of 'killing' and all other offences, and distributed according to how many words each trial contained – from the shortest, at 8 words, to the longest, at 157,000 words. By doing this, we discovered that the nineteenth-century trial came to be marked by large numbers of very short trials, as a result of the rise of plea bargaining, even for those accused of serious crimes like killing. For many, 'justice' had moved from the courtroom to the police cell.[17]

This graph provides a good example of how 'distant reading' allows us to discover new facts about familiar sources, but it did not result in popular history. And the same could be said of many of the important projects that are beginning to use sophisticated techniques such as formal network analysis, topic modelling, Text Frequency/Inverse Document Frequency measures and, most influentially, approaches derived from Bayesian probability – all generally thought of as forms of 'big data'

---

[17] 'Digging into Data Challenge Conference', *With Criminal Intent* (http://criminalintent. org/2011/06/digging-into-data-challenge-conference/, 28 Apr. 2015).

analysis.[18] The challenge is to link the individual to the complex patterns of data we can generate – to put Sarah Durrant back into the picture.

While some forms of academic *research* are in danger of turning their back on the rich opportunities digital history presents for bridging academic and popular history, academic history *writing* has been slow even to embrace the new possibilities of the digital as a means of dissemination. We continue to prioritise our traditional publication genres – the monograph, the journal article, the chapter in an edited collection. These are what we submit to the Research Excellence Framework (REF) in the UK, where in the most recent exercise websites and electronic databases accounted for just 0.5 per cent of the 6,431 submitted outputs in history.[19] They are also what we list on our CVs, and focus on when making decisions about promotion. We even resolutely ignore the electronic editions we consult when we write our footnotes and compile our bibliographies, choosing instead to cite the print versions. Similarly, we routinely fail to acknowledge our use of keyword searching as a research method.[20]

The 'e-book' is a good example of how slowly the academic history world, and its partners in the publishing sector, is changing. While academic monographs are now frequently published in e-book editions, alongside the traditional hardback and sometimes paperback, the e-book is typically little more than an online pdf document – taking advantage of only the most basic of the numerous opportunities the internet offers for making knowledge accessible and fostering dialogue. This failure to exploit the potential of the digital is particularly frustrating in the case of published editions of primary sources, such as tax and legal records and diaries. Despite the fact that these editions are often unrewarding to read in book form, and require very detailed indexes to be useful, they are still rarely delivered in an electronic format which would enable the keyword and structured searching necessary to maximise their usefulness.

---

[18] For a recent discussion of these approaches, see Tim Hitchcock, 'Big Data for Dead People: Digital Readings and the Conundrums of Postitivism', *Historyonics* (http://historyonics.blogspot.co.uk/2013/12/big-data-for-dead-people-digital.html, 28 Apr. 2015).

[19] Research Excellence Framework 2014: Overview Report by Main Panel D and Sub-panels 27 to 36 (Jan. 2015), pp. 51–2 (www.ref.ac.uk/media/ref/content/expanel/member/Main%20Panel%20D%20overview%20report.pdf, 1 May 2015).

[20] Jonathan Blaney, 'The Problem of Citation in the Digital Humanities', in Clare Mills, Michael Pidd and Esther Ward, *Proceedings of the Digital Humanities Congress 2012* (Sheffield: HRI Online Publications, Studies in the Digital Humanities, 2014) (www.hrionline.ac.uk/openbook/chapter/dhc2012-blaney, 17 July 2015); Tim Hitchcock, 'Confronting the Digital, or How Academic History Writing Lost the Plot', *Cultural and Social History*, 10.1 (2013), 12, 19.

In a book published in 2015, we tried to push the boundaries of the e-book, by designing it so that it is most productively read online.[21] Thousands of embedded hyperlinks take the user from relevant places in the text directly to the free online editions of the primary sources we have cited or quoted from, or the complete databases which underlie our tables and graphs, or catalogue entries of the printed primary source texts we cite, or e-book editions in Google Books of the secondary sources. These links are intended not only to make real the traditional purpose of a footnote – to allow the relevance of a specific piece of evidence to be confirmed by the reader, and the research journey of the authors to be made explicit – but also to encourage a new kind of reader engagement with our research. This is not a book that needs to be read sequentially from pages 1 to 450 (how many of us do that anyway?); instead, readers are encouraged not only to dip in and out of the book as they wish, but also to follow research threads back into the sources, where they can conduct their own research and consider other interpretations and lines of argument that we have not even thought of.

Bringing our publisher along on this journey proved difficult. While they were keen on the approach when we initially approached them, the production processes publishers use to generate books are not readily adaptable to new formats. They are still framed in terms of the production of a printed book, and the generation of basic pdfs from this printed text. It is difficult to work outside this system; the structures of academic publishing change very slowly.

While the online and the digital have fundamentally reshaped the landscape of historical research, bringing into being a new audience, and a new class of practitioners, the practices of academic research and writing threaten to ignore these new possibilities, heading in entirely different directions. Developments in the analysis of big data have tended to make digital history inaccessible, technocratic and in some ways irrelevant for a wider audience, while academic publishing is resistant to innovation. There are very real challenges to overcome if we are to achieve the potential for the internet to bridge the divide between academic and public history, and let history serve its primary function as a form of social memory, while also taking advantage of new methodologies created by big data. And in our estimation, the answer to this conundrum is provided by the internet itself.

First and most obviously, ease of publication means that historians can put the results of our research into the public domain almost instantly, and in innovative formats which are more readable by a wide audience.

---

[21] Tim Hitchcock and Robert Shoemaker, *London Lives: Poverty, Crime and the Making of a Modern City, 1690–1800* (Cambridge, 2015).

The academic blog is a good example of this. While some blogs explicitly address a public rather than academic audience (the 'History Matters' blog at the University of Sheffield is a good example of this), other historians use blogs to disseminate findings, or try out emerging arguments, for their peers as well as a wider audience.[22] Many, particularly younger, scholars are beginning to use social media and blogs as part of the process of developing ideas, collecting evidence and perhaps most importantly, ensuring that once complete, the history they have written has an audience of eager readers who have followed the research process from day one. One way of viewing the research blog is thus as the first draft of history; one can use one's blogs, and any comments received, as a starting point for writing more formal publications. This is the approach we are adopting on our latest project, the Digital Panopticon.[23]

Perhaps the best example of this is Ben Schmidt's hugely influential blog, *Sapping Attention*.[24] Schmidt's blog posts analysing nineteenth-century word frequency and authorship contributed to his doctorate, and will form part of his first book. Helen Rogers maintains two blogs: *Conviction: Stories from a Nineteenth-Century Prison*, on her own research; and a collaborative blog, *Writing Lives*, created as an outlet for the work of her undergraduates. These blogs bring together research and teaching, and in the process are building a substantial community of interest.[25] The list could go on. The *Many Headed Monster*, the collective blog authored by Brodie Waddell, Mark Hailwood, Laura Sangha and Jonathan Willis, is rapidly emerging as one of the sites where seventeenth-century British history is being re-written.[26] Others have a longer pedigree: Sharon Howard has been overseeing the *History Carnival* for over a decade, allowing historians from around the world to bring together themed content about early modern history.[27] For many historians, Twitter is where a lot of the ongoing discussion, in at least some corners of history, is taking place.[28] Following the hashtag #Twitterstorians, created by Katrina Gulliver,

[22] *History Matters: History Brought Alive by the University of Sheffield* (www.historymatters.group. shef.ac.uk/, 28 Apr. 2015).

[23] www.digitalpanopticon.org (1 May 2015).

[24] Ben Schmidt, *Sapping Attention: Digital Humanities: Using Tools from the 1990s to Answer Questions from the 1960s about 19th Century America* (http://sappingattention.blogspot.co.uk/, 28 Apr. 2015).

[25] Helen Rogers, *Conviction: Stories from a Nineteenth-Century Prison* (http://convictionblog. com/, 28 Apr. 2015); *Writing Lives* (http://www.writinglives.org/, 28 Apr. 2015).

[26] Broddie Waddell *et al.*, *The Many-Headed Monster: The History of 'the Unruly Sort of Clowns' and Other Early Modern Peculiarities* (https://manyheadedmonster.wordpress.com/, 28 Apr. 2015).

[27] Sharon Howard, *The History Carnival* (http://historycarnival.org/, 28 Apr. 2015).

[28] Laura O'Brien, 'Twitter, Academia and Me', *The Society for the Study of French History* (http://frenchhistorysociety.co.uk/blog/?p=348, 28 Apr. 2015).

which aggregates the 'tweets' of hundreds of individual historians, for a few days reveals a wild world of debate and engagement.

The relationship between these 'publications' and more formal academic outputs and reward procedures is unclear. At the moment, blogs listed on an academic CV are unlikely to be taken seriously as research publications, though they may well be seen as evidence of public engagement, which *is* starting to be recognised within promotions procedures.

Internet publication leads us to the controversial topic of Open Access, and the emerging requirements in the UK to make research publications freely available online. We do not propose to rehearse the various objections to Open Access, except to observe that it is hard to resist the conclusion that many academics have lost the plot on this issue. By focusing on economic costs, business models and copyright licensing, and insisting on ring-fencing the forms of dissemination used for traditional methods of scholarship, we are in danger of undervaluing the opportunities Open Access creates to widen the audiences for academic writing, to rethink the content of that writing and to develop new styles and genres – not just blogs, but more interactive or iterative forms of writing, where there is a dialogue between the writer and a broad audience.[29]

Many experiments in this area have failed to gain real traction, but journals such as *Digital Humanities Now* (http://digitalhumanitiesnow.org/) and the online platform *Open Library of Humanities* (www.openlibhums.org/about/) are pioneering new forms of cooperative peer review, pre-review publication and Open Access that point the way towards more useful, re-usable, transparent and open form of scholarly communication.

Innovative forms of communication can also be used to address the problems of the growing sophistication and lack of transparency of computer-based forms of analysis and the persistent divide between statistically and computer literate academics (still a small subset of the discipline) and everyone else interested in history. New presentational methods can be used to summarise both large bodies of data and the complex relationships identified through data analysis, and present them in an accessible form. A straightforward example is any graph produced by the Ngram viewer, which provides a visual summary of the language contained in millions of books. Even more user-friendly possibilities can be found via the in-vogue practice of 'visualisations' – pick up any newspaper today and you will find plenty of examples, presented with varying

---

[29] For a wider discussion of the role of social media in modern academic discourse, see Tim Hitchcock, 'Doing it in Public: Impact, Blogging, Social Media and the Academy', *Historyonics* (http://historyonics.blogspot.co.uk/2014/07/doing-it-in-public-impact-blogging.html, 1 May 2015).

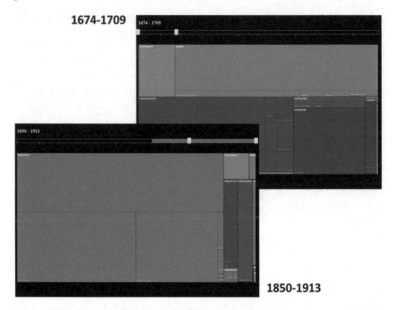

Figure 7 (Colour online) The distribution of punishment sentences for Old Bailey convicts, 1674–1709 compared to 1850–1913 (Digital Panopticon project: http://www.digitalpanopticon.org/datavis/punishment_treemap.html, 17 July 2015).

degrees of effectiveness. Used properly, visualisations (more precisely, infographics) provide an accessible form of 'distant reading', allowing anyone quickly to see broad patterns, identify trends and note anomalous cases – all of which can then be investigated in greater detail using a variety of research methods, including more traditional forms of 'close reading'.

For example, in the Digital Panopticon project, we are using visualisations to summarise judicial and penal experiences of felons in order to identify patterns in the thousands of life stories we are tracing of those convicted at the Old Bailey between 1780 and 1875. The project is still in its early phases, but Figure 7 illustrates, in the form of a 'treemap', an interactive visualisation of punishment sentences at the Old Bailey over the entire period of the *Proceedings*, demonstrating more effectively than a table or graph ever could the dramatically changing penal policy of Old Bailey judges. By using the sliding bar at the bottom of the page, the online user can watch the composition of punishment sentences change over the period from 1674 to 1913, revealing the transformation from

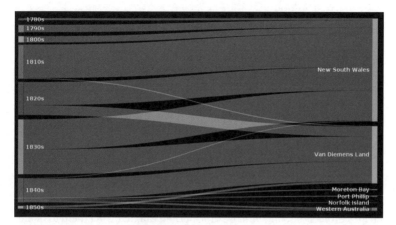

Figure 8 (Colour online) Destinations of transportees to Australia by decade. Each line represents one or more convicts, with the thickness of the line denoting the number of convicts in each decade who were sent to each colony (Digital Panopticon project: http://www.digitalpanopticon. org/datavis/sankey.html?data=linksdecade, 17 July 2015).

a penal system dependent on hanging, branding and whipping to one predominantly reliant on imprisonment.

The interactive user can then rapidly move from this 'distant reading' to individual stories – by clicking through from the relevant box to individual trials, to find Sarah Durrant.[30]

Another useful form of visualisation is a 'Sankey diagram', which maps relationships between two different variables. Figure 8 documents a key stage in the convict story – from sentence at the Old Bailey to transportation to Australia – showing how the date of conviction largely, but not exclusively, determined the colony to which convicts were sent. Ultimately, we will be charting the entire lives of these convicts (or as much as we can document), and our visualisations will chart various life courses from birth, through previous convictions, the Old Bailey trial and sentence, actual punishments experienced and subsequent life events (reoffending, marriage, death). When you are tracing the lives of some 90,000 convicts, the only way of summarising and analysing this evidence is through visualisations like this; and they should also be effective in communicating our findings to a wider audience.

[30] This feature is already available when using the statistical function on the Old Bailey Online: http://www.oldbaileyonline.org/forms/formStats.jsp (17 July 2015).

Mapping, using Geographical Information Systems (GIS), is another increasingly popular form of visualisation.[31] This kind of display has wide contemporary resonance as a result of the use of features such as Google Maps in day to day life, but it is also a widely used and accessible research tool. There are numerous examples, but to highlight a single one, the French Book Trade in Enlightenment Europe project spent some ten years developing interactive online maps that allow a user to interrogate the detailed records of a Genevan publisher and bookseller, the Société Typographique de Neuchâtel, from 1769 to 1794.[32] The Société sold books to purchasers all over Europe, and this website's mapping function (one of a number of types of visualisation on the site) allows the distribution of particular titles and authors to be mapped – reflecting a total of 70,000 sales transactions. Users can create their own maps by selecting particular book titles, authors, subject matter, types of publication, languages and client's professions, and limit by time period, thus allowing them to define their own research questions.[33] Unfortunately, it is not possible to drill down from the resulting maps to the individual records which form the underlying data.

Two terms have recently been widely used in relation to the internet – 'affordances' and 'disruption'. The first comes from the world of design, and refers to the uses that any bit of technology – any object – can be put. In writing history online, we are confronted with a remarkable set of new 'affordances', in terms of genres of publication and communication, as well as a wide variety of methodological approaches, from big data and distant reading to the simple but magical power of keyword searching on the infinite archive. But as an ever growing list of industries has discovered, every new affordance brings in its train 'disruption'. New career paths, Open Access, MOOCs and the empowerment of people outside the academy to produce their own histories, cut to their own cloth, challenges the historical profession to re-think how WE do history online. It is not a challenge we can afford to ignore.

Our belief is that we are in a fantastic age of new and popular historical engagement, and while it is not being led by academic historians (nor should it be), we need to be actively involved, and make sure that we add

---

[31] Ian Gregory, 'Using Geographical Information Systems to Explore Space and Time in the Humanities', in *The Virtual Representation of the Past*, ed. M. Greengrass and L. Hughes (Aldershot, 2008), 35–46.

[32] *FBTEE: The French Book Trade in Enlightenment Europe* (http://fbtee.uws.edu.au/main/, 28 Apr. 2015).

[33] Simon Burrows and Mark Curran, 'The French Book Trade in Enlightenment Europe', *Journal of the Digital Humanities*, 1.3 (2012) (http://journalofdigitalhumanities. org/1–3/the-french-book-trade-in-enlightenment-europe-project-by-simon-burrows-and-mark-curran/, 17 July 2015).

our tuppence to the pot. As academics, we should do our bit to ensure that academic history is remade more open, more democratically accessible and ever more able to do the business of allowing society to question itself, to question its values in light of its past, its politics and its inherited principles. Despite the 'disruptions', as long as we keep in mind these underlying purposes of history writing, we can't go far wrong.

Transactions of the RHS 25 (2015), pp. 95–112 © Royal Historical Society 2015
doi:10.1017/S0080440115000043

RICHARD WAGNER AND THE GERMAN NATION
The Prothero Lecture

By Tim Blanning

READ 2 JULY 2014

ABSTRACT. Richard Wagner's relationship with the German nation was inconsistent and often contradictory, veering between pride and distaste. One constant feature, however, was his intense hostility to the German princes. He held them responsible for the decline of German culture after the Reformation and, more especially, after the Thirty Years War. Their imitation of Italian and French models amounted to cultural treason in his view. The great revival of the 'German spirit' in the eighteenth century, he asserted with characteristic vehemence, came from the common people. It was they too who rose in revolt against Napoleonic tyranny in the great 'War of Liberation' of 1813–15. Yet once again the princes betrayed them, restoring despotic rule once the French yoke had been removed and resuming the patronage of French plays and Italian operas. In forming this narrative, Wagner was strongly influenced by Friedrich Schiller, who ranks with Shakespeare and Beethoven in his rather limited pantheon. It found its way into several of his music dramas, most explicitly in *The Mastersingers of Nuremberg*, whose political message has often been misunderstood.

On 28 November 1863, Richard Wagner dined with his friends Hans and Cosima von Bülow at the Hotel Brandenburg in Berlin. Wagner was in high spirits, having just relieved his usual financial worries by selling for ninety talers a gold snuff-box, a present from the grand duke of Baden. After dinner, Hans went off to prepare for a concert, while Cosima and Richard went for a drive 'in a handsome carriage'. After a while, the latter recorded in his autobiography, they fell silent:

> we gazed mutely into each other's eyes and an intense longing for the fullest avowal of the truth forced us to a confession, requiring no words whatever, of the incommensurable misfortune that weighed upon us. With tears and sobs we sealed a vow to belong to each other alone. It lifted a great weight from our hearts.[1]

Although the relationship was consummated in the following June and a daughter, appropriately named Isolde, was born nine months later, they did not start living together until the spring of 1866. To lessen the pain of separation, Cosima presented her lover with a magnificent note-book,

---

[1] Richard Wagner, *My Life*, ed. Mary Whittall, trans. Andrew Gray (Cambridge, 1983), 729. This is the best translation available, although bizarrely it has no index.

bound in brown leather, decorated with twelve gems of malachite and protected against prying eyes by a stout lock. In this *Brown Book*, Wagner recorded his most intimate thoughts and feelings for her to read later. As he was not writing with one eye on posterity (unlike when dictating his autobiography *My Life* to Cosima), it enjoys special authority.

On 11 September 1865, while living in Munich, Wagner wrote for Cosima: 'I am the most German being. I am the German spirit. Question the incomparable magic of *my* works, compare them with the rest; and you can, for the present, say no differently than that – it is *German*.'[2] That seems unequivocal enough as an assertion of national identity, but – as so often with Wagner – complexity, if not confusion, lurked behind confident assertion. He went on:

> But what is this German? It must be something wonderful, mustn't it, for it is humanly finer than all else? – Oh, heavens! It should have a soil *this German*! I should be able to find my people! What a glorious people it ought to become. But to this people only could I belong.[3]

As this anguished doubting implies, Wagner's 'Germany' was an ideal construction which he despaired of ever seeing actually created.

Absence had not made the heart grow fonder. In August 1860, Wagner returned to Germany after eleven years in exile, but felt no patriotic emotion. To his friend and benefactor (and Cosima's father) Franz Liszt he wrote:

> It is with a real sense of horror that I now think of Germany . . . May God forgive me, but all I see there is pettiness and meanness, the semblance and conceit of solidity, but without any real ground or basis. Half-heartedness in everyone and everything . . . I must also confess that setting foot on German soil again made not the slightest impression upon me, except, at most, a sense of surprise at the foolishness and unmannerliness of the language that was being spoken all around me. Believe me, we have no fatherland! And if I am 'German', it is no doubt because I carry my Germany around with me.[4]

Wagner wrote so much, especially about himself, that all manner of conflicting views can be ascribed to him. In what follows, I shall address one particular aspect of his relationship with Germany that has not attracted the attention it deserves. It relates to his reading of recent German history. The context of the entry in the *Brown Book* just cited was a report published in an illustrated magazine of the jubilee celebrations of the Students' Association (*Burschenschaft*) at Jena, the first and most famous of many similar organisations founded in German universities as Napoleon's empire in Germany collapsed. Liberal, democratic and nationalist, they soon fell victim to the reaction which followed the

---

[2] Richard Wagner, *The Diary of Richard Wagner: The Brown Book 1865–1882*, ed. Joachim Bergfeld (1980), 73.

[3] *Ibid.*

[4] *Selected Letters of Richard Wagner*, ed. Stewart Spencer and Barry Millington (1987), 503.

assassination of August Kotzebue in 1819, 'the single most sensational act of the post-war decades in Germany'.[5] A popular playwright, Kotzebue was also a notorious reactionary and was suspected of being a Russian agent to boot. His assassin, Karl Ludwig Sand, was a member of the Jena *Burschenschaft* and became *the* great martyr-figure of the German student movement following his public execution by decapitation.

Wagner was sympathetic to Sand and hostile to Kotzebue, whose plays he regarded as the ultimate in philistine superficiality. It was a prejudice which may have dated back to his idolisation of his uncle Adolf, a prominent Leipzig intellectual who had nursed a special loathing for Kotzebue for both political and aesthetic reasons.[6] Richard Wagner was only two years old when the Jena *Burschenschaft* was founded and only six when it was suppressed, but the jubilee of 1865 brought the memories flooding back: 'I gave way to gentle tears', he recorded in the *Brown Book*.[7] That the memories were imagined did not make them any the less powerful, for they were underpinned by a political narrative. In Wagner's view, the 'War of Liberation' of 1813–15 which threw off twenty years of French tyranny had been a popular rising in the cause of liberty and independence: 'Anno 1813 in Germany... 14-year-old boys, and 60-year-old men, went running to camp! It was a fervent, sacred cause: to which were sung songs that sounded almost pious. That was hope! A Germany was to come into being.'[8]

It was a crusade which also had a musical dimension in Wagner's memory. Among the visitors to his widowed mother's house in Dresden during his childhood was Carl Maria von Weber, *Kapellmeister* to the Saxon court. In his autobiography, Wagner recorded:

> when my mother introduced the nine-year-old boy to him, and he asked what I wanted to become and hinted that it might even involve music, my mother said that, while I was wild about [Weber's opera] *Der Freischütz*, she had nevertheless noticed nothing in me that might suggest a talent for music.[9]

Weber was a fervent nationalist, who set to music the most popular of all patriotic songs of the period – Theodor Körner's 'Lützow's wild, audacious pursuit'. This celebrated the feats of a force of volunteers led by Ludwig Adolf Wilhelm von Lützow, from whose black uniforms with red piping and gold epaulettes come the black–red–gold colours of the German national flag.[10] The final verse of Körner's poem runs:

[5] Christopher Clark, *Iron Kingdom. The Rise and Downfall of Prussia 1600–1947* (2006), 399.
[6] Carl Friedrich Glasenapp, *Life of Richard Wagner* (6 vols., 1900–8), I, 493. On Wagner's idolisation of Uncle Adolf, see Robert W. Gutman, *Richard Wagner: The Man, his Mind and his Music* (1968), 16.
[7] Wagner, *The Diary of Richard Wagner*, 73.
[8] *Ibid.*
[9] Wagner, *My Life*, 28.
[10] John Warrack, *Carl Maria von Weber*, 2nd edn (Cambridge, 1976), 163.

It is a wild pursuit, it is a German pursuit:
Its quarry are murderers and tyrants.
So you who love us, do not grieve or complain,
For the land is free and dawn is breaking,
Even if it cost us our lives.
So from generation to generation let it be repeated:
That was Lützow's wild, audacious pursuit!

This was the first piece of music that the young Wagner transcribed.[11] For contemporary Germans, the poem was given added piquancy by the knowledge that Körner himself had been killed in action as a member of the Lützow *Freikorps* at the age of twenty-one. His posthumous fame was assured by the quality of his *œuvre*, which proved to be one of the most anthologised of the nineteenth century, and also by the visual tribute paid by his friend and comrade-in-arms Georg Friedrich Kersting when he included him in his celebrated painting of 1815 'At the Advance Guard' (*Am Vorposten*) as one of the three soldiers who gave their lives in the war against Napoleon.[12] All three are wearing the large black velvet berets, the emblematic headgear of German patriots and favoured by Wagner throughout his life.

Weber's *Freischütz*, which aroused the young Wagner's wild enthusiasm, was more than an opera. In the verdict of the leading musical periodical of the day, the *Allgemeine Musikalische Zeitung*, it was 'a national event'. So colossal was its success that everything else was driven from the stage: 'and where does this appeal, this awesome power come from? It comes from the national character which inspires the opera and from its uniquely German qualities.'[13] If it owed much of its appeal to its numerous attractive melodies and brilliant orchestration, it had a special resonance because of the contemporary context. If the nominal setting of the opera is Bohemia in the aftermath of the Thirty Years War, everyone in the audience knew that it was really about Germany in the aftermath of the Napoleonic wars.[14] Although there is no overt political message, most of the characters are simple country people and the music they sing is steeped in a folk idiom. Extra nationalist spice was added to the premiere

---

[11] Wagner, *My Life*, 29.
[12] Hannelore Gärtner, *Georg Friedrich Kersting* (Leipzig, 1988), 89–103.
[13] *Allgemeine Musikalische Zeitung*, 7.28, 10 July 1830, 222–3.
[14] This was well put by the director David Pountney in the course of an interview with Hilary Finch, published in the *Times* on 8 Sept. 1999. Asked what *Der Freischütz* could do for the future of opera, he replied: 'Well, it happens to be exactly the type of piece we should be trying to create in a modern context. It was written in essentially popular language; and it addressed a subject which was in its day absolutely contemporary – and still is. Weber wrote it within five years of the end of the Napoleonic wars which had been so deeply traumatic for Germany. This highly sophisticated and civilised country found itself being marched over by an arrogant dictator, and realised it had no social or civil apparatus to resist him.'

in Berlin on 18 June 1821 by the location. It was staged, not at the Court Opera House on Unter den Linden, where the Italian Gasparo Spontini ruled the roost, but at the new Playhouse on the Gendarmenmarkt.[15]

Just how much of an impact *Der Freischütz* had made on Wagner was revealed by a review he wrote of the work in Paris in June 1841 for the *Dresden Evening News*. It reveals so eloquently his immersion in romantic-nationalist semiotics that it deserves to be quoted rather than paraphrased:

> Oh, my magnificent German fatherland, how can I help loving you, how can I help adoring you, even if only because it was on your soil that *Der Freischütz* was written! How can I help loving the German people, the people that loves *Der Freischütz*, that even today still believes in the wonder of the most naïve fairy-tale, that even today, when it has reached its maturity, continues to experience that sweet, mysterious trembling which made its heart throb when it was young! Oh, how wonderful is German dreaming, with its visions of forests, of the evening, of the stars, of the moon, of the clock on the village church striking seven! Happy is the man who can understand you, who can believe, feel, dream and share your rapture with you! How happy I am to be German![16]

Sitting in the auditorium of the Paris Opera, these thoughts had 'pierced my heart like a thrust from a voluptuous dagger' (a very Wagnerian image) and had prompted him to burst into tears. The French, he went on, would have found the reason for this emotional outburst simply risible; only the Germans would understand, when he told them that it happened at the end of Act One, when the troubled huntsman is left alone brooding as the rest of the peasants dance their way into the inn to the strains of the *Walzer*, the most folksy of all the folksy tunes in *Der Freischütz*.

The setting of *Der Freischütz* shortly after the end of the Thirty Years War played an important part in Wagner's historical narrative of Germany, for it was then, in his view, that an existing pernicious development had become irreversible. He set out his version of German history since the sixteenth century on several occasions, most explicitly in the 'diary entries' he wrote for the benefit of King Ludwig II of Bavaria. The rot had set in, he opined, with Charles V, the multi-national, unGerman emperor who had supported the decadent papacy against Luther's Reformation. Until then, the German princes had marched largely in step with the German spirit but now, with very few exceptions, they increasingly whored after foreign models and fashions. Any remaining ties with the people were then severed by the devastation inflicted by rampaging foreign armies after 1618: 'from the end of the Thirty Years War Germany in effect ceased to

---

[15] Norbert Miller, 'Der musikalische Freiheitskrieg gegen Gaspare Spontini. Berliner Opernstreit zur Zeit Friedrich Wilhelms III.', in *Preußen - Versuch einer Bilanz*, ed. Manfred Schlenke (5 vols., Hamburg, 1981), IV: *Preußen – Dein Spree-Athen. Beitrage zu Literatur, Theater und Musik in Berlin*, ed. Hellmuth Kühn (Hamburg, 1981), 209.

[16] Richard Wagner, '*Der Freischütz*: a Report to Germany', in *Sämtliche Schriften und Dichtungen*, 5th edn (12 vols., Leipzig, n.d.), I, 220.

exist'.[17] Chief among the princely renegades arraigned by Wagner was Frederick the Great of Prussia, who despised his people and everything to do with Germany, devoted himself exclusively to French culture, spoke only French and even thought only in French. His example was followed by all the other princes, great and small, the only variation being that those in the south followed Austria in finding Italian and Spanish models more seductive.[18]

This collective act of cultural treason had persisted until Wagner's own day. The great movement of the eighteenth century, which had brought forth, among others, Bach, Lessing, Goethe, Schiller, Haydn, Mozart, Beethoven and Kant, went unnoticed by the rulers, with very few exceptions. It was from the reviving spirit of the German *people* that this revival came and, between 1813 and 1815, it inspired them to rise up and throw off the yoke imposed by their French conquerors. Alas, the princes failed to understand what was happening: like Frederick the Great, they viewed their subjects merely as cannon fodder and so expected them to return to their subservient status once the Napoleonic wars ended. They judged everything by French standards and so saw in the enthusiasm of the German people only Jacobin subversion. From 'this terrible misunderstanding', Wagner lamented, Germany had gone on suffering until the present day, leaving the princes just as purblind as they had ever been. In all of history, he thundered, there could be no blacker story of ingratitude than the treason of the German princes: the German people had got rid of the French oppressors only to find that their princes had reinstated French civilisation!

The battlefields which had resounded to Körner's songs were still reeking of the blood of martyred German patriots when the princes resumed their addiction to foreign fashions. It was Italians such as Rossini and Spontini who were summoned to Vienna and Berlin to provide entertainment. Nothing had changed since then: still today (in 1865), he complained, if the king of Prussia or the emperor of Austria wished to lay on a gala for a visiting dignitary, then it was always a French play or an Italian opera that was staged. The great Schiller celebrations of 1859, when nearly 500 German towns had commemorated the centenary of the great poet's birth, had shown what could be done, but none of Germany's rulers had noticed. Only in Bavaria, Wagner flatteringly told

---

[17] *König Ludwig II. und Richard Wagner Briefwechsel*, ed. Otto Strobel (Karlsruhe, 1936), IV, 8. Reprinted here are the diary entries Wagner made for Ludwig to read and which he later rewrote as *What is German?* in 1878 – Jürgen Kühnel, 'The Prose Writings', in *Wagner Handbook*, ed. Ulrich Müller and Peter Wapnewski, trans. John Deathridge (Cambridge, MA, 1992), 612–13.
[18] *König Ludwig II. und Richard Wagner Briefwechsel*, ed. Strobel, IV, 9.

Ludwig II, had successive kings recognised a mission 'for the salvation of the German people'.[19]

This was actually more than flattery, for the most spectacular tribute to German culture sponsored by a German prince had indeed been made by a Wittelsbach. Between 1830 and 1842, Ludwig's grandfather, King Ludwig I, had built 'Walhalla', a classical temple on the banks of the Danube near Regensburg, containing ninety-six busts of great Germans. Its purpose was proclaimed by its creator at the opening: 'May Walhalla foster the strengthening and expansion of German feeling. May all Germans, from whatever region they may come, always feel that they share a common fatherland, of which they are proud and to which they contribute with all their might for its greater glory.'[20] Among the original honorands was of course Schiller. Although Shakespeare and Beethoven are usually given pride of place on the rather short list of people Wagner admired unequivocally, Schiller must also be included. In all the voluminous writings by and about Wagner, his name appears again and again. For example, *Opera and Drama* (1851), the most important of the 'Zürich reform writings', reveals that Wagner knew Schiller's works inside out. He observed Schiller's birthday on 10 November every year ceremonially. The exception that proved the rule was 1869 when it got forgotten in the intensive work on the composition of *Twilight of the Gods*. Reminded by Cosima a day later, Wagner had a good answer: 'well, yesterday was the very day on which, while I was working, I felt inwardly pleased by Schiller's picture hanging on the wall opposite me, and I pictured to myself his whole essence'.[21] Perhaps the ultimate tribute he offered was to consider staging Schiller's trilogy *Wallenstein* at Bayreuth.

Most fundamentally, Wagner admired Schiller because of his advocacy of an aesthetic approach to politics, best summarised in his two celebrated aphorisms: 'the jurisdiction of the stage begins where the realm of secular laws ends' and 'if man is ever to solve the problem of politics in practice, he will have to take the aesthetic route, because it is only through beauty that man makes his way to freedom'.[22] Wagner also shared Schiller's fundamental aversion to utilitarian considerations playing any role in

---

[19] *Ibid.*, 9–10.

[20] Thomas Nipperdey, 'Nationalidee und Nationaldenkmal in Deutschland im 19. Jahrhundert', in *idem*, *Gesellschaft, Kultur, Theorie* (Göttingen, 1976), 150.

[21] *Cosima Wagner's Diaries*, ed. Martin Gregor-Dellin and Dietrich Mack, I: *1869–1877* (1978), 163.

[22] 'Die Gerichstbarkeit der Bühne fängt an, wo das Gebiet der weltlichen Geseze sich endigt', quoted in Peter-André Alt, *Friedrich Schiller*, 2nd edn (Munich, 2009), 38: '[I hope to convince you] . . . daß man, um jenes politische Problem in der Erfahrung zu lösen, durch das ästhetische den Weg nehmen muß, weil es die Schönheit ist, durch welche man zu der Freiheit wandert.' 'Über die ästhetische Erziehung des Menschen in einer Reihe von Briefen', *Sämtliche Werke*, V: *Erzählungen, theoretische Schriften*, ed. Wolfgang Riedel (Munich and Vienna, 2004), 573.

culture. In his *Letters on the Aesthetic Education of Mankind* of 1794, from which the second of the two aphorisms just quoted is taken, Schiller excoriated utility as 'the great idol of our age, for which all forces must slavishly labour and all talents must worship'.[23] He took Kant's definition of aesthetic experience as 'pleasure without any practical interest' and built on it a programme for moral and, eventually, political liberation.[24] Wagner took this further but gave it a nationalist twist. It had been a German achievement, the achievement of Winckelmann, Lessing, Goethe and, of course, Schiller, to rediscover the non-utilitarian aesthetics of classical antiquity. Whereas the Italians had just plundered it for what they could easily imitate, and the French had then taken from the Italians what suited their national obsession with elegant forms, the Germans had recognised what was 'purely human' (*reinmenschlich*) and completely divorced from utility.[25] In *The Artwork of the Future*, Wagner stated firmly that the arts 'can only initiate creative work in partnership with artistic humans, not with those who are bent on utilitarian ends'.[26]

But Wagner's sense of affinity with his hero also derived from a sense of fellow-suffering. Born a subject of the duke of Württemberg, Schiller had been given a good education at an elite military school but had also felt the heavy hand of princely despotism, including a ban on any further publications after his first sensational success, *The Robbers*. In 1782, he had fled, eking out a wandering existence until settling in Jena in 1787. This unhappy history intensified Wagner's often-expressed loathing of the German princes. It was of course enhanced by his own perceived persecution by the king of Saxony, which in 1849 sent him into exile pursued by an arrest warrant. Cosima's diaries contain many irate expostulations about the princes. In July 1869: 'a violent outburst against the German princes, who lend their support to nothing, to neither talent nor natural gifts, they let everything truly German die of neglect'. In August 1869:

> when one thinks that our courts are nothing but imitations of the court of Louis XIV, which meant something in the France of his day, and now all these little Napoleons can think of is to surround themselves with the same hocus-pocus! No nobler ambitions, in art only what is most vulgar; and for that they spend all their money, yes, even spill blood.

In November 1871: 'in the evening read Plato's *Republic* to R. with much enjoyment. – before that R. read from Freytag's book about the times of

---

[23] *Sämtliche Werke*, V: *Erzählungen, theoretische Schriften*, ed. Riedel, 572.
[24] T. J. Reed, *Schiller* (Oxford, 1991), 67–9.
[25] *König Ludwig II. und Richard Wagner Briefwechsel*, ed. Strobel, 17.
[26] *Sämtliche Schriften und Dichtungen*, III, 149. Translation from *The Artwork of the Future*, trans. Emma Warner, a special issue of *The Wagner Journal* (2014), 71.

the war of liberation, always delighting in the German people and being shocked by the wickedness of the German princes'.[27]

Wagner's version of recent German history was both populist and radical. It found expression in his operas in a number of ways. Chronologically, the first was *Rienzi, the Last of the Tribunes*, based on the novel by Edward Bulwer Lytton. Later disowned by Wagner himself, never performed at Bayreuth, mischievously dubbed 'Meyerbeer's best opera' by Hans von Bülow and invariably presented as a fascist parable whenever it *is* staged, it nevertheless contains much memorable music, notably the overture, the conclusion to Act Two and 'Rienzi's prayer' which opens Act Five. It also gave Wagner an early opportunity to portray the German princes in all their brutal selfishness, lightly disguised as the noble factions competing for the domination of fourteenth-century Rome. In Act One, as the Orsinis try to ravish Rienzi's sister Irene, a street brawl threatens to erupt when they are stopped by the rival Colonnas. Rienzi intervenes and takes the opportunity to denounce all noble factions:

> What crime is there left to you? You have turned Ancient Rome, the Queen of the World, into a den of thieves, desecrating the Church, so that the Pope had to flee to distant Avignon. No pilgrim dares to make his way to Rome to celebrate the great festivals of the Church, for like highwaymen you lie in wait to rob them. Exhausted, impoverished, once-proud Rome is wasting away, and you even take from the poorest of the poor what little they still possess. Like criminals, you break into homes and places of work, cutting down the men and ravishing the women. Just look around you and see what you have done. Look around you – these ancient temples, these great columns, tell you of the time when Rome was free and great, when it ruled the world and its citizens could call themselves the kings of kings. Tell me, you bandits, are there still Romans?[28]

Opposed by the nobility, betrayed by the church and deserted by the people, Rienzi dies with Irene at the end of the opera, as the Capitol goes up in flames, but not before he has made one last declaration of love for his fatherland. In response to Irene's jibe that he does not know what it is to renounce a love because he has never loved a woman, he furiously responds:

> Oh yes I have loved - Oh Irene
> Can you still not know the name of my beloved?
> I have loved my sublime bride with ardour
> ever since I began to think, to feel,
> ever since the splendour of the ancient ruins

---

[27] *Cosima Wagner's Diaries*, ed. Gregor-Dellin and Mack, I, 128, 136, 431–2. He would have enjoyed Treitschke's comment on the German princes competing for territory when Napoleon destroyed the Holy Roman Empire: 'they battened on the bleeding wounds of the fatherland like a swarm of hungry flies': Heinrich von Treitschke, *Deutsche Geschichte im 19. Jahrhundert* (5 vols., Leipzig, 1927), I, 178.

[28] *Dokumente und Texte zu 'Rienzi, der letzte der Tribunen', Richard Wagner Sämtliche Werke*, ed. Reinhard Strohm, XXIII (Mainz, 1976), 156.

told me how great she had once been.
I have loved my bride with a feeling of pain,
for I have seen her brought so low,
so shamefully mistreated, so terribly mutilated,
disgraced, dishonoured, ravished and despised!
Oh, how the sight of her aroused my fury!
Oh, how her suffering strengthened my love!
I have dedicated my life to her alone,
my youth and all my adult powers;
Yes, I wanted to see my sublime bride
crowned as queen of the world –
for let me tell you that the name of my bride is *Rome!*[29]

'Or *Germany*', Wagner might well have added. The vision of a once great nation torn apart by factional feuding kept recurring, although it would of course be reductionist to try to include every one of his operas in this interpretive scheme, or even to present it as his main concern. In *Tannhäuser* (1844–5) it is apparently peripheral. The ruler of thirteenth-century Thuringia, Landgrave Hermann, is presented sympathetically as an eirenic patron of the arts. In his address to the knights of his court before the singing contest, however, he reminds them of the recent bad times, when they had been forced to wage bloody war to assert the majesty of the German Empire against the ferocious Guelphs and domestic discord.[30] Moreover, it soon becomes clear that all is not well in Thuringia. Tannhäuser has returned from the fleshpots of the Venusberg (*mons veneris*) to find a complacent, hidebound, inward-looking society which mistakes the formal expression of love for the real thing. No great acumen is needed to spot that this is Wagner returning from Paris to Dresden in 1842. Just as Tannhäuser was expelled from the Wartburg for telling the truth about the essential carnality of love, so was Wagner driven into exile by the king of Saxony for joining the revolution in 1848–9.

He took his critique a step further in *Lohengrin*, written and composed in Dresden between 1846 and 1848, although not performed until 1850 (at Weimar by courtesy of his friend Franz Liszt). Although set in an even earlier period, it was also more topical. In 932 AD, the German king and duke of Saxony Henry the Fowler has terminated a truce with the Hungarians. To rally support for the impending war, he goes to Brabant, the westernmost territory of the German Empire, to rally support. On arrival, he proceeds to berate the local nobility, assembled on the banks of the river Scheldt outside Antwerp:

[29] *Ibid.*, 200–1.
[30] *Sämtliche Schriften und Dichtungen*, II, 21.

How painful and distressing it must be for me
To find you at each other's throats and leaderless,
Fighting among yourselves in frenzy.

But his ringing appeal – 'The time has come to defend the honour of the Empire, and that applies in equal measure to everyone, east and west!' – falls on deaf ears. His Saxon and Thuringian followers shout their support, but the Brabanters stay glumly silent: Hungary is a long way away, and what business is it of theirs? It is only when the charismatic hero, Lohengrin, appears from nowhere, defeats the evil Frederick of Telramund in single combat and adds his voice in support of Henry's crusade that they respond. Even then, there remains a dissenting group:

First Noble: Listen to him! Does he mean to take us away from our land?
Second Noble: To fight an enemy who has never been a threat to us?
Third Noble: We must not let him get this underway!
Fourth Noble: But who will stop him when he orders us to march?
Frederick of Telramund: I shall.

They fail. When King Henry musters the men of Brabant in the final scene, he is greeted with unanimous shouts of 'Hail!' His speech of thanks which follows is one of the few overtly nationalist passages in all of Wagner's *œuvre*:

I thank you, trusty men of Brabant!
How proudly will my heart swell
when I find in every part of Germany
such a mighty and numerous band of warriors!
Now let the Empire's enemies draw near,
we look forward to giving them a warm reception:
so that never again will they dare
to venture forth from the barren wastes of the East.
The German sword for German lands
So let the power of the Empire be upheld![31]

All present then roar out the last two lines. Unsurprisingly, this passage has proved problematic for many present-day directors and is often cut, as is the assurance given a little later by Lohengrin to Henry when explaining that he will not be able to join him in the campaign against the Hungarians: 'Great king, let me predict to you that you will win a great victory, and that from now until the end of days the hordes of the East will never prevail!'[32] Wagner, of course, was not thinking of the Hungarians of the tenth century but of the Russians of the nineteenth, whose tsar, Nicholas I, had the well-deserved reputation of being the most

[31] *Ibid.*, 107.
[32] *Ibid.*, 112.

tyrannical of all European sovereigns. It was also well known that he kept the German princes (he was married to a sister of King Frederick William IV of Prussia) on the straight and narrow path of reaction. Wagner made the connection explicit in a crucial passage in his autobiography:

> Now that I had finally completed *Lohengrin*, I had for the first time the leisure necessary to look about and study the course of events, and thus I could no longer remain personally indifferent to the lively ferment in which the idea of Germany and the hopes for its realisation had plunged everybody . . . Instead of speeches, I wanted deeds, specifically deeds from our princes whereby they would break irrevocably with their old ways, so injurious to wider German interests. To this end I got excited enough to write a popular appeal in verse, calling upon the German princes and their peoples to launch a great military undertaking against Russia, the apparent source of the pressure in favour of those policies of the German princes that had so fatefully alienated them from their subjects. One stanza ran:

It's the old war against the East
Coming home to us today:
The people's sword must never rust
When freedom is at bay.[33]

His own freedom in Germany came to an abrupt end with the failure of the rising in Dresden in May 1849, almost the last episode in the abortive German revolutions of 1848–9. Sparked off by the king of Saxony's refusal to accept the new (and equally abortive) German constitution, it was quickly put down with Prussian help.[34] Wagner had been deeply involved. Indeed, the Saxon prosecutor's indictment accused him of being one of the leaders and, more specifically, of holding meetings at his home to plan the insurrection; of ordering the manufacture of hand-grenades; of manning an observation-post on the tower of the Church of the Cross (*Kreuzkirche*); and of raising support in the countryside around Dresden.[35] On 9 May, just as the Prussians were regaining complete control of the city, he succeeded in escaping, in the company of the Russian anarchist Mikhail Bakunin. Pursued by a warrant for his arrest, he made his way, first to Weimar, where he was helped by the ever-generous Franz Liszt, and then to Switzerland, which he reached by the end of the month.

When dictating his autobiography to Cosima for the benefit of the autocratic King Ludwig II in the mid-1860s, Wagner was at pains to play down his revolutionary activism, claiming that he had just decided 'to let the tide of events carry me wherever it might . . . to surrender myself to the stream of events'.[36] This exculpation was contradicted both by his actions

---

[33] Wagner, *My Life*, 362.
[34] Volker Ruhland, 'Der Dresdner Maiaufstand von 1848/49', in Hans-Peter Lühr, 'Der Dresdner Maiaufstand von 1849', *Dresdner Hefte*, 43 (1995), 27–36.
[35] *Wagner. A Documentary Study*, ed. Herbert Barth, Dietrich Mack and Egon Voss (New York, 1975), 174–5.
[36] Wagner, *My Life*, 390, 402.

during 1848–9 and by his continuing commitment to violent revolution after he had fled. Indicative of his radicalism was – among many other inflammatory tirades – a newspaper article published in April 1849 in which a personification of 'Revolution' proclaims:

> I will utterly annihilate the established order in which you live, for it springs from sin, its flower is misery and its fruit is crime; but the seed has ripened and I am the reaper. I will destroy every wrong which has power over men. I will destroy the domination of one over the other, of the dead over the living, of the material over the spiritual, I will shatter the power of the mighty, of the law and of property. Man's master shall be his *own* will, his *own* desire his only law, his *own* strength his only property, *for only the free man is holy and there is nought higher than he.* Let there be an end to the wrong that gives one man power over millions, which subjects millions to the will of one individual, to the evil which teaches that one has the power to give happiness to all others. Equals may not rule equals, equals have no higher power than equals, *and since all are equal I shall destroy all dominion of one over the other.*[37]

There is much more in the same vein. His correspondence of the period was equally extreme, for example: 'I have no money but an enormous desire to commit acts of artistic terrorism' (to Franz Liszt); 'My business is to bring about revolution wherever I go' (to Theodor Uhlig); and 'I long passionately for the revolution, and the only thing that gives me the will to live is the hope of surviving long enough to see it and to take part in it' (to Ernst Benedikt Kietz).[38]

Although Germany was to be the first port of call for his 'sublime Goddess of Revolution', Wagner was looking for nothing less than a *world* revolution that would emancipate all humanity, for she promises, among other things: 'I shall destroy the existing order of things which divides mankind into hostile nations.'[39] In October 1848, the actor Edward Devrient recorded in his diary: 'Wagner brought me a sketch for an opera; he still has these great socialist ideas in his head. Now it is not enough for him to have a united Germany, now it has to be a united Europe, a united humanity indeed.'[40] Expelled from Germany and, as it turned out, not able to return for eleven years, his horizons widened. Neither his numerous 'Zürich reform writings' nor the tetralogy *The Ring of the Nibelung* are informed by a nationalist perspective. Even the most notorious of the former – *Judaism in Music* – ends with the injunction: 'take part in this work of redemption through self-denial, for then we are one and indivisible'.[41] This universalism was then given a powerful impetus by his acquaintance with the philosophy of Arthur Schopenhauer, made in 1854, which had a profound, if sometimes over-stated, influence on his

[37] *Wagner. A Documentary Study*, ed. Barth, Mack and Voss, 172.
[38] *Selected Letters of Richard Wagner*, ed. Spencer and Millington, 171, 183, 226.
[39] *Wagner. A Documentary Study*, ed. Barth, Mack and Voss, 172.
[40] *Eduard Devrient aus seinen Tagebüchern*, ed. Rolf Kabel (2 vols., Weimar, 1964), I, 451.
[41] *Richard Wagner. Stories and Essays*, ed. Charles Osborne (1973), 39.

subsequent works.[42] Characteristically, Wagner claimed that he had been a Schopenhauerian intuitively even before reading his *magnum opus The World as Will and Idea*.[43]

The Ring of the Nibelung (whose text he did not alter but reinterpreted to fit his new *Weltanschauung*), *Tristan and Isolde*, *The Mastersingers of Nuremberg* and *Parsifal* deal with great universal themes such as the incompatibility of love and power, domination-free discourse, sexual and social revolution and the renunciation of desire. Yet Wagner's old hatred of the decadent world of the German nobility was never far away. In *Twilight of the Gods*, it appears as the court of the Gibichungs, where the degenerate Gunther and his pathetic sister Gutrune are unable even to find mates by their own efforts. They have to rely on the trickery of their half-brother, the evil Hagen, and so are drawn into a web of deceit, treachery and murder. Hagen's father is the capitalist plutocrat Alberich, who half-seduced and half-raped Queen Grimhilde, a *mésalliance* epitomising the unholy marriage of new money and old blood in nineteenth-century Europe. Hagen is thus the polar opposite of Siegfried, the product of the loving union between the twins Siegmund and Sieglinde, a hero without fear, malice or ambition and so doomed to succumb to the wiles of his enemy.

The theme of the charismatic hero coming from outside to redeem the tired world of the old regime was one of Wagner's favourites – Rienzi, Tannhäuser, Lohengrin, Siegfried, Walther von Stolzing, perhaps Tristan, certainly Parsifal, all qualify.[44] The most explicit criticism of the nobility is to be found in *The Mastersingers*, specifically in the final peroration of Hans Sachs. Having won the singing competition and thus the hand of the beautiful (and rich) Eva Pogner, Walther at first refuses to enter the guild of mastersingers, not unreasonably perhaps, given his earlier treatment by them. Hans Sachs then steps forward to save the day by giving Walther a sharp reminder that he had won not because of the length of his noble pedigree but by his merit as an artist. It was the mastersingers, he goes on, who had kept the flame of true German art burning in the dark days, which, alas, were about to return:

> Beware! Evil deeds threaten us;
> once the German people and the German empire
> fragment under false foreign domination,
> then soon no prince will be able to relate to his people,
> and foreign delusions and baubles

---

[42] Barry Millington, *Richard Wagner. The Sorcerer of Bayreuth* (2012), 83. Wagner's debt to Schopenhauer is discussed with exceptional clarity and cogency in Bryan Magee, 'Wagner and Schopenhauer', in *idem*, *The Philosophy of Schopenhauer* (Oxford, 1983), 326–78.

[43] Wagner, *My Life*, 510.

[44] I have discussed this in 'Richard Wagner and Max Weber', *Wagnerspectrum*, 2 (2005), 93–110.

will take hold of Germany;
and no one would know any more
what was German and genuine,
if it didn't live on in the tradition of the German masters.[45]

This passage has been denounced for being 'chauvinistic'[46] or even 'a summons to a racial war on the Latins'[47] but was not directed against foreigners at all, as the context (and a careful reading of the text) reveals. The work is set in the newly Protestant city of Nuremberg in the mid-sixteenth century (the historical Hans Sachs's dates were 1494–1576). Sachs is looking forward with anxiety (and Wagner is looking back in anger) to a period of civil strife driven by religious hatreds, culminating in the Thirty Years War of 1618–48. Sachs is of course right to be alarmed. The Holy Roman Empire will indeed fragment as Spanish, Danish, Dutch, Swedish and French armies rampage across German-speaking Europe, aided and abetted by the German princes. Even after military conflict has come to an end, foreign domination will persist in the form of the French and, to a lesser extent, Italian culture imitated by the deluded princes, slaves to alien fashions. Only the authentic, if unsophisticated, culture of the mastersingers will keep the native flame burning. In other words, Sachs is not targeting foreigners, nor is he asserting German superiority; his anger is reserved for the *German* princes. Although Wagner certainly had a low opinion of contemporary French culture, he blamed its materialism and superficiality not on the French nation but on the oppression of Napoleon III's Empire.[48] If 'chauvinism' is defined as 'exaggerated patriotism of a bellicose sort, blind enthusiasm for national glory or military ascendancy' (as it is by the *Oxford English Dictionary*), there is nothing chauvinistic about this speech.

Hans Sachs would have been even more upset had he been able to look into the future and see what happened when German native culture did find its feet again in the course of the eighteenth century. The great cultural revival was accompanied by a new political catastrophe after 1792 when the French Revolutionary and Napoleonic wars turned Germany into a French colony to be exploited at will. In 1813, Wagner believed, the German people rose in revolt in a great war of liberation and threw off the foreign yoke, only to find that the German princes had not changed one jot. The traitors were still inside the gates and still wedded to 'foreign delusions and baubles'. In November 1878, Cosima recorded in her diary:

[45] *Sämtliche Schriften und Dichtungen*, II, 270.
[46] Thomas Grey, 'Wagner's *Die Meistersinger von Nürnberg* as National Opera (1868–1945)', in *Music and German National Identity*, ed. Celia Applegate and Pamela Potter (Chicago and London, 2002), 83.
[47] Gutman, *Richard Wagner*, 282.
[48] 'Deutsche Kunst und deutsche Politik', *Sämtliche Schriften und Dichtungen*, VIII, 31–2.

'R. says that the 1813 uprising, so misinterpreted by the ruling princes and thus crushed, was as much a disaster for Germany as the Thirty Years War.'[49] That few historians would accept the Wagner version of modern German history does not matter. It enjoyed wide popularity at the time, not least because it was popularised by Friedrich Schiller. Wagner himself cited Schiller's poem 'The German Muse', in which a sense of grievance about the lack of princely patronage was outweighed by the pride the German people could take in the knowledge that they had created their culture by their own unaided efforts. In an unpublished draft of a poem, written partly in prose and partly in verse, of the same period (1801) which was later given the title 'German Greatness', Schiller returned to the theme:

> At a time when two arrogant nations [France and Great Britain] have their feet on his neck, can the German hold up his head ... and take his place with pride among the peoples of the world? Yes he can! He may suffer misfortune in war, but he has not lost what constituted his real value. The German Empire and the German nation are two quite different things. The majesty of the German never rested on the heads of his princes. The German has founded his own true value away from politics and even if the Empire were to go under, German dignity would remain inviolate. For it is a moral form of greatness and resides in culture and the character of the nation, which is quite independent from its political fate
>
> . . . .
>
> Heavy chains oppressed all peoples on the earth
> When the Germans broke them asunder
> By entering the lists against the Vatican and
> Declaring war on the illusion ['*Wahn*']
> Which held the whole world in thrall.
> The greater victory is won
> By him who unleashes the blaze of truth,
> And who liberates minds
> To win freedom to use reason
> Is a victory for all nations
> And stands for all eternity.
>
> . . . .
>
> Germany's majesty and honour
> Never rested on the heads of princes
> And even if Germany's Empire
> Were to perish in the flames of war,
> German greatness would remain intact.[50]

---

[49] *Cosima Wagner's Diaries*, ed. Gregor-Dellin and Mack, I, 431–2.
[50] *Deutsche Grösse: ein unvollendetes Gedicht Schillers 1801*, ed. Bernard Suphan (Weimar, 1902), 5–8. This includes the original *in facsimile*. For a modern edition, see *Friedrich Schiller: Sämtliche Werke*, I: *Gedichte, Dramen I*, ed. Albert Meier (Munich, 2004), 473–8. Here, the work is headed

Hans Sachs'a final speech in *The Mastersingers*, in other words, sounds almost like Schiller set to music. Although Wagner cited 'The German Muse', he cannot have known the longer version, which was not published until 1871 in volume XI of Schiller's complete works published in 1871. Although this was in Wagner's library at Wahnfried, he had finished his libretto nine years earlier.[51] In any event, the uncanny resemblance between the two texts reveals how close were their conceptions of modern German history.

Of all the traitorous German princes, the most toxic were the Prussians. As a Saxon, Wagner had special reason to hate them. The end of the Napoleonic wars brought victory for the Germans but defeat for the Saxons. As their king, Frederick Augustus I, stayed loyal to Napoleon until the end, Saxony had been punished with the loss to Prussia of more than 40 per cent of its population and more than half of its territory. That gave a special piquancy to *Lohengrin*, for in the tenth century, when Saxony was the dominant force in Germany and the German king was a Saxon, Brandenburg did not even exist. It was only for a brief period during and after the Franco-Prussian War of 1870–1 that Wagner felt anything positive about Prussia and even then – like most non-Prussian Germans – it was for the negative reason that Prussia was putting the French to the sword. On 22 January 1871, Cosima recorded:

> Regarding the outcry in the press against the bombardment of Paris, R. says: 'Now at last I understand the Prussians and their stiff, buttoned-up character; it used to annoy me to see the King of Prussia in that uniform buttoned right up to the neck, even in his workroom. But now I can understand it; if it had been otherwise, we should be lost.'[52]

This enthusiasm did not last long. In 1871, he proclaimed: 'Wonderful progress is being made in establishing the new Reich... Anyone who does not understand figures such as Bismarck, Roon & Moltke around this King Wilhelm – is very much to be pitied' but five years later he was complaining: 'The world, and more especially "Germania", is becoming increasingly repugnant to me!'[53] As for Bismarck, when he met him in 1871, Wagner was 'utterly enchanted with the genuine charm of his character'.[54] By 1878, he was commenting 'no good star is watching over

---

'1797', although the explanatory note on p. 954, following Suphan, states that 1801 is more likely.

[51] *Schillers sämmtliche Schriften*, XI: *Gedichte*, ed. Karl Goedeke (Stuttgart, 1871), 412–14. I am most grateful to Barry Millington for supplying me with a copy of the Wahnfried catalogue. Barry Millington drew attention to the similarity between the speech of Hans Sachs and Schiller's fragment in *Wagner* (1986), 255. On Wagner's debt to Schiller, see my article 'Hans Sachs and Friedrich Schiller', in *Richard Wagner. Die Meistersinger von Nürnberg*, ed. Gary Kahn (2015), 40–6.

[52] *Cosima Wagner's Diaries*, ed. Gregor-Dellin and Mack, I, 325.

[53] *Selected Letters of Richard Wagner*, ed. Spencer and Millington, 780, 853.

[54] *Cosima Wagner's Diaries*, ed. Gregor-Dellin and Mack, I, 362.

Bismarck's creation' and later the same year was finding him guilty of 'great superficiality!'.[55] By the end of the year, Bismarck was dismissed as 'a bad man', although with the characteristic proviso that 'the princes are entirely to blame'.[56] In October 1880, Cosima recorded, 'he expresses to me his utter antipathy to Bismarck' and the following March he called him 'a brutal barbarian'.[57] The bellicose Francophobia of 1870–1 was by now very much a thing of the past. On 6 September 1880, Cosima made the following revealing entry in her diary:

> Yesterday a poem by E. Geibel in celebration of [the battle of] Sedan aroused utter disgust, and today a 'Germania' in the *Illustrirte* the same feeling; R. says 'I have only to see a fellow in a winged helmet and I feel sick.' – And the description of the battle itself produces from him an outburst of indignation: 'The dead horses alone are enough! And it all shows the barbaric times in which we live.' – The Emperor's latest speech to the army, which ends with the words that his final thoughts will always be for the army, evokes from R. the exclamation, 'I should have thought for the ballet – a person like that is nothing more than a dim-witted soldier, and that's about all they know!' He wonders how to save Fidi [their son Siegfried] from having to do military service – through naturalisation elsewhere? Continual thoughts of America, above all in order to gain independence for himself and particularly for *Parsifal*.[58]

In conclusion, I must repeat my recognition that Wagner's attitudes to the German nation cannot be reduced to admiration of Friedrich Schiller and hostility to the German princes and nobility. From all the immense riches of his work, there is a great deal more to be mined on this subject, as so many analysts have demonstrated. I hesitate to say that this particular niche has been left unexplored because so much more has been written about Wagner than even the most diligent and uninterrupted scholar can hope to master or even be aware of.[59] However, in view of a persistent tendency to write about Wagner's politics as if an indictment for a war crimes tribunal were being prepared, it bears restating.

---

[55] *Ibid.*, II, 84, 196.

[56] *Ibid.*, 229.

[57] *Ibid.*, 551, 644.

[58] *Ibid.*, 533–4.

[59] 'The number of books and articles written about him, which had reached the ten thousand mark before his death, overtook those about any other human being except Jesus and Napoleon' – Bryan Magee, *Aspects of Wagner*, 2nd edn (1988), 33.

Transactions of the RHS 25 (2015), pp. 113–134 © Royal Historical Society 2015
doi:10.1017/S0080440115000055

TRAITORS AND THE MEANING OF TREASON IN AUSTRIA-HUNGARY'S GREAT WAR

By Mark Cornwall

READ 26 SEPTEMBER 2014

ABSTRACT. Treason is a ubiquitous historical phenomenon, one particularly associated with regime instability or wartime loyalties. This paper explores the practice and prosecution of treason in the last decades of the Habsburg monarchy with a special focus on some notorious wartime treason trials. It first sets the rhetoric and law of treason in a comparative historical context before assessing the legal framework supplied by the Austrian penal code of 1852. Although the treason law was exploited quite arbitrarily after 1914, the state authorities in the pre-war decade were already targeting irredentist suspects due to major anxiety about domestic and foreign security. In the Great War, the military were then given extensive powers to prosecute all political crimes including treason, causing a string of show-trials of Bosnian Serbs and some leading Czech politicians. By 1917–18, however, this onslaught on disloyalty was backfiring in the wake of an imperial amnesty: as loyalties shifted away from the Habsburg regime, the former criminals themselves proudly began to assume the title of 'traitor'. The paper is a case-study of how regimes in crisis have used treason as a powerful moral instrument for managing allegiance. It also offers a new basis for understanding instability in the late Habsburg monarchy.

In early 1919, a few months after Czechoslovakia declared independence from the Austro-Hungarian empire, a former Habsburg military judge travelled by train from Prague to Vienna. During the war, Jaroslav Kunz had headed one of Vienna's military courts, but he was now in Czechoslovak service and keen to assert his new patriotism. He was visiting the Austrian capital to collect his mother and sister and repatriate them but he was also there on a special mission. The Czechoslovak prime minister, Karel Kramář, and others in the government had asked him to locate the archive of the notorious Czech treason trials of 1914–17 and to claim it as Czechoslovak property. When Kunz finally tracked down the records to the court house where he himself had worked, he was horrified at what he found. Not only were thousands of court documents – protocols, letters and photographs – strewn all over the floor. They were being fed by soldiers into a stove in order to heat the building. 'It was a true picture of Austrian disintegration', wrote Kunz later: 'So ended the infamous work of Austrian military justice!'[1] He finally found fragments

---

[1] Jaroslav Kunz, *Náš odboj v zrcadle rakouské vojenské justice* (Prague, 1930), 6–10.

of Czech treason material, had them packed in boxes and sent back to Prague. Over the next decade, he would reproduce them in colourful reminiscences, peering behind the black and yellow Habsburg curtain so that, as he said, 'we do not forget the cage in which we lived'.[2]

Many documents from the wartime trials in Vienna had been destroyed, or – in the case of the most famous Russophile trial[3] – never seem to have undergone archival repatriation. In the Czech case, since 1919, most have remained unsorted in Prague and ignored by historians. In part, this document-diaspora explains why the history of high treason (*Hochverrat*) in wartime Austria-Hungary has been so neglected. Usually in the past century, those writing about the subject have had a national-political agenda – on behalf of the 'national traitors' – to demonstrate their righteous struggle under the Habsburg yoke. This was especially true in the mass of Czech memoirs that surfaced in the interwar period, recalling Czech martyrdom in Vienna's so-called 'Prison of Death'. From that 'Viennese bastille' the traitors had survived *en masse* to tell their story, to bolster a new Czech national narrative, while the voices of their accusers were silent since the Habsburg regime had lost its legitimacy. In contrast, in the new state of Yugoslavia after the Great War, there was a much fainter echo of the court trials conducted against Bosnian Serb traitors.[4] In fact it was not until the late 1980s, when Serbian nationalism was suddenly resurgent in Yugoslavia, that some popular and academic interest was aroused in the mass treason trials of Bosnian Serbs.[5] Some Serbian historians then rekindled the subject to meet a contemporary agenda, showing how the myth of the traitor has often been cyclically exploited in nationalist narratives.

To paraphrase the German journalist Margret Boveri, let us take a walk in this Austro-Hungarian 'landscape of treason', for it is a very instructive ramble for any historian.[6] Treason, of course, is historically ubiquitous and the ultimate political crime. It always involves some kind of power struggle, a perceived challenge to existing authority, or a threat to an established political community that may endanger state security. The cry of 'treason' or 'traitor' has consistently been invoked over the centuries as a linguistic device with which to disarm a political opponent, a way of publicly branding some disloyalty to a cause or community. But more

[2] Jaroslav Kunz, *Za černožlutou oponou. Z Vídeňských vzpomínek* (Prague, 1921), 5.

[3] That of the Ruthene politician Dimitrij Markov in the summer of 1915.

[4] For example, Vladimir Ćorović, *Crna knjiga. Patnje Srba Bosne i Hercegovine za vreme svetskog rata 1914–1918* (Belgrade and Sarajevo, 1920).

[5] See the useful proceedings of a Bosnian conference from 1986, collected in *Veleizdajnički proces u Banjaluci. Zbornik radova*, ed. Galib Šljivo (Banjaluka, 1987); and the more popular nationalist work by Djordje Beatović and Dragoljub Milanović, *Veleizdajnički procesi Srbima u Austro-Ugarskoj* (Belgrade, 1989).

[6] Margret Boveri, *Der Verrat im 20. Jahrhundert* (Reinbek bei Hamburg, 1976), 7.

concretely, the concept of treason was and is embedded in most states' criminal codes, constituting there 'the heaviest and most cumbersome weapon in the fight for political power'.[7]

Whether rhetorically or judicially, treason has always been pronounced as the most abominable act. Just as the thirteenth century English jurist Henry de Bracton advised that it exceeded all other crimes, so Edward Coke when condemning the Gunpowder plotters in 1606 piled up his metaphors to describe the insidious, covert world of the traitor: 'For Treason is like a tree whose root is full of poison, and lyeth secret and hid within the earth'; it required the severest punishment imaginable (hanging, drawing and quartering).[8] Three centuries later, at the trial of Roger Casement in 1916, another attorney general F. E. Smith opened his prosecution by stressing treason as 'the most heinous crime', while the judge later directed the jury: it was 'the gravest known to the law' and (in wartime) 'almost too grave for expression'.[9] An Austrian jurist around the same time defined *Hochverrat* as a peculiar crime which, because of its special dangers and unforeseeable consequences, deserved the harshest penalty.[10]

The treason trial well into the twentieth century was the ultimate theatre for a public power struggle, where regimes would don a mask of legality in order to eliminate those identified as traitors. In this process, the traitor was always demonised, for in all cases of treason the struggle for power is interpreted in moral terms: allegedly, the moral universe of the community, the collective, has been violated by one of their own who has become a traitor.[11] In the sixteenth century, the traitor might still be interpreted as Satan's agent working against God's anointed.[12] By the twentieth, he was more likely, as in the case of Casement's 'homosexual depravity', to be simply stigmatised or pathologised for his base character traits. The violent language deployed for this purpose crossed all borders and cultures. It could be extreme when the final contest was actually a show-trial with minimal defence and no redress. Thus, in Hungary in 1950, the traitors in one Stalinist show-trial were described as the 'scum

---

[7] Otto Kirchheimer, *Political Justice: The Use of Legal Procedure for Political Ends* (Princeton, 1961), 76.

[8] Coke's words, in *A True and Perfect Relation of the Whole Proceedings against the Most Barbarous Traitors* (1606), D4; J. G. Bellamy, *The Law of Treason in England in the Late Middle Ages* (Cambridge, 1970), 7.

[9] *Trial of Roger Casement*, ed. H. Montgomery Hyde (1960), 7, 179. See similarly: *The Trial of William Joyce*, ed. C. E. Bechhofer Roberts (1946), 30.

[10] *Das Strafgesetz über Verbrechen, Vergehen und Uebertretungen: nebst den hiezu erflossenen Nachtragsgesetzen*, Oesterreichische Gesetzeskunde, II, ed. Ludwig Altmann (Vienna, 1913), 62.

[11] Nachman Ben-Yehuda, *Betrayals and Treason: Violations of Trust and Loyalty* (Boulder, CO, and Oxford, 2001), 125.

[12] Lacey Baldwin Smith, *Treason in Tudor England. Politics and Paranoia* (1986), 129–38.

of society' who had turned to treason 'because of their cowardly and vacillating characters'.[13] In 2013, the uncle of North Korea's dictator was executed because he was 'despicable human scum, worse than a dog [who had] perpetrated thrice-cursed acts of treachery'; history would never forget his 'shuddering crimes'.[14]

In all these cases, though the treason was socially constructed and peculiar to its era, the regime usually defined the crime in universal terms, emphasising a timeless morality which the traitor had transgressed. Sometimes – rarely – the power struggle ended with the traitor's victory. More often, the moral construction of treason was turned on its head by the accused. The traitors – whether the earl of Strafford in 1641, Casement in 1916 or the Norwegian fascist Vidkun Quisling in 1945 – might at their trial take a final stand for posterity, publicly appealing to history or some higher power in order to challenge the court's moral superiority and foster some posthumous legacy of their own.[15] Many traitors, if given a voice, pointed the finger of treason at their accusers, identifying them as the real traitors to the wider community.

I

In the late Habsburg monarchy, we can find many features of this generic landscape of treason. Those put on trial were usually stigmatised as 'depraved' and misguided individuals who had no moral compass. Not only had they cunningly plotted for years to undermine the natural order, but the entangled roots of their treason finally flourished in some monstrous enterprise. Thus, in 1916, the prosecutor at the trial of Karel Kramář would claim that the seeds of his 'ignominious treason' had effectively caused the First World War.[16] The fact that such treason trials were so prolific in Austria-Hungary's final decade requires an explanation. It fully matches a pattern where traitors are usually sought and found during periods of regime instability or in wartime, when loyalty to the state has to be publicly displayed, and an example made of any prominent individuals who seem to be disloyal.

A deeper consideration is where we should place the late Habsburg monarchy in the broader landscape of treason (where the historiography

---

[13] The concluding speech of the prosecutor Gyula Alapi, in *László Rájk and his Accomplices before the People's Court* (Budapest, 1949), 272–3: 'The only defence against mad dogs is to beat them to death.'

[14] *Guardian*, 14 Dec. 2013, 3.

[15] See for example Strafford's defence in J. P. Kenyon, *The Stuart Constitution. Documents and Commentary* (Cambridge, 1966), 194–5; *Casement*, ed. Montgomery Hyde, 200–4; Oddvar Hoidal, *Quisling: A Study in Treason* (Oslo, 1989), 754, 764.

[16] Archiv Ústavu TGM (AÚTGM: Archive of the T. G. Masaryk Institute, Prague), Fond Maffie, karton 39, XIII: Markus Preminger's concluding speech at the Kramář trial, 3845–6.

is singularly weak for the modern era).[17] Austria-Hungary in the early twentieth century sat on the edge of two worlds, with treason still mainly signifying disloyalty to the Habsburg monarch and his empire. In contrast, treason for the rest of the twentieth century was increasingly interpreted ideologically, as a question of allegiance to a political system, whether communist, fascist or democratic-capitalist. By the twentieth-first century, with Edward Snowden labelled alternatively as a traitor or a 'whistle-blower', it has become far more problematic to find the meaning of treason or to pinpoint where individuals owe their loyalty in a global world. In short, as Britain has recently found with young jihadists, treason has become far harder for states to police.

The charge of *Hochverrat* in wartime Austria-Hungary gained its power because, alongside a strong rhetoric about treason from July 1914, the accusation lay within a firm legal framework. This matched the idea of the Austro-Hungarian monarchy after 1867 as a *Rechtsstaat*, a state where its citizens had equal protection under the law. The major penal code remained the Austrian code of 1852, completed during the decade of dynastic neo-absolutism. Hungary issued its own criminal code in 1878, relying heavily on German and French models, but it was the Austrian that remained valid for most treason trials of the First World War.[18]

Under this code, the relevant paragraph was §58. Like all treason laws on the European continent, §58 incorporated major threats to both internal and external state security, and especially matched imperial Russia's definition of the crime.[19] Treason under §58 had three key objects. The first clause (§58a) protected the monarch's physical safety, defining it as treason to injure or endanger the person of the emperor. Unlike in England or Italy, this did not cover other members of the imperial family, so the assassination of Archduke Franz Ferdinand at Sarajevo in 1914 was not in itself a treasonable act. Nor did simple abuse or disrespect towards the monarch constitute treason: since the 1780s, *Majestätsbeleidigung*, which

[17] There have been few attempts to conceptualise the modern history of treason, but see Ben-Yehuda, *Betrayals and Treason*, and Thomas Noetzel, *Die Faszination des Verrats. Eine Studie zur Dekadenz im Ost-West-Konflikt* (Hamburg, 1989). Cf. the plentiful studies for early modern England, such as John Bellamy, *The Tudor Law of Treason: An Introduction* (1979), and Lisa Steffen, *Defining a British State: Treason and National Identity, 1608–1820* (Basingstoke, 2001).

[18] Josef Prušák, *Rakousko právo trestní* (Prague, 1912), 14. The territory of Croatia-Slavonia (autonomous under Hungary) retained the Austrian 1852 code with some Croatian amendments. The code was also introduced in Bosnia-Hercegovina after its occupation in 1878.

[19] For the following, see the comparative discussion by Franz van Calker, 'Hochverrat und Landesverrat', in *Vergleichende Darstellung des deutschen und ausländischen Strafrechts. Vorarbeiten zur deutschen Strafrechtsreform*, ed. Karl Birkmeyer, Fritz van Calker, Reinhard Frank *et al.*, Besonderer Teil, 1 (Berlin, 1906), 2–71. Also, *Das Strafgesetz*, ed. Altmann, 60–5, and Wolfgang Pfeifer, 'Der Hochverrat im österreichischen Strafrecht vom 18.Jahrhundert bis zur Gegenwart' (Ph.Diss, Graz, 2008), 120–30.

might include refusing to shake the emperor's hand as well as more open hostility in word or deed, had been down-graded and codified separately.[20] The second clause (§58b) made it treason to instigate a violent change of government; most famously it was employed in 1870 against Austrian socialists who had demonstrated in the streets of Vienna and were deemed to have a violent revolutionary purpose.[21] Both of these clauses had existed since the Austrian criminal code of 1803. Both conceived treason as the attempted as well as the completed act, so there was no such thing as 'attempted treason'.

But it was the third clause (§58c) which the Habsburg authorities would wield most persistently during the Great War since it tied the empire's existence to an external threat. All the major wartime trials were based on this rubric of territorial treason (*Gebietshochverrat*) which had originated in the mid-nineteenth century in the unstable aftermath of the 1848 revolutions. Under §58c, treason was defined vaguely not only as causing a danger to the external security of the state (as in the 1803 code), but as fomenting civil war at home or – most significantly – as working to detach a part of the imperial territory.[22] The attempted act was again akin to the act itself; the crime might be committed in speech, word or deed, with or without violence. So there was ample scope in §58c for clever lawyers to twist treason to match the state's political objectives. Even if many of these clauses had exact parallels in other European penal codes (Russian or Italian for example), Austrian law was still one of the severest in Europe, prescribing execution by hanging for all forms of treason. Traitors in the Magyar half of the empire were luckier since Hungarian law, though similar, was more precise and only a physical attack on the king required the death penalty.[23]

It was therefore §58 which was the major legal basis for *Hochverrat* and, as with the English Treason Act of 1351, its vagueness or potential for politicised 'construction' laid it open to abuse. Indeed, in the decade before the Great War, several Austrian jurists had pointed out the dangers inherent in §58 and argued for a complete overhaul of a penal code much of which was over a century old. In 1913, the Austrian minister of justice

---

[20] Philip Czech, *Der Kaiser ist ein Lump und Spitzbube. Majestätsbeleidigung unter Kaiser Franz Joseph* (Vienna, Cologne and Weimar, 2010), 66–80.

[21] Herbert Steiner, 'Der Wiener Hochverratsprozess 1870', in *Sozialistenprozesse: Politische Justiz in Österreich 1870–1936*, ed. Karl R. Stadler (Vienna, 1986), 13–30.

[22] Pfeifer, 'Der Hochverrat im österreichischen Strafrecht', 120–1, 128–9. Contemporary legal commentaries noted that Austrian law, unlike German, French or Italian, had no specific conception of *Landesverrat* (betraying state security), but partly subsumed it into *Hochverrat* in §58c: see Calker, 'Hochverrat und Landesverrat', 11, 63.

[23] See the Hungarian Criminal Code of 1878 (§126–38). §126–7 covered almost exactly the same fields as the Austrian §58 but were more detailed with special protection for Hungarian territory. For a German translation: *Das ungarische Strafgesetzbuch über Verbrechen und Vergehen*, trans. Gustav Steinbach (Budapest, 1878), 30–3. My thanks to Attila Barna for this source.

had told the Upper House of the Austrian Reichsrat that the law failed to reflect the major transformation that had occurred in the past century in relations between citizens and the state.[24]

Yet apart from §58, the Austrian penal code supplied other ways to prosecute acts which some might term 'treason' as a threat to state security. These included the vague political crime of 'disturbing public order' (equivalent to English 'sedition') through refusing to obey state law or inciting hatred of the regime. But most sinister was §67, the so-called 'crimes against the war power of the state'. This covered a range of precise acts such as espionage, but also any behaviour designed to benefit the enemy in time of war.[25] In short, it was a licence for arbitrary justice against civilians when the wartime state was anxious about disloyalty. We can glimpse this extended treason early in Jaroslav Hašek's novel *Good Soldier Švejk*, when Švejk is suddenly arrested for 'high treason' by the wily detective Bretschneider. Švejk had hardly violated §58 but a vigilant security officer might well interpret his mad pronouncements as falling within a constructed definition. In contrast, the words Švejk uttered later in a casual conversation with a fellow-soldier over coffee were more clearly treacherous: 'A monarchy as idiotic as this ought not to exist at all.'[26]

II

Hašek's main target for satire – the vigilant Habsburg policeman or army officer – appears quite accurate. For with the outbreak of war in 1914, the Habsburg state, armed with new emergency powers to curb dissent, was paranoid about any outsiders to the patriotic community. A statistic for Vienna alone suggests that cases of political crime including treason, normally eighteen per year, rose twelve-fold in 1914.[27] The reality was not that more *Hochverrat* was being committed, but that the army from July 1914 was overwhelmingly responsible for interpreting and prosecuting this crime. The military always claimed that they were impartial because they were supposedly non-political in their exercise of justice.[28] But

---

[24]AÚTGM, Fond Maffie, karton 39, XIII: Eduard Körner concluding speech at the Kramář trial, 4230–2.

[25]*Das Strafgesetz*, ed. Altmann, 65–6. The 'Verbrechen wider die Kriegsmacht des Staates' (§67) found greater exposition in the military penal code of 1855, §304–31. See *Das Militär-Strafgesetz über Verbrechen und Vergehen vom 15 Jänner 1855 samt den einschlägigen und ergänzenden Gesetzen und Verordnungen*, ed. Alexander Koller (2nd edn, Vienna, 1901), 229–40.

[26]Jaroslav Hašek, *The Good Soldier Švejk* (Harmondsworth, 1974), 13, 207–8. Bretschneider (p. 50) had vainly tried to inveigle Švejk into admitting that the empire was doomed to extinction.

[27]Franz Exner, *Krieg und Kriminalität in Österreich* (Vienna, 1927), 26.

[28]See Jonathan Gumz, *The Resurrection and Collapse of Empire in Habsburg Serbia, 1914–1918* (Cambridge, 2009), 117–18, 126ff.

their behaviour matched an obsessive wartime agenda of safeguarding efficiency at the expense of civilian freedom, as well as a very entrenched set of pre-war national prejudices. For most of the war, at least until the summer of 1917, they could control the machinery of treason due to the powers they suddenly acquired.

With the empire now split into 'war zone' and 'hinterland', it was in the former that the military authorities assumed quasi-dictatorial powers. This eventually meant a huge swathe of territory, excluding only greater Hungary and four of the Austrian crownlands but including those regions closest to the enemy. It is true that martial law was not absolute in the war zone: the military authorities were still supposed to work with the civilian, and concepts of the *Rechtsstaat* were never wholly abandoned.[29] Even so, the powers transferred by imperial decree in July 1914 placed all civilians under military jurisdiction for all political crimes, including treason, espionage, 'disturbing public order' and even *Majestätsbeleidigung*.[30] The result was an arbitrary interpretation of these crimes with devastating results for any civilians who obstructed the army machinery. In the first months of the war, the Army High Command (*Armeeoberkommando*: AOK) simply abandoned the military judicial rulebook introduced in 1912; it returned to an inquisitorial form of trial and widespread use of the court-martial or 'summary justice' (*Standrecht*). The court-martial required no preliminary investigation of the case, the advantage was wholly with the prosecution; the only sentence for a guilty verdict was the death penalty which had to be carried out within two hours.

This draconian procedure was now applied to all those officially charged with political crimes in the war zone. One calculation, based on the cases registered by the War Ministry in Vienna, suggests about 1,900 court-martial deaths, of which 60 per cent were civilian. About 88 people were executed for *Hochverrat*, but 351 for the much vaguer crime against the war power of the state.[31] Some would die for the most minor forms of disloyalty. Thus, a man from Ljubljana, who in June 1915 publicly praised Italy and called the Germans pigs, was found guilty under §65 ('disturbing public order'); he was executed despite pleading intoxication at the time.[32] These summary trials fell mainly in 1915–16. We can compare them with a far more alarming figure for those civilians who, in the first months of hostilities, were called traitors and executed without trial. It is now accepted that as the front initially wavered against

---

[29] See Christoph Führ, *Das k.u.k. Armeeoberkommando und die Innenpolitik in Österreich 1914–1917* (Graz and Vienna, 1968), 21 (n. 49), 88, 181; and Gumz, *Resurrection*, 140.

[30] Joseph Redlich, *Austrian War Government* (New Haven, 1929), 81–2.

[31] Karl Platzer, *Standrechtliche Todesurteile im Ersten Weltkrieg* (Berlin and Stuttgart, 2004), 71–8.

[32] *Ibid.*, 160.

the Serbian and Russian armies, the Habsburg forces committed mass atrocities against Serb and Ruthene (Ukrainian) civilians who seemed to be in collusion with the enemy. It seems hard to believe a staggering figure of 30,000 Ruthene executions, even if in September 1914 the chief of the general staff himself declared Ruthene territory to be an enemy land. But in the south, the empire's Serbs were certainly stereotyped as constituting a 'mass mobilization of high treason'; as Habsburg troops advanced and retreated, over 3,000 Serb civilians near the frontline were summarily executed in a few weeks.[33] Only later did this chaos give way to the legal device of the summary court-martial.

For the military, the ultimate traitors were those who colluded with the enemy and especially dangerous were those suspected of an openly irredentist ideology. Here, the most notorious traitor to suffer summary justice was the Italian Cesare Battisti. His case reveals well the regime's dilemma of how best to manage prominent displays of treason.[34] Battisti's story was mythologised at the time and since because of the post-war division of Austrian Tyrol in Italy's favour. For Italians, and Mussolini's fascist state, the treason could be celebrated as national martyrdom. For German-Austrians, Battisti personified 'perfidious Italy', the ally that had betrayed Austria-Hungary by changing sides in May 1915; in their eyes, he had been legally tried and deserved his fate. Battisti was certainly unusual as a well-known irredentist who met his end on the scaffold. At the start of the war, like some other outspoken parliamentary deputies – the Croat Frano Supilo or the Czech Tomáš Masaryk – he had crossed the imperial frontier, feeling like them that Austria-Hungary was doomed; it could not be reformed and the solution was national liberation at the side of the western Allies. For all these public traitors, Austrian military intelligence began to amass files of incriminating evidence, and an indictment of *Hochverrat* under §58c was slowly pieced together. Only in Battisti's case was the effort rewarded, for on 11 July 1916 he was captured fighting for Italy on Monte Corno and immediately taken to Trento to be court-martialled.

Subsequent events showed how gingerly the regime needed to tread when processing state betrayal. For if the public arraignment of a treacherous leader might act as a deterrent, as the military insisted, it could also produce a martyr.[35] In Battisti's case, the authorities typically had tried to discredit him beforehand, leaking tales of embezzlement

---

[33] For an exaggerated claim of up to 30,000 Ruthene executions: Alexander Watson, *Ring of Steel: Germany and Austria-Hungary at War 1914–1918* (2014), 155. For Serb persecution: Gumz, *Resurrection*, 34–58.

[34] For the following, see Oswald Überegger, *Der andere Krieg. Die Tiroler Militärgerichtsbarkeit im Ersten Weltkrieg* (Innsbruck, 2002), 366–86.

[35] See Kirchheimer, *Political Justice*, 7–8.

although in fact it was a cast-iron case of treason under §58 (with the added sin that Battisti had deserted to Italy when liable for conscription at home). The verdict after the brief court-martial on 12 July therefore spoke of the 'worst and most ignominious treason to the fatherland'. It was the dénouement that then backfired, for Battisti was publicly humiliated when alive and dead. Led out to execution only two hours after the verdict, he was surrounded by troops who shouted abuse, scoffing and jeering when the condemned man cried out that he died as an Italian not as an Austrian. While the news of this scene soon leaked out to the public, even more damning were the postcards that circulated displaying Battisti's corpse alongside grinning faces. The Austrian satirist Karl Kraus condemned this grisly display of 'self-satisfied cosiness (*Gemütlichkeit*)'. But the Austrian military welcomed the postcards as a useful propaganda tool, to justify very starkly why the empire had gone to war with Italy.[36] The picture's mixed reception showed that by 1916 it was impossible to bridge the divide in how treason was being interpreted across Austro-Hungarian society.

While the military prosecuted treason in the war zone quite arbitrarily, albeit with a legal veneer, in the Austrian 'hinterland' – the four Bohemian and Austrian crownlands – they had no such special powers and had to act more cautiously. Repeatedly in the first year of the war, the AOK pressed Count Stürgkh, the Austrian prime minister, to extend martial law into the hinterland in order to deal with treacherous civilian elements. Czech traitors in Bohemia should just be court-martialled with no right of appeal.[37] Although this campaign was always rebuffed, it is not true that the AOK lacked any power outside the war zone.[38] Since all political crimes now fell under military jurisdiction, in the hinterland too those crimes had to be tried in military courts. The result was substantial military control even if the civilian judiciary could try to temper the proceedings; from 1914 to 1916, the number of cases tried by military courts in the hinterland rose from 2,000 to 23,000.[39]

III

How this affected the prosecution of traitors is clear from the large-scale treason trials to which we now turn. Those organised in Bosnia, in the war zone, had a foregone conclusion. In the hinterland, in Vienna or Zagreb, the military authorities had to work harder to secure a conviction but still had overriding legal control. In particular, through the wartime

[36] Überegger, *Der andere Krieg*, 384–6.
[37] See Führ, *Armeeoberkommando*, 34ff, 91–7.
[38] Cf. *ibid.*, 22.
[39] Manfried Rauchensteiner, *Der Erste Weltkrieg und das Ende der Habsburgermonarchie* (Vienna, 2013), 452.

emergency laws, they found ways to intervene and preemptively arrest suspected traitors. This occurred usually with Czech suspects, like the Czech National Socialist leader Václav Klofáč, who was arrested in September 1914 and incarcerated without trial for almost three years. By 1917, he was being earmarked for a monster treason trial that never took place.[40]

The essence of the treason trial, like all political trials, was not just about enforcing the law, but about incriminating domestic enemies so that they could be eliminated. Under §58, this was terminal since the death penalty always applied. By convicting key public figures from either the Czech or Serb communities, the regime also aimed to deter, to sound a warning-shot, to assert a normative Habsburg patriotism at the expense of any other competing allegiances. It might be argued that under the law many of those indicted were indeed traitors (for instance Klofáč), but even so – as in the trials of Casement in England or Joseph Caillaux in France – there was considerable 'construction' of the law to secure a conviction. And some of the Habsburg prosecutors went even further. Determined to convict, they stretched the evidence and sometimes in the courtroom manufactured an 'alternative reality' to explain traitors' behaviour. This foreshadowed the techniques of totalitarian show-trials later in the century. The difference in Austro-Hungarian treason trials was that a defence lawyer was permitted, so there was some slight chance of acquittal.[41]

Yet the monarchy's political trials were not a wartime novelty nor a purely military instrument. In peacetime before 1914, several high-profile treason trials had been staged, notably against Serbs and Ruthenes. They suggest an empire already in crisis, which needed publicly to arraign the 'disloyal' in order to shore up its security. They also showed the real difficulty of defining treason, an uncertainty which could work to the advantage of both protagonists. In the notorious Zagreb treason trial of 1909, which lasted 150 days, 53 Serbs from Croatia were charged with treason under §58c and 31 were eventually found guilty.[42] The prosecutor's remit was to stigmatise a broad swathe of Croatia's Serbs and he twisted the evidence accordingly. Among the observers was R. W. Seton-Watson (a later president of the Royal Historical Society) who sat in the courtroom for three weeks. Calling it 'one of the grossest travesties of justice in modern times', on a par with the Dreyfus scandal, he found it hard to

---

[40] *Obžalovací spis proti Václav Klofáčovi a Rudolfu Giuniovi pro zločin [velezrády] dle §58c tr. z.*, ed. Zdeněk V. Tobolka (Prague, 1919), viii–x.

[41] Kirchheimer, *Political Justice*, 46–8.

[42] For context, especially on the rhetoric of treason, see Mark Cornwall, 'Loyalty and Treason in Late Habsburg Croatia: A Violent Political Discourse before the First World War', in *Exploring Loyalty*, ed. Jana Osterkamp and Martin Schulze-Wessel (Götingen, forthcoming, 2016).

believe that high treason in Austria-Hungary had 'not yet been consigned to the lumber-room of medieval phrases'.[43] The Czech Tomáš Masaryk agreed, warning the Austrian parliament in May 1909 about the danger of using the term *Hochverrat*, an anachronistic phrase from a bygone age.[44]

In fact, many statesmen and army officers in the Habsburg regime did see treason as a very present danger. In early 1914, two major trials were held of radical 'old Ruthenes', Russophile Ukrainians from the empire's eastern provinces. They were all accused of plotting with pan-Slavists from Russia to detach Austro-Hungarian territory. Although the evidence pointed strongly towards a guilty verdict, a conviction depended on whether simply spreading propaganda was equivalent to treason.[45] At the second trial held in Lwow (Lemberg) in Galicia, the prosecutor argued that the cultural-humanitarian work of the 'traitors' (using Russian funds) had simply been a cover for a political plot. Typically, the Austrian press described the accused as outsiders: one as a character from a Dostoevsky novel, another as 'a shabby little man' whose eyes one would never forget.[46] In the end, however, the jury composed of Poles proceeded to acquit these 'traitors'. It was a set-back for the civilian authorities, a sign that wielding the treason law was a risky business. Vienna's leading newspaper advised 'that political trials generally do not tend to achieve their aims'; intensive education in Galician villages was the real solution.[47] But it was a warning from peacetime not heeded when the war began. Military courts then could envisage more success, for no juries would be involved in the proceedings.

Of the main wartime treason trials, those against Serb and Czech civilians gained most notoriety and have left the most evidence. The charge of §58c, where the domestic traitor was conspiring with an external danger, now had real resonance as Austria-Hungary was facing attack on three military fronts. As the military authorities gathered evidence and made new paranoid connections, the phenomenon of treason snowballed. By 1917, they imagined it as one monstrous enterprise spanning the empire, a tree with deep pre-war roots whose poisonous buds were only just blossoming. In the vivid simile of Edward Coke, these buds needed

---

[43] R. W. Seton-Watson, *The Southern Slav Question* (1911), 184, 208.

[44] Thomas G. Masaryk, *Der Agramer Hochverratsprozess und die Annexion von Bosnien und Herzegovina* (Vienna, 1909), 30–1: speech to the Reichsrat on 14 May 1909.

[45] For context, see Z. A. B. Zeman, *The Break-Up of the Habsburg Empire 1914–1918: A Study in National and Social Revolution* (London, New York and Toronto, 1961), 3–11.

[46] 'Russophile Agitatoren vor den Lemberger Geschworen', *Neue Freie Presse* (Abendblatt), 3 June 1914, 4; Berthold Merwin, 'Bilder vom Lemberger Hochverratsprozess', *ibid.* (Abendblatt), 9 June 1914, 3.

[47] 'Freispruch der Angeklagten im Lemberger Hochverratsprozeß', *ibid.* (Morgenblatt), 7 June 1914, 2.

'blasting and nipping' before they ripened and brought 'utter destruction and desolation upon the whole State'.[48]

It was in Sarajevo in October 1914 that the first of the political confrontations was staged. On trial were Gavrilo Princip, Nedeljko Čabrinović and twenty-three other men associated with the assassination of Archduke Franz Ferdinand and his wife. The charge, however, was not one of murder, but *Hochverrat* under §111 (the Bosnian equivalent of §58) as this would carry the death penalty for those who had both planned and executed the treacherous deed.[49] In this setting, the broader political objective was clear. The accused were brought to the courtroom in chains and surrounded by soldiers with bayonets at the ready; in the distance the echo of gunfire from the front was a constant reminder that this treason had led to war.[50] For the prosecution, it was vital to show that the assassins were not lone fanatics but pawns in a vast plot organised by the Serbian enemy to detach Bosnia from the Habsburg monarchy. Their conviction would not just be a matter of justice: it would publicly justify Austria-Hungary's war against that international traitor, Serbia. It was with this aim that behind the scenes the Habsburg foreign minister, Count Berchtold, wanted pressure put on the court so that it was mindful of the current clash with Serbia.[51] The prosecutor duly argued that the assassins were revolutionaries committed to violence, unfortunate wretches who resembled an ulcer in a healthy body. But above all, they were tools of a huge Serbian plot, which had operated for years in Bosnia-Hercegovina via a range of allegedly 'cultural societies' like *Narodna Odbrana* or the Sokol (gymnastics) association. The prosecution equated membership of one of these societies with the preparation of treason. In short, 'Great Serb propaganda [was] in itself treason.'[52]

In this atmosphere, the defence lawyers had an impossible task, for a guilty verdict seemed inevitable. The presiding judge even rebuked one lawyer for being too solicitous of criminals 'who by tomorrow would be condemned to death for treason'.[53] Nor did the young assassins help themselves for most were determined to confess their guilt. Typically, they inverted the label of 'traitor' by claiming to have acted in response to the treachery of Habsburg rule; due to that tyranny in Bosnia, they wanted to destroy the empire and achieve South Slav unification. Their case was

[48] *A True and Perfect Relation of the Whole Proceedings*, D4.

[49] The most accurate trial transcript is in *Sarajevski atentat. Stenogram Glavne rasprave protiv Gavrila Principa i drugova*, ed. Vojislav Bogićević (Sarajevo, 1954). Some historians have used unreliable transcripts: e.g. Christopher Clark, *The Sleepwalkers: How Europe Went to War in 1914* (2012), 51–5.

[50] Rudolf Zistler, *Kako sam branio Principa i drugove 1914 godine* (Ljubljana, 1937), 4, 17.

[51] Vladimir Dedijer, *The Road to Sarajevo* (1966), 336.

[52] Speech of prosecutor Franjo Švara: *Sarajevski atentat*, 332–42.

[53] Zistler, *Kako sam branio Principa*, 4.

also not aided by many of their own defence lawyers. One, who was a Croat, spent a long time lambasting the Serbs, regretting that he had to represent men who had dug the grave not only of Franz Ferdinand but of the Croatian nation.[54] A general defence argument, however, was to question the defendants' actual intentions. It had not been proven that the assassins, let alone their accomplices, had intended to commit *Gebietshochverrat* when murdering the heir-apparent. As silly teenagers, with heads in the clouds, they did not really know what they were doing.

On the defence team, it was the lawyer Rudolf Zistler who tried most diligently to challenge the prosecution case. He too focused on the issue of intent, arguing that under Austrian law treason required an overt act to be committed; instead, the prosecutor was 'constructing' treason through mere association with Serb propaganda or Yugoslav dreams. As Zistler vividly noted, 'If you say you are a supporter of Plato's ideal state or the utopia of Thomas More – that does not make you a traitor.'[55] The act of killing Franz Ferdinand in fact could only be defined as 'political murder', not 'treason', for despite what Princip and others were now claiming, there was no clear proof that they expected the murders to result in the secession of Bosnia from the state.

Zistler, however, then probed even more deeply, challenging the indictment's whole political and legal framework. First, he urged the court to see the trial in the context of recent national developments, for 'in our monarchy unfortunately treason trials recur in a steady periodic cycle, like a chronic illness'.[56] He then delivered his legal *coup de grâce*. Although Bosnia had been annexed by Austria-Hungary in 1908, the union had never been formally ratified by the Austrian or Hungarian parliaments. As a result, he argued, Bosnia was still not yet legally part of the empire, so it was impossible to commit the crime of treason in breaking it away from the state.[57]

Zistler's clever stance did not save his defendants from the gallows. Instead, it earned him several rebukes from the presiding judge and led to his expulsion from Bosnia after the trial because of his 'hostile disposition'. At the end of his speech, he had appealed to history and to justice, but the courtroom in the belligerent context of October 1914 ignored this, leaving him to describe the overall result as 'legal murder'.[58] Not surprisingly, a century later (2014) Zistler's arguments would be exploited by Bosnian Serb nationalists, including the film director Emir Kusturica, in a crude

---

[54] Speech of Konstantin Premužić: *Sarajevski atentat*, 351–4. See also the minimal defence given to the assassin Trifko Grabež: *ibid.*, 364.

[55] Zistler speech: *Sarajevski atentat*, 378.

[56] *Ibid.*, 368.

[57] *Ibid.*, 369–72. See also Zistler, *Kako sam branio Principa*, 13: 'The verdict could not construct a treasonable intention to destroy the annexation [which was] an illegal situation.'

[58] *Ibid.*, 15.

campaign to try to overturn the court verdict and canonise their Serb hero Gavrilo Princip.[59]

While the Sarajevo trial was at least one of criminal assassins, the mass treason trials that mushroomed across Bosnia in 1915–16 were legally far more questionable. It is unclear how many were caught up in this judicial hysteria but it certainly reached into the hundreds. Serbian historians have struggled to explain the political meaning, suggesting even that behind the trials lay some grand purpose by the Habsburg military to wipe out Serb intellectuals as a prelude to reforming the empire radically.[60] The reality was probably more prosaic: a military regime convinced that the Bosnian Serb population was riddled with *staatsfeindliche* elements. Certainly, the Sarajevo trial, after an intense inquiry into Serb irredentism, gave the authorities obvious 'traitors' to pursue. The new trials that started the following spring were in two main groups. The first targeted the Serb *omladina* or youth organisations, seeing in them the hothouses that had produced fanatics like Princip. The second – three major trials – were more politically weighty, indicting several hundred of the Bosnian Serb intelligentsia. All these court-cases interpreted propaganda as treason: that working to raise Serb national consciousness, via societies like *Narodna Odbrana* or Sokol, was akin to plotting the annexation of Bosnia by Serbia. That link might be tendentious, dependent on a construct of the treason law, but there is no doubt that the military authorities believed in their own arguments. They thought (wrongly) that *Narodna Odbrana* was the terrorist organisation that had planned the archduke's murder. Mistrust of all Serbs was ubiquitous: according to one of Bosnia's wartime governors, only a third were loyal while another third were trying to give the impression of loyalty.[61]

Yet there was a deeper meaning to this political theatre, organised in the war zone by a military power that could manipulate the court personnel to its advantage. Alongside the brutal arrests there was, as even one of the Sarajevo assassins noted, some evidence of the *Rechtsstaat* in operation.[62] The larger purpose, glimpsed already in the Sarajevo trial, was to justify publicly Austria-Hungary's war in the Balkans, consistently underlining the traitors' place in Serbia's international plot. Thus, in the

---

[59]See for example, http://www.invest-in-serbia.com/archive/general/1391910600-kusturica-to-seek-annulment-of-gavrilo-princip-s-trial.html (accessed 31 Aug. 2014).

[60]Milorad Ekmečić, "'Žalosna baština iz godine 1914" (Političke namjene sudskih procesa u Bosni i Hercegovini za vrijeme prvog svjetskog rata)', in *Veleizdajnički proces u Banjaluci*, 13, 40.

[61]*Ibid.*, 32. See also the memoirs of Stefan Freiherr Sarkotić von Lovćen, 'Der Hochverrats-Prozeß von Banjaluka', *Berliner Monatshefte für internationale Aufklärung*, 7/1 (Jan. 1929), 33–4.

[62]Vasa Čubrilović, 'Razmišljanja o veleizdajničkim procesima u prvom svetskom ratu', in *Veleizdajnički proces u Banjaluci*, 4.

famous Banjaluka trial, which arraigned 156 intellectuals over six months, the seeds of treason had supposedly been planted over a decade earlier and had flourished through espionage and propaganda before the war. The actual evidence at the trial was slight and wholly circumstantial: a list of names in some documents seized by Habsburg troops in Serbia. Yet none of the defence arguments had any effect in the face of political manipulation from Vienna and Sarajevo. In April 1916, sixteen men were handed the death penalty, commuted to life imprisonment a year later.[63]

IV

It is useful now to juxtapose how Austria-Hungary treated Czech traitors compared to Serb. After the war, much of this national treason lost its pejorative edge, the traitors became heroes, and in their memoirs they took care to minimise their wartime opportunism. In August 1914, the Czech population, in comparison to Serbs or Ruthenes, was not immediately suspect to the military authorities for there was no obvious irredentist threat. Even so, according to §58 certain Czech politicians were indeed already traitors. Václav Klofáč for example was not just a virulent pre-war critic of the empire but in early 1914 had plotted in Russia to organise an underground Czech resistance should war break out; in September, after returning from an American lecture tour full of treasonable speeches, he was arrested and locked up without charge.[64] Only thereafter did the military begin to stigmatise Czechs as unreliable. The main reason was clear evidence that some Czech troops were performing weakly at the front, seemingly due to Czech civilian disloyalty in the hinterland. After repeatedly failing to impose martial law on Bohemia, the AOK in May 1915 finally pounced.[65] Two key Czech politicians, Karel Kramář and Alois Rašín, were arrested. A treason case was carefully constructed against them in Vienna, resulting in the most impressive European treason trial of the whole war.

Much later in the 1920s, when the young actor Otto Preminger (the later film director) appeared in a play in the Czechoslovak capital of Prague, he decided temporarily to change his surname. For his father Markus had been Austria's public prosecutor, a hate figure to many Czechs as chief prosecutor in the Kramář trial. Markus Preminger was an outsider in many ways. A Jew, from the eastern-most province of the

[63]See *ibid.*: Dženana Čaušević, "'Veleizdajnici" na sudskom procesu u Banjaluci i u zatvorima', 369–85.

[64]See Bohuslav Šantrůček, *Václav Klofáč (1868–1928)* (Prague, 1928), and Milada Paulová, *Dějiny Maffie. Odboj Čechů a Jihoslavanů za světové války 1914–1918*, I (Prague, 1937), 27ff, 113–15.

[65]Führ, *Armeeoberkommando*, 47–8; Rauchensteiner, *Der Erste Weltkrieg*, 355–60, 444. For the mythology around Czech military treason: Richard Lein, *Pflicherfüllung oder Hochverrat? Die tschechischen Soldaten Österreich-Ungarns im Ersten Weltkrieg* (Vienna, 2011).

monarchy, he had taken part in early 1914 in prosecuting Russophile traitors and had then fled westwards as the Russian armies invaded. He would always divide opinion for he publicly personified a supranational German-Jewish loyalty in the face of nationalist treachery. One Czech historian described him as 'a marvellous speaker, a master of rhetoric, but an unscrupulous and egotistical Bukovina Jew'.[66] One English supporter noted in retrospect Preminger's 'sharp mind and acid wit', a man hardened to anti-Semitic abuse who had 'led the prosecution of Dr Kramarz (which in German rhymes with "arse")'.[67]

In May 1915, Karel Kramář was targeted by the military as the leading Czech traitor. The timing coincided with Italy's entry into the war, but also with a notorious case of Czech 'mass-desertion' on the eastern front (infantry regiment 28). Kramář's arrest in fact was a knee-jerk reaction after months of military anxiety. The last straw was news that he had secretly (and stupidly) met the Italian consul in Prague, but most significant was his political background, as a leading Czech statesman who had constantly been advocating Slav unity and Russian friendship. Kramář was married to a Russian and regularly holidayed in the Crimea. Before 1914, he had been the leading promoter of so-called 'Neo-Slavism', a cultural movement to foster closer Slav cooperation across Eastern Europe in the face of German dominance. 'Neo-Slavism' was not inherently anti-Habsburg, but it had an underlying political agenda as Kramář hoped to re-balance the Austro-Hungarian empire in favour of its Slav majority. Yet its real prerequisite was a much closer international alliance between Austria and Russia, a dream that was scuppered because of the Bosnian crisis of 1909 followed by the Balkan Wars.[68] Just as Neo-Slavism rapidly disintegrated before 1914, so for Kramář the outbreak of a European war was a disaster: Russia, his chief Slav ally, was now the official state enemy. He felt it impossible publicly to espouse loyalty to the monarchy alongside the German empire. It was on this basis, and a retrospective interpretation of Kramář's pre-war behaviour, that Preminger would try to unmask him as a long-term traitor.

From the start, Preminger felt that Kramář could certainly be accused of 'crimes against the war power of the state', for 'as leader of the Czech people he has undoubtedly failed to fulfil the heighted patriotic obligation of these serious times'. But a charge under §58 for *Hochverrat* was also likely. Already on Kramář's arrest in Prague, evidence had been seized showing his links to the Czech resistance movement now organised abroad by Tomáš Masaryk. The reality was that Kramář was not a major player

---

[66]Paulová, *Dějiny Maffie*, 154. See also František Soukup, *28. říjen 1918*, I (Prague, 1928), 172: Preminger advanced in Austria as 'a great legal star of the war'.
[67]Willi Frischauer, *Behind the Scenes of Otto Preminger* (1973), 26, 29, 40.
[68]See Paul Vyšný, *Neo-Slavism and the Czechs 1898–1914* (Cambridge, 1977).

in the Czech Maffie (the name assumed by the small resistance group at home) and was struggling with his own loyalties. However, on his arrest the police found incriminating material at his house: apart from twenty-four copies of the English *Daily Mail*, an edition of *Nation Tchèque*, the Czech independence journal produced in Paris by the historian Ernst Denis. Preminger saw treason in the mere possession of these enemy papers. But then there was Kramář's highly suspicious meeting with the Italian consul, as well as a letter from Mrs Kramář, asking her husband to purchase a copy of Edward Gibbon's *Decline and Fall*: clearly, she was expecting the downfall of the Austro-Hungarian empire. All this suggested to Preminger that Kramář had a 'disloyal mentality' which was probably criminal; further investigation was now needed to uncover the full extent of his conspiracy.[69]

While Preminger meticulously set about preparing the indictment, Kramář and other Czech traitors were moved to the garrison prison in Vienna. The AOK had decided that all Czech political trials should be staged at the military court in Vienna, not in Prague. It ensured less collusion with Czech officialdom, and facilitated the coordination of treason material at the centre (for in the summer the major Russophile trial, which could not be staged in Galicia, took place in Vienna).[70] After the war, the garrison prison, the 'Prison of Death', gained notoriety as epitomising Czech martyrdom and Austrian barbarism, even if by the standard of later regimes it was mildly oppressive. The traitors were left in solitary confinement for months, fully cut off from the world and wholly unsure about their fate while evidence was gathered against them. Some like Kramář did not cope well. Others like Alois Rašín remained stoical, quietly considering a martyr's end. As a lawyer, he could smile at how the law was being reinterpreted, and took solace from reading *War and Peace* where man was portrayed as just a 'speck of dust raised on the wheel of history'. Rašín sensed that the trial was a historic watershed and hoped (vainly) that historians would later pay it due notice.[71]

The trial of Kramář and Rašín finally opened in December 1915 and lasted for a full six months.[72] Like a theatre premiere, many flocked to get

[69]AÚTGM, Fond Maffie, karton 44, Preminger to AOK (A 2162/15), 31 May 1915, enclosing report.

[70]Kunz, *Náš odboj*, 57; Paulová, *Dějiny Maffie*, 607.

[71] *Paměti Dr. Alois Rašín*, ed. Ladislav Rašín (Prague, 1994), 127, 129, 135. See also the memoirs of Jan Rezníček, *Ve věži smrti* (Prague, n.d.), 48ff.

[72] There is no historical analysis of this trial in any language although the full transcript was quickly translated into Czech: *Proces dra Kramáře a jeho přátel*, ed. Zdeněk V. Tobolka (5 vols., Prague, 1918–20). A rare study is Tomáš W. Pavlíček, 'Politicum a martýrium v nejdelším trestním procesu první světové války. Stylizace a strategie během procesu s Karlem Kramářem', in *Karel Kramář (1860–1937). Život a dílo*, ed. Jan Bílek and Luboš Velek (Prague, 2009), 344–66.

seats although press coverage was outlawed. On trial was the fundamental question, personified by Kramář, of what constituted loyalty to the Habsburg monarchy in peace or war. The prosecution, after translating thousands of Czech documents into German and researching widely in university libraries, had an overwhelming amount of circumstantial evidence and fielded experts on military intelligence to prove that Kramář's treason had damaged the army. For the defence, while Kramář himself pleaded his innocence at length, an array of Habsburg statesmen lined up to endorse his pro-Austrian character, including the former foreign minister Count Berchtold and the Austrian prime minister Count Stürgkh.

Preminger argued[73] that these notable witnesses were irrelevant, for Kramář was a wily and manipulative individual who had been playing a double game for years; any support he had given the Austrian government before 1914 was purely opportunistic and a mask for treason. Crucial to the prosecution case was to tie together Kramář's behaviour before and during the war in one enormous conspiracy. His Neo-Slavist movement was depicted retrospectively not as a failure, but as a successful plot to unite all Slavs under Russian leadership and destroy Austria-Hungary; his many speeches, his pre-war trips to Russia or Serbia, were trawled over to prove his close plotting with the monarchy's Serb and Ruthene traitors. Indeed, the plot was Europe-wide, a 'large criminal design' if one factored in his ties to France and Italy and obvious sympathy for the arch-traitor Masaryk. While colluding with these enemies to violate §58, he had then set a depraved example for all Czechs at home, failing to display any patriotic loyalty. This had resulted in large numbers of Czech civilians being prosecuted for 'political crimes', and in mass desertions at the front. History, said Preminger, would judge this disgraceful example of treacherous seduction.[74]

Kramář's defence lawyer, Eduard Körner, proceeded to pick large holes in an indictment that rested on so many assumptions.[75] His legal summing up typically attacked the vagueness of §58, asking like so many jurists before him whether it was appropriate for a modern state. He then questioned whether the crime had actually been committed either subjectively or objectively. Subjectively, there was little proof that Kramář through his actions was intending to transgress §58c. But objectively

---

[73] The following draws on AÚTGM, Fond Maffie, karton 39, XIII, Preminger's speech, 3790–846; and the indictment: Militäranwalt des Militärkommandanten in Wien (A 2162/15/960), *Anklageschrift* (Vienna, 1915).

[74] *Ibid.*, 111. Preminger referred here to official data for prosecutions under §58 which showed that Czechs were most likely to be accused: AÚTGM, Fond Maffie, karton 2, Glivitzky to Preminger, 27 May 1916.

[75] See AÚTGM, Fond Maffie, karton 39, XIII: Körner speech, 4227–47.

too the criteria were lacking. For as in England the crime of treason required an 'overt deed', and Körner – like lawyers in the Bosnian trials[76] – queried whether spreading propaganda or writing newspaper articles could constitute a treasonable act. Nor was there proof that Kramář's behaviour had actually influenced the Czech population as the prosecution maintained. There seemed to be no 'causal nexus' between Kramář and Czech rebellion but just the 'vague construction of a connection'.[77]

On 3 June 1916, the military court gave its verdict: Kramář and Rašín were both found guilty of treason and sentenced to death pending appeals. As this was simply announced in the press without any comment, it stirred strong public emotions. Two Czech leaders, even if their loyalties were dubious, had been judged traitors to the community. Their Czech compatriots in Prague were now cowed and alarmed about future persecution; many would later claim that the verdict had been a judgement on the whole Czech nation, something that Preminger in court had precisely denied.[78] German nationalists meanwhile tended to gloat, noting that, just like France's Dreyfus affair, this moment was a fatal watershed for the Czech nation.[79] The real danger however, in the middle of the war, was how this public stigmatisation might affect imperial cohesion. As the Austrian liberal Josef Redlich observed, the hostility of the Czechs would not be defused by death sentences, only by the state intervening wisely and sensitively; thus he predicted, the Kramář verdict was likely to be 'the starting point for the most dangerous internal battles in the Austro-Hungarian monarchy'.[80]

V

The climax of our stroll in the landscape of treason brings us to the rehabilitation of these traitors. Usually, for such rehabilitation to be effective, it takes place after a full regime change when the traitor's fortunes are reversed, or when the state sees fit to grant a magnanimous pardon from a position of strength. In July 1917, a year after the Kramář sentence, the new Habsburg emperor Karl suddenly announced a full amnesty for all those found guilty of political crimes. It meant the immediate release of Kramář and Rašín, and a halt to the other trials Preminger was organising for Czech traitors like Klofáč or the

---

[76] For example, the defence lawyer Danilo Dimović at the Banjaluka trial: Čaušević, 380.
[77] Körner speech, 4244–5.
[78] For a typical Czech nationalist reaction: Jan Hajšman, *Česká Mafie. Vzpomínky na odboj doma* (Prague, 1932), 222.
[79] Soukup, *28. říjen 1918*, I, 177–82.
[80] Josef Redlich, *Schicksalsjahre Österreichs. Die Erinnerungen und Tagebücher Josef Redlichs 1869–1936*, II (Vienna, 2011), 171.

exiled Masaryk. From November 1916, Emperor Karl's regime had been pursuing an idealistic new direction, dismantling military powers and reintroducing constitutional government. The amnesty, as his own personal decision after months of agonising about tendentious military justice, was meant to foster national reconciliation at home.[81] Yet as many of his ministers warned, it seemed a foolhardy move when the ground had not been carefully prepared. Not only was a full amnesty granted with no preconditions to make the 'traitors' conform. The new regime acted from a position of weakness, when powerful national groups still existed who could publicly reject the rehabilitation. Most notably, could Kramář really be pardoned, a man whom many German-Austrians felt to be the 'incarnation of an anti-German policy'?[82] The move further destabilised the state, for the regime failed to follow it up with a concerted policy of national reconciliation.

Indeed, in the last year of war, the accusations of treason moved from the private courtroom back into the public domain and were particularly virulent between Czech and German-Austrian agitators. German-Austrian nationalists, having attacked the amnesty from the start, proceeded to publicise all examples of Czech wartime treason; they reproduced Preminger's arguments and publicly labelled Kramář as 'the dark demon who unleashed the world war'.[83] The released Czech prisoners meanwhile were fêted in their communities and could pose as national martyrs. Since the Austrian government increasingly backed a 'German course', banking on victory at the side of the German Reich, most Czech leaders began to narrow their allegiance in a national direction: moving from dual Czech-Austrian loyalty to simply backing Czech state independence. The result was clear by April 1918, when the Habsburg foreign minister Count Czernin made a tactless speech attacking Tomáš Masaryk and warning of other such Czech traitors at home. In reply, the domestic Czech leaders rejected the label of traitors, but added that in fact there was no difference between themselves and Masaryk.[84] In other words, the badge of treachery was one they were now proudly brandishing as their own.

---

[81] *Kaiser Karl. Persönliche Aufzeichnungen, Zeugnisse und Dokumente*, ed. Erich Feigl (Vienna and Munich, 1984), 206–7; and especially the vivid discussion in Arthur Graf Polzer-Hoditz, *Kaiser Karl. Aus der Geheimmappe seines Kabinettschefs* (Vienna, 1929), 421–33.

[82] Joseph Maria Baernreither, *Der Verfall des Habsburgerreiches und die Deutschen. Fragmente eines politischen Tagebuches 1897–1917* (Vienna, 1938), 231–3. Also Kirchheimer on political amnesties: *Political Justice*, 405–6, 410–11.

[83] Friedrich Wichtl, *Dr. Karl Kramarsch, der Anstifter des Weltkrieges* (Munich, 1918), 4.

[84] Viktor Dyk, 'Czernin', *Národní listy*, 4 Apr. 1918, 1; and speech of František Staněk, quoted in *ibid.*, 14 Apr. 1918, 1. Also Zeman, *Break-Up*, 175.

Many have questioned the 'meaning of treason', often with unsatisfactory or vague conclusions.[85] If we search for its meaning in wartime Austria-Hungary, we discover a fundamental conflict over allegiance within the state. Before 1914, a lively discourse of treason already existed and the regime was wielding this ultimate legal weapon to silence irredentist enemies within. The war intensified this trend as the empire, under military dominance, fought a largely defensive battle for survival. Once identified, the traitors were publicly paraded as monstrous 'outsiders' who had supposedly plotted their evil schemes for decades. The aim was to assert a restricted version of imperial patriotism against any alternative visions, but also to justify to a European audience why Austria-Hungary had been forced to fight this total war. Ultimately then, treason meant a high-risk and dangerous power struggle. By 1918, it was the traitors who were gaining the upper hand and proudly turning the accusation on its head. Thus, as Jaroslav Kunz discovered when he went in search of those documents in Vienna, treason is always a transitory and constructed phenomenon. It constitutes an ideal subject for the historian who wishes to explain a regime in crisis.

---

[85] See Rebecca West, *The Meaning of Treason* (1982), 413–20, who took a firm moral stance against the traitor. One reviewer questioned whether she had actually explained 'the meaning': *Journal of American History*, 52.2 (1965), 421–2.

Transactions of the RHS 25 (2015), pp. 135–158 © Royal Historical Society 2015
doi:10.1017/S0080440115000067

THE USES OF FOREIGNERS IN MAO-ERA CHINA: 'TECHNIQUES OF HOSPITALITY' AND INTERNATIONAL IMAGE-BUILDING IN THE PEOPLE'S REPUBLIC, 1949–1976

By Julia Lovell

READ 10 MAY 2014

ABSTRACT. This paper focuses on the inner workings of Mao-era China's 'foreign affairs' system (*waishi xitong*): the complex, comprehensive web of bureaucracy woven after 1949 to monitor and control Chinese contact with the outside world. It explores one of the channels along which the People's Republic between 1949 and 1976 tried to project international, soft-power messages beyond conventional diplomatic channels: the inviting of so-called 'foreign guests' (*waibin*) on carefully planned tours around China, often with all or at least some expenses paid. Earlier accounts of this hospitality have evoked a machine of perfect control, carefully judged to manipulate visitors and rehearsed to ensure flawless performances by Chinese hosts. Using memoirs and Chinese archival documents, the paper discusses the attitude of top-level leaders to such visits, the way in which trips were prepared and planned, and the successes and weaknesses of the system. It argues that the People's Republic of China's hosting programme had a domestic as well as an international purpose. Although foreigners were the official target (and indeed, Maoist China's 'techniques of hospitality' garnered some rich international political dividends) the government also used the preparation for and execution of hosting duties to underscore at home the triumph of the revolution.

In the contemporary UK, where politicians crave big-spending Chinese tourists and investors, and access to Chinese markets, we are familiar with the idea of the People's Republic of China (PRC) exercising hard, economic power.[1] But China's leaders also yearn for the country's cultural influence, its soft power, to match its financial clout; and they are prepared to spend lavishly to achieve this aim. In 2009 alone, China spent

[1] I would like to thank several people who commented on this paper and helped with materials: especially Thelma Lovell (for extensive and invaluable assistance with Italian and German-language sources, and for insights on the European engagement with Maoist politics and culture), Matthew Johnson, Li Jigao, Jiang Tao, Yao Shuyi, You Lan, Robert Macfarlane and Michael Schoenhals. I wish to thank also the audience of the Royal Historical Society for their constructive and stimulating comments when this lecture was delivered on 10 May 2014. I am especially grateful for a Philip Leverhulme Prize which enabled me to visit China and obtain materials for this paper which are unavailable in the UK.

$6.6 billion on a media group that would give China a stronger international voice.[2] The year before, China spent $44 billion hosting its international coming-out party: the 2008 Olympic Games.

The state's latest soft-power campaign is the so-called 'China Dream', designed to market globally the idea of a strong, successful, happy China. China's propaganda tsars are certainly serious about communicating their message. The posters have been splashed over China's major cities; international conferences are being held to debate and communicate the slogan's meaning; for weeks in the summer of 2013, a ballad entitled 'The Chinese Dream' performed by a song-and-dance combo from China's nuclear-missile corps topped the charts.[3]

China's aspirations for global cultural influence only started to make international headlines in the past decade or so, when the publicly divulged sums of money involved became eye-watering. But the impulse is much older, stretching all the way back through the twentieth century.[4] And among some non-Chinese audiences between the 1950s and the 1970s, China enjoyed perhaps its greatest international soft power since the Enlightenment. The culture and politics of Maoist China permeated global radicalism during these decades. Mao and his ideas of continuous, peasant revolution appealed to leftwing rebels, and civil-rights and anti-racism campaigners in the US, Australia, France, Germany, Holland, Belgium, Italy, Norway and Sweden. Across the developing world (in Asia, South America and Africa), Maoist politics inspired post-colonial nations with idioms such as self-reliance, party rectification and revolutionary spontaneity.[5] The list of those who found in favour of Maoist China is a bewilderingly various one: Quakers, sinologists, French philosophers, Venezuelan pirate revolutionaries, West German Dada hippies, Congolese feminists, Algerian guerrillas[6] – and Shirley

---

[2] See, for example, Vivian Wu and Adam Chen, 'Beijing in 45b Yuan Global Media Drive', *South China Morning Post*, 13 Jan. 2009, at http://www.scmp.com/article/666847/beijing-45b-yuan-global-media-drive (accessed 12 Jan. 2015). For a discussion of China's quest for soft power in the early twenty-first century, see Joshua Kurlantzick, *Charm Offensive: How China's Soft Power is Transforming the World* (New Haven, 2007).

[3] 'Chasing the Chinese Dream', *Economist*, 4 May 2013, at http://www.economist.com/news/briefing/21577063-chinas-new-leader-has-been-quick-consolidate-his-power-what-does-he-now-want-his (accessed 12 Jan. 2015).

[4] For twentieth-century China's preoccupation with international 'face' as represented by sporting achievements, see Susan Brownell, *Training the Body for China: Sports in the Moral Order of the People's Republic* (Chicago, 1995); Xu Guoqi, *Olympic Dreams: China and Sports, 1895–2008* (Cambridge, MA, 2008). For an exploration of the literary dimensions of this search for global prestige, see Julia Lovell, *The Politics of Cultural Capital: China's Quest for a Nobel Prize in Literature* (Hawai'i, 2006).

[5] For an informative introduction to this context, see *Mao's Little Red Book: A Global History*, ed. Alexander Cook (Cambridge, 2014).

[6] A sampling of issues of *Peking Review* from the mid-1960s indicates the international flavour of the enthusiasm for Maoist China and the Cultural Revolution. For more balanced

Maclaine, who in 1975 wrote an adulatory account of a six-week visit to Mao-era China during which she found her way out of a mid-life crisis.[7]

Where did this global enthusiasm for Maoism come from? The dominant view of, say, Western Europe's engagement with Maoism is to see it largely as a home-grown phenomenon – as an eccentric youthful experiment in alternative politics, an intellectual and cultural outburst divorced from China itself. Consider this recollection by a former Italian Maoist sympathiser during the 1960s:

> [Maoist] China was a challenge to the society in which we lived: to our authoritarian education, our oppressive factories, our conciliatory and bureaucratic communism. This spurred the young of the European New Left movement to take the Cultural Revolution as a point of reference, without worrying too much about learning what kind of thing it really was . . . We had a vague, confused feeling of the anti-authoritarian and libertarian character of the initial phases of the Cultural Revolution, which chimed with the contemporary need for a modernisation of European society.[8]

This quotation expresses the way in which Maoist China was conveniently remote and unknown to many of its young leftwing worshippers in Europe and the United States. In the utopian, politically polyglot phase of the late 1960s and early 1970s, many radical students in Germany, France, Italy and Norway picked up on the superficial aspects of Maoism that appealed, and overlooked the rest. Richard Wolin, in his acute and informative book on French Maoism, makes the following sharp comment about the creative, adaptive qualities of the French interpretation of Chinese communism in the 1960s and 1970s: 'if the

---

assessments, see for example: Andreas Kühn, *Stalins Enkel, Maos Söhne: Die Lebenswelt der K-Gruppen in der Bundesrepublik der 70er Jahre* (Frankfurt, 2005); Sebastian Gehrig, '(Re-) Configuring Mao. Trajectories of a Culturo-Political Trend in West Germany', *Transcultural Studies*, 2 (2011), 189–231; *Die Kulturrevolution als Vorbild: Maoismen im Deutschsprachigem Raum*, ed. Sebastian Gehrig, Barbara Mittler and Felix Wemheuer (Frankfurt, 2008); Gerd Koenen, *Das Rote Jahrzehnt: Unsere Kleine Deutsche Kulturrevolution 1967–1977* (Cologne, 2001); Christophe Bourseiller, *Les Maoïstes: la folle histoire des Gardes Rouges Français* (Paris, 1996); Richard Wolin, *The Wind from the East: French Intellectuals, the Cultural Revolution and the Legacy of the 1960s* (Princeton, 2010); Roberto Niccolai, *Quando la Cina era vicina: la rivoluzione culturale e la sinistra extraparlamentare italiana negli anni '60 e '70* (Pistoia, 1998).

[7] Shirley Maclaine, *You Can Get There From Here* (New York, 1975).

[8] Lisa Foa, 'Perché fummo maoisti: la Cina è un giallo', *Limes* (1995), 237–8. Jon Rognlien, the scholar of Norwegian Maoism, confirms this view: interview by author, Skype (Cambridge and Copenhagen), 3 Feb. 2014. For an almost exclusively light-hearted take on the engagement with Maoism by French youth of the late 1960s and early 1970s, which again emphasises the playful, imagined nature of this enthusiasm, see Gerard Miller, *Minoritaire* (Paris, 2001), 76–123. He writes, for example: 'It's impossible to understand the passionate interest in China that thousands of French teenagers of my generation felt if you imagine that we were in love with the idea of the iron fist. Quite the contrary: what dazzled us about Mao was his spirit of mischief, his insubordination . . . To me, Mao's China at the end of the 1960s was much more "olé-olé" [than the doctrines of the Trotskyites] . . . [D]uring these years there was frankly nothing better to do in France than to be enraged; and nothing better for the enraged than to be Maoist' (79, 80, 97).

Cultural Revolution did not exist, the gauchistes [the French leftists] would have had to invent it'.[9]

But this conclusion – that global Maoism was nothing to do with Chinese Maoism – underestimates the skill and hard work that the PRC put into disseminating its soft power globally between 1949 and 1976. This paper aims to complicate the stereotype of a closed-off, isolated Maoist China, shunned by the international community, that has long persisted in popular impressions of the period.[10] Using memoirs and Chinese archival documents, it will describe some of the ways in which Mao-era China reached out to the world beyond conventional diplomatic channels: the agencies that strove to spread Chinese cultural and political influence and how successful they were. For the limited opening of Chinese archives over the past decade and a half has enabled us to glimpse more of the inner workings of China's so-called 'foreign affairs' system (*waishi xitong*): the complex, comprehensive web of bureaucracy woven after 1949 to monitor and control Chinese contact with the outside world.

Mao-era China and Cold War cultural diplomacy: an overview of recent scholarship

This paper does not make claims to be revisionist in arguing that the politics and culture of Mao-era China had international reach: any historian of (for example) 1960s France, Germany, Italy, Scandinavia, India, Southeast Asia, Peru and so on will be well aware of engagement with Maoist political theory and practice outside China.[11] Yet until relatively recently, few scholars considered the international spread of ideas about Maoist China between the 1950s and 1970s in a bilateral or transnational way: the extent to which the enthusiasm for Maoism was driven by what non-Chinese imagined Maoism to be; the extent to which impressions of China were actively shaped by Maoist China. Paul Hollander's *Political Pilgrims* undertook an acute, comparative analysis of Western 'fellow-travellers' to Communist regimes including the USSR, the PRC, Vietnam and Cuba, but without accessing

---

[9] Wolin, *The Wind from the East*, 3.

[10] Over the past two decades, a plethora of memoirs of Mao-era China published in English, often focused on the political and xenophobic extremism of the Cultural Revolution, has powerfully influenced non-specialist understandings of this period of history: the best known and most successful has probably been Jung Chang's *Wild Swans* (1991).

[11] Consider, for example, the rich secondary literature on the engagement with Maoist politics and culture within individual countries, particularly India, Nepal, Peru and France: Sumanta Banerjee, *In the Wake of Naxalbari: A History of the Naxalites Movement* (Calcutta, 1980), and *India's Simmering Revolution* (New Delhi, 1984); Aditya Adhikari, *The Bullet and the Ballot Box: The Story of Nepal's Maoist Revolution* (London, 2014); *The Shining Path of Peru*, ed. David Scott Palmer (1992); Wolin, *The Wind from the East*; and Belden Davis, 'French Maoism', in *The 60s without Apology*, ed. Sohnya Syres *et al.* (Minneapolis, 1984), 148–77.

Chinese-language sources.[12] For decades, moreover, study of Cold War politics, diplomacy and culture in the West remained largely Eurocentric in focus, preoccupied with the USSR–US axis. Although many international histories of communism and the Cold War have been written in European languages, for years they tended to treat Maoism as little more than a case-study within a Eurocentric whole.[13] As a result, the importance of Maoist China in this conflict as offering a genuine alternative to USSR communism, providing intellectual and practical support to rebels throughout the world, was until recently relatively neglected in mainstream scholarship on the Cold War.[14]

Scholarship on the Cold War of the past fifteen years has, however, steadily acknowledged more fully the Asian and specifically Chinese influence. Odd Arne Westad has crucially expanded previously Western-centric perspectives on the Cold War, bringing the study of the role played by the Third World into mainstream scholarship on the conflict.[15] As part of this greater globalisation of Cold War history, manifested also in the journal *Cold War History* and in *The Cambridge History of the Cold War*, we have in recent years seen a welcome increase in the participation of mainland Chinese scholars in international and Anglophone debates about Maoism and the Cold War, in for example Chen Jian's *Mao's China and the Cold War* and Qiang Zhai's *China and the Vietnam Wars, 1950–1975*.[16]

[12] Paul Hollander, *Political Pilgrims: Travels of Western Intellectuals to the Soviet Union, China and Cuba 1928–1978* (Oxford, 1981). As another example, consider Tom Buchanan's thorough but unilateral account of the links between China and British leftists, in *East Wind: China and the British Left, 1925–1976* (Oxford, 2012), and a review by Qiang Zhai (a prominent archival historian of Chinese foreign relations during the Cold War) expressing reservations about the one-sided nature of Buchanan's treatment: 'Buchanan's treatment would have been fuller if it had incorporated some coverage of Chinese reception and manipulation of the British Left. Buchanan would have presented his readers with an international history if he had examined how the Chinese, both the Nationalists and Communists, used foreigners, including the British Left, to "sell" their images and win international endorsement abroad.' Available at: http://www.h-net.org/reviews/showrev.php?id=36957 (accessed 12 Jan. 2015).

[13] See, for example, Archie Brown, *The Rise and Fall of Communism* (2010); Robert Service, *Comrades: Communism, a World History* (2008); David Priestland, *The Red Flag: Communism and the Making of the Modern World* (2010). Of these three general histories (all of which are sound and informative), Priestland's book is probably the most expansive in perspective.

[14] See Yinghong Cheng, 'Beyond Moscow-Centric Interpretation: An Examination of the China Connection in Eastern Europe and North Vietnam during the Era of De-Stalinization', *Journal of World History*, 15.4 (Dec. 2004), 487–518. For the early findings of an exciting forthcoming book on Soviet and Chinese competition for influence in the Third World, see Jeremy Friedman, 'Soviet Policy in the Developing World and the Chinese Challenge in the 1960s', *Cold War History*, 10.2 (2010), 247–72.

[15] Odd Arne Westad, *The Global Cold War: Third World Interventions and the Making of Our Times* (Cambridge, 2005).

[16] *The Cambridge History of the Cold War*, ed. Melvyn P. Leffler and Odd Arne Westad (Cambridge, 2010); Chen Jian, *Mao's China and the Cold War* (Chapel Hill, 2001); Qiang Zhai, *China and the Vietnam Wars, 1950–1975* (Chapel Hill, 2000).

Since 2000, China historians and political scientists such as Zheng Yangwen, Anne-Marie Brady, Alexander Cook, Cagdas Ungor and Matthew Johnson have pioneered a more transnational approach to China's approach to cultural diplomacy in the Cold War. *The Cold War in Asia: The Battle for Hearts and Minds* (edited by Zheng Yangwen, Liu Hong and Michael Szonyi) argued for the importance of the Asian theatre in general, and of the impact of Mao-era China in particular, to Cold War culture and diplomacy.[17] *The Cold War in Asia* was therefore particularly timely in offering wide-ranging and practical insights into the cultural and political channels along which Maoism played an international role, in countries including Burma, Indonesia, Mexico and Sweden. Alexander Cook's 2014 volume of essays, *The Little Red Book: A Global History*, furthermore provided an illuminating selection of national case-studies describing the international reception of Mao's Little Red Book.

With her two monographs *The Friend of China: The Myth of Rewi Alley* and *Making the Foreign Serve China*, Anne-Marie Brady trail-blazed study of Chinese-language sources on the PRC's foreign affairs system.[18] Particularly in the latter volume, Brady provided a thorough history of this system and its Soviet antecedents, while making innovative use of internal foreign affairs publications and manuals, and analysing the cases of specific individuals (such as Edgar Snow) courted by Beijing as useful 'international friends'. Matthew Johnson's recent research into the visits of black American writers to the PRC through the 1950s and 1960s (making use of both Chinese- and English-language sources) has illuminated Mao-era China's attempts to assert a leading role in the global revolutionary, anti-imperialist movement.[19] Cagdas Ungor's doctoral dissertation on the PRC's 'external propaganda' (*duiwai xuanchuan*) machinery has cast important light on the network of foreign-language broadcast and print media, such as Peking Radio and periodicals including *Peking Review* and *China Reconstructs*, through which Mao-era China attempted to win global influence.[20]

In sum, recent work on Mao-era China's foreign relations has used Chinese-language archival materials made newly accessible over the past two decades to suggest that during the 1950s and 1960s China poured large amounts of money and expertise into a painstaking and

---

[17] *The Cold War in Asia: The Battle for Hearts and Minds*, ed. Zheng Yangwen, Liu Hong and Michael Szonyi (Leiden, 2010).

[18] Anne-Marie Brady, *The Friend of China: The Myth of Rewi Alley* (2002), and *Making the Foreign Serve China: Managing Foreigners in the People's Republic* (Lanham, 2003).

[19] Matthew Johnson, 'From Peace to the Panthers: PRC Engagement with Africa–America Transnational Networks, 1949–1979', *Past and Present*, 218 supplement 8 (2013), 233–57.

[20] Cagdas Ungor, 'Reaching the Distant Comrade: Chinese Communist Propaganda Abroad (1949–1976)' (Ph.D. dissertation, Binghampton University, 2009).

at times sophisticated soft-power programme. Not all this money and effort was wisely spent: Ungor's analysis of Maoist China's often clumsily designed external propaganda substantially undermined earlier, Cold War-era portrayals of China's foreign-language publications as highly effective ideological weapons. Nonetheless, both older and more recent research indicates that some of the PRC's efforts at cultural diplomacy garnered rich political dividends, in both hard- and soft-power terms. Greater understanding of Maoist China's cultural diplomacy could have an impact on our view of the exercise of both hard and soft power on both sides of the Cold War divide. If the international enthusiasm for Maoist China was substantially engineered by the Chinese government itself, what does this phenomenon tell us about the priorities of the Chinese state and leadership at the time? How important was China as a cultural and political actor in the Cold War?

Several aspects of Mao-era China's international soft and hard-power programmes would reward further investigation: the efficacy of public overtures such as external propaganda; the workings of shadowier organisations, especially the International Department (*Zhonglianbu*), which directed crucial relationships between the Central Committee of the Chinese Communist Party (CCP) and other national communist parties.[21] But for reasons of space, this paper will consider just one of the channels along which the People's Republic between 1949 and 1976 tried to project international, soft-power messages: the inviting of so-called 'foreign guests' (*waibin*) on carefully planned tours around China, often with all or at least some expenses paid and with the bonus of one-on-one conversations with leaders such as Mao Zedong or Zhou Enlai, the country's charming, urbane foreign minister then premier between the 1950s and 1970s.

The government of Mao-era China hoped that, back in their own countries, these travellers would return the favour of hospitality through speeches, articles, books and political briefings that would spread positive propaganda for the People's Republic. Until 1954, the People's Republic was officially recognised by only twenty-one other states. In this situation, courting non-diplomatic delegations was an essential part of China's campaign to improve its international image, at a time when its official avenues for exercising influence were narrow. How, then, was this hospitality planned and carried out? And what results did it produce?

---

[21] This department's archives have not been declassified, and the prospects for access at present seem non-existent. In 2013, an official history of the organisation was published: *Zhongguo gongchandang duiwai jiaowang 90 nian* (A history of the Chinese Communist Party's interactions with the outside world over the past ninety years), ed. Wang Jiarui (Beijing, 2013).

Contemporary accounts evoke a veritable foreign delegation industry in Mao-era China. Travelling troupes – of both the famous and the obscure – flooded Beijing: rumour had it that fourteen hotels in the capital alone were dedicated to the delegation trade through the 1950s. This is what one witness wrote about such establishments in 1958:

> These hotels have an atmosphere of their own, for nobody is ever seen to pay a bill...Japan had sent a Trade Union delegation, a Youth and Women's Delegation, a Scholars' Mission, a Writers' Mission and a Fertilisers' Delegation...There was a Burmese Women's delegation, a Norwegian Students' Delegation, a French Film Delegation, a Singapore Trade Mission, an Italian Socialist Party Agricultural Mission, a Hong Kong Industrial Delegation, a Finnish Trade Union Mission.[22]

To give a sense of the scale of the enterprise: perhaps as many as 100,000 such delegates visited in the first decade of the People's Republic alone.[23]

Reports written from both sides of the encounter evoke a machine of perfect control, judged to play to the individual weaknesses of particular visitors, and rehearsed to ensure flawless performances by Chinese hosts. In his 1962 memoir *Escape from Red China* (written after fleeing China in 1957 via Hong Kong) Robert Loh, a Shanghai factory manager, gave a view from inside the system. His role was to play the part of a gently reformed capitalist to foreign visitors to Shanghai in the 1950s. He was to reassure foreigners that the Communists' humanity and moderation had won over even bourgeois industrialists to Chinese socialism. He wrote: 'The process of deceiving the foreigners resembles theatrical production. Each little play is carefully staged and rehearsed.'[24] By 1954,

> the entertainment was staged with a high degree of efficiency...Before each entertainment program, the performers were briefed on the background of the guests and were told how to answer the questions they could expect to be asked. The performers and the entertainment officials together worked out the acts and arranged for the props that would create the planned impression on the visitors.

These could include, Loh recounted, elegantly bourgeois ornaments, books and records, and luxuries such as imported food, cigarettes and alcohol.[25]

Loh underlined the political sensitivity of the work: 'even a small slip...could have international repercussions...Thus, whenever I was chosen to entertain a group of foreigners, I would be informed at least a week in advance. I would then attend meetings in which I would receive "guidance".' Every aspect of every 'performance' was minuted

[22] Michael Croft, *Red Carpet to China* (1958), 7, 39.
[23] Herbert Passim, *China's Cultural Diplomacy* (New York, 1962), 1.
[24] Robert Loh, *Escape from Red China* (New York, 1962), 153.
[25] *Ibid.*, 155–6.

by 'interpreters' (in reality, politically reliable cadres) who subsequently produced full reports of everything seen and discussed.[26]

The Communists, Loh concluded, 'rarely blundered once they had perfected their means of deceiving foreigners.

> They took infinite pains to see that the entertainment went smoothly. Emphasis was placed on making it seem casual and spontaneous. This was easier than it may sound, because almost all visitors wanted to see the same things; rarely did a foreigner ask to see something for which a showpiece had not been carefully prepared . . . Moreover, each visitor was studied with such care that generally his behaviour could be anticipated. He was shown only what would impress a person of his type the most. He also stayed in only the best hotels . . . at the end of his visit he usually was given expensive and carefully chosen gifts, so that he would leave with a warm feeling of regard for his hosts.[27]

In a depressingly effective appeal to vanity, hosts often reassured visiting authors of the canonical status of their books in China: for how could such a writer then accuse such a country of intellectual repression?[28]

The scenarios were sometimes planned far in advance, especially if children were involved. Loh remembered how the authorities ordered that, weeks before the household received some African visitors, the daughter of one of his closest friends, also an industrialist, be given a doll painted black to accustom her to the idea of dark skin. When two African ladies eventually visited the family, the little girl had been trained to rush up to them both and give them a kiss. Loh wrote: 'It was remarkably successful. The two ladies were so touched that they had tears in their eyes.'[29]

Loh's account is backed up by selected Western eye-witnesses, who affirmed that 'nothing was left to chance' in orchestrating foreign visits to Maoist China. Jacques Marcuse, a Belgian journalist in Beijing through the 1950s, observed that 'the special correspondent is given the VIPP (Very Important Potential Propagandist) treatment . . . you do not allow visitors to see anything but that which you want them to see'.[30] The political scientist Paul Hollander, in his analysis of Western 'political pilgrims' to Communist countries, has described the 'techniques of hospitality' rolled out by Maoist China to make the very best impression on visitors: flowers, cars, banquets, elite healthcare, luxurious hotels. On her 1954 visit to the PRC, Simone de Beauvoir was apparently particularly taken by her Beijing hotel room's two brass double beds and pink silk sheets.[31] Loh, Marcuse and Hollander, therefore, all coincide in painting a picture of a

[26] *Ibid.*, 156.
[27] *Ibid.*, 159.
[28] Hollander, *Political Pilgrims*, 361–2.
[29] Loh, *Escape from Red China*, 169.
[30] Jacques Marcuse, *The Peking Papers* (New York, 1967), 8, 19.
[31] Hollander, *Political Pilgrims*, 363. See also Passim, *China's Cultural Diplomacy*, 12.

remarkably effective state hospitality machine, dedicated to manicuring international views of China.

At this point, it would be reasonable to interject that there was little special about the great care with which the PRC received foreign guests. All governments research and brief on visitors, and strive to put their best foot forward. Consider the elaborate preparations for Irish president Michael Higgins's 2014 state visit to the UK, or the vast security apparatus built around the presidential travels of George W. Bush after 9/11. But I would like to argue that officially micromanaged foreign visits to Maoist China are a little different, because they represented one of a very few channels by which one could gain access to China during these years. Contemporary Irish visitors to the UK, by contrast, can draw their impressions from a much wider range of sources and contacts. To the Maoist government, these visitors offered a crucial opportunity to construct and control the country's international image. An early scholar of the PRC's cultural diplomacy, Herbert Passim, wrote:

> Every foreign visitor is another feather in [China's] cap, a mark of recognition, another milestone on the road to acceptance and respectability, another blow to the American policy of non-recognition. The overwhelming majority are drawn from the most influential and articulate strata of their home countries, so that their impact value is incomparably greater than that of ordinary tourists.[32]

Non-political, non-diplomatic visitors were often indulged by Maoist China as state guests, not tourists: many were met at the airport by ministers, they enjoyed audiences with Mao and Zhou and their visits were publicised on the front pages of newspapers.[33] And because contemporary visitors to, and information on, the People's Republic were scarce outside China, the eye-witness reports of such travellers enjoyed a greater prestige and influence back in their home countries. One sometimes encountered the strange spectacle of a non-specialist visitor to China regarding themselves or being regarded, on his or her return, as an expert on the country, merely by virtue of having been there.[34] Indeed, through the 1950s the Chinese government often showed an inclination to refuse visas to people with a background in Chinese studies or Chinese language skills, indicating a preference for visitors without prior or independent knowledge of China.[35]

And now that provincial and Foreign Ministry archives in China are partially open, we can read some of the plethora of reports written before and after many foreign visits, cataloguing plans, successes and deficiencies. We can see a little into the internal workings of the system: its scope and

---

[32] Passim, *China's Cultural Diplomacy*, 8.
[33] *Ibid.*, 9, 38.
[34] *Ibid.*, 30.
[35] *Ibid.*, for example 79, 80–4, 94–5, 107, 109–10.

capacity. Was it as seamlessly choreographed as our witnesses cited above describe? What were its stand-out public relations coups? And when did it fail?

There can be no doubt that, in the minds of leaders like Zhou Enlai, Liu Shaoqi and Mao Zedong, hosting foreign visitors represented high-level, confidential political work. In 1950, while Communist armies were still quashing the last remnants of opposition in the south and while the country was hammered by hyper-inflation, the Foreign Ministry focused on taking control of all contact between Chinese institutions and foreign visitors: 'From now on, any institution that receives foreign guests must first contact the Foreign Ministry. This is mandatory.'[36] A report from 1954 declared that 'receiving foreign guests is... an extremely significant political job, crucial for warming up the international situation... If rightists don't come, they'll always be saying bad things about us. If we do let them come, they'll find that difficult.'[37] Documents from 1958 and 1964 reiterated: 'To receive foreign guests well, politics must take command'[38] and such work must be supervised only by 'politically reliable cadres with a high level of policy and professional competence'.[39] 'Any mistake will result directly in political losses', emphasised a 1953 circular.[40]

Documents outlining even mundane arrangements – numbers of guests, details of invitations, banqueting plans – were annotated by Zhou Enlai and Liu Shaoqi, indicating the leadership's micromanagement of such issues. All the way up to his death, Zhou personally received thousands of foreign visitors: not just high-level dignitaries, but also

[36] Archive of Chinese Foreign Ministry (ACFM) 117–00110–02 (1950), 'Zhou Zongli "Zai lingzhi ge jiguan zhaodai waiguo shijie ji waibin jun xu shixian yu waijiaobu lianxi" ji bu gei Zongli de baogao' (Premier Zhou once more orders every organisation to contact the Foreign Ministry before receiving foreign diplomats or guests, and a report made to the premier).

[37] Shanghai Municipal Archive (SMA) A-42–1–20 (1954), 'ZhongGong Shanghaishi zhonggongye weiyuanhui guanyu jiedai waibin gongzuo yijian' (Opinions on the reception of foreign guests, by the Heavy Industry Committee of the Shanghai Municipal Branch of the CCP).

[38] Beijing Municipal Archive (BMA) 100–001–00465 (1958), 'Jiedai waibin de zongjie, jiedai Sukeji gongzuozhe daibiaotuan, qingnian daibiaotuan, qingzhu SuGong qingtuan jianguo 40 zhounian huodong, wei zai jing geguo liuxuesheng juban lianhuanhui de jihua, zongjie, jianghua deng' (Summary of reception of foreign guests: plans, summaries and talks for receiving the Youth Delegation of Soviet Technology Workers, the Youth Delegation, for congratulating the CPSU Youth League on its 40th anniversary and for parties for foreign students in Beijing).

[39] BMA 088–001–00160 (4 Sept. 1964), 'Shishe youguan jiedai waibin gongzuo de wenjian' (Documents on the reception of foreign guests).

[40] SMA A-47–2–10–37 (1953), 'ZhongGong Shanghaishi wei guanyu waibin fang Hua canguan jiedai gongzuo de tongzhi' (Notice from the Shanghai Municipal Branch of the CCP about the reception of foreign guests visiting China).

journalists, students, teachers, trade delegations, sports teams. At one point, Zhang Wentian – deputy foreign minister through the 1950s – ridiculed Zhou's focus on such work, objecting that Zhou ought to spend his time on more important, strategic matters and that he was spending too much of the Ministry's budget on drinking Maotai – a kind of Chinese liquor commonly used for banqueting toasts – with foreign journalists. Zhou disagreed: he responded that he was willing to pay for the food and drink himself, but that he was determined to continue. In diplomacy, he once remarked, 'there's no such thing as a small detail' (*waijiao wu xiaoshi*).

Logistical preparations for visits were strenuous. In the words of one report, 'every link must be pulled tight': from the drawing up of propaganda, to the preparation of accommodation and food.[41] There was a strong psychological logic underpinning the material care with which visits were managed. Paul Hollander places adroit emphasis on the importance of 'hospitality' as a technique for making individuals feel guiltily indebted to their Chinese hosts and inclined to reciprocate positively. In the archives, short-term foreigners in China are never described as 'visitors' or 'travellers': they are always 'foreign guests' (*waibin*), with all the implications of indebtedness that the word brings. Given the numbers of foreign visitors travelling to China even during the Mao era, not all had their costs covered by Chinese state organisations. Yet evidence in archival reports and eye-witness accounts suggests a strong cosseting principle at work: visitors were to be showered with attention and goodies, leaving them as gratefully dependent on their hosts as possible. Even at the toughest of times, the appropriateness of such expenditure was not questioned. Queen Elisabeth of Belgium visited in 1961, near the apogee of the post-Great Leap Forward famine, a predominantly manmade disaster generated by radical collectivisation after 1957. Nonetheless, all Queen Elisabeth's costs (including hairdressing and laundry) were covered by China, and thousands of *yuan* spent on presents. The cadres in charge reasoned: 'We must dispel their suspicions about our country, for example that we are having a famine and that the communes have collapsed and that Chinese people are warmongers.'[42]

Dossiers were compiled on the political background of every guest: to understand and exploit their vulnerabilities. Again in preparation for Queen Elisabeth's arrival, the Beijing government undertook research into the interpersonal complexities of the Belgian royal retinue of a thoroughness worthy of *Paris Match*. These files were then diligently

---

[41] SMA A-47–1–154 (1) (1953), 'Er ge yue lai Shanghai waibin zhaodai gongzuo de zongjie baogao: juemi' (Top secret: summary report on reception of foreign guests in Shanghai over the past two months).

[42] BMA 102–001–00190 (1961), 'Zhongdian waibin zai jing canguan' (Visits of VIP foreign guests to the capital).

studied by all cadres who had contact with particular foreigners: 'to imagine in advance all the kinds of questions that foreign guests might ask'.[43] One directive acknowledged that 'This kind of work is very stressful, it's easy to get tired and irritated . . . the questions asked by foreign guests are sometimes limited but sometimes limitless. Sometimes you need an encyclopedia to satisfy them.'[44] Words of welcome, introductory remarks and question-and-answer sessions were to be scripted in advance and censored first by the work unit's senior leadership, and then by at least two cadres in the Propaganda Department of the Committee for Receiving Foreign Guests. Once approved, all this material was turned into secret, internal pamphlets, again to be studied by hosting cadres.

There was a handy eight-syllable slogan to express the appropriate political approach: 'seem relaxed on the outside, but be tense inside, and don't give anything away' (*waisong neijin, bulu henji*).[45] The levels of vigilance demanded verged on the obsessive compulsive. As one report hectored: 'Planning, arrangement and checking: all three are essential. There can be no exceptionalism. Once you have checked everything, check it again.'[46]

Reports written before and after visits evoke a system of military discipline, a discipline that applied equally regardless of the political affiliations of the visitors. In some cases, the ratio of minders to delegates was almost one-to-one. A miscellaneous group of 214 visitors to Shanghai in 1953 (from Western Europe, the United States and non-socialist Asia) was accompanied by 212 cadres dispatched by the Central Committee.[47] When Kim Il-sung visited Shanghai in 1958, the welcoming party was 6,900 strong, and every member had to be 'politically pure'. In advance of Kim's arrival, almost eighty 'suspicious elements' were arrested or put under intensified surveillance; twenty-three were sent off for labour reform. The ranks of those selected to be shown to the Koreans were also checked and cleansed: for example, the children of landlords and rightists were purged, again 'to guarantee political purity'.[48]

Security was deemed essential: on a 1953 visit, the special operatives detailed to a foreign delegation disguised themselves variously as messengers, odd-jobbers, room attendants, receptionists and guides; they

[43] See *ibid.* and SMA A-42–1–20.

[44] SMA A-47–1–154 (1).

[45] SMA A-42–1–20.

[46] SMA A-47–1–154 (1).

[47] *Ibid.*

[48] SMA A-72–2–4 (9 Sept. 1958), 'Shanghai xian jiedai guobin zhihuibu guanyu yi Jin Richeng shouxiang wei shou de Chaoxian zhengfu daibiaotuan fang Hu qijian jiedai gongzuo zongjie baogao' (Report by the Shanghai county headquarters for receiving state guests, on the work done to receive the government delegation from North Korea led by Prime Minister Kim Il-sung while visiting Shanghai).

wiped baths, they piled bedding, they brought refreshments, but their true function, apparently, was never identified by the foreign guests.[49] Secrecy and organisation became all the more pressing at moments of political and social crisis. Despite the fact that much of China was starving in 1960, the government went ahead with its plans to invite more than 2,000 foreign guests to attend National Day celebrations. But planning was beset by fundamental logistical problems. A Foreign Ministry directive warned: 'The task of providing their food will be very onerous. Recently, because of the tensions surrounding food supply, we have discovered that bad elements have broken into food supplies for foreign guests in food trucks... Reduce as far as possible the number of cities that the foreign guests visit.'[50]

Still the show went on: a banquet, a reception on the Tiananmen rostrum and a fireworks display hosted by Zhou Enlai and Liu Shaoqi, to which all foreign guests, experts and journalists in Beijing were invited.[51] Indeed, through the famine years of 1959 to 1961, both foreign visitors and residents complained – with unwitting grotesquerie – of how hard it was to keep the pounds off in China. Rewi Alley, a long-term New Zealand resident in China, wrote to his nephew in 1961: 'How does one get weight down? I am 200 and should be 170. Only one way I suppose. That strong push away from the table!!'[52]

Internal Chinese reports claimed that all this work won major PR triumphs for the CCP. Chinese write-ups of visits are scattered with approbatory comments: Sri Lankan agronomists, Polish economists, Indian and Greek Communists who exclaimed that China was now their model. One Argentian hugged his host cadre with delight after a visit to a commune.[53]

---

[49] SMA A-47-1-154 (1).

[50] ACFM 117-00742-01 (1960), '1960 nian Zhongguo guoqing, zhongyang guanyu jiedai de zhishi, zhuwai shiguan, youguan difang waishichu guanyu guoqing gongzuo de qingshi ji laiwang wendian' (Central Committee Directives and telegrams on instructions for the reception of foreign guests, embassies abroad and local foreign affairs departments for National Day 1960).

[51] *Ibid.*

[52] Brady, *Making the Foreign Serve China*, 117.

[53] See, for example, SMA A-72-1-24 (1959), 'ZhongGong Shanghai shiwei nongcun gongzuo weiyuanhui, Shanghaishi renmin weiyuanhui nongcun gongzuo weiyuanhui 1959 nian jiaoqu renmin gongshi jiben qingkuang ji renmin gongshe gaikuang he chuli dui Maqiao renmin gongshehua de fanying' (The basic situation and general survey of People's Communes in the suburbs, and a summary of responses to Maqiao People's Commune, from 1959, by the rural work committee of the CCP Shanghai municipal committee and the rural work committee of the Shanghai municipal people's committee); SMA A-72-2-3 (1959), 'ZhongGong Shanghaishi nongchang gongzuo weiyuanhui, Shanghaishi renmin weiyuanhui nongcun gongzuo weiyuanhui guanyu waibin canguan qingkuang (The CCP

One of the remarkable aspects of this system is how willingly – according to both Chinese and non-Chinese accounts – many foreign visitors drew conclusions about the general superiority of the system from a carefully choreographed visit to a single model commune, school, farmer or temple. Even the handlers for a 1952 delegation that included Nehru's sister, Mrs Pandit, seemed surprised by how easily convinced the visitors were after seeing just one temple in Shanghai that Chinese people enjoyed freedom of religious belief.[54]

Yet the real proof of the system lay not in what guests politely said to their expectant minders, but in how they responded when they were far beyond China. A good example can be seen in the response of Edgar Snow, the American journalist upon whom the CCP first developed many of their foreigner-handling techniques.

In 1936, Zhou Enlai and Liu Shaoqi, in consultation with one of the Communists' most useful and influential Chinese fellow-travellers Song Qingling, had carefully picked Snow as the ideal mouthpiece for taking their story to the international world. Song Qingling occupied an unusual and highly prestigious role in Chinese politics of the 1920s to 1940s. As the widow of the veteran revolutionary and first president of the republic, Sun Yat-sen (who died in 1925), she had impeccable revolutionary credentials. In 1927, the Chinese revolution split between left and right, when Chiang Kai-shek, leader of the Nationalist Party, ended the Soviet-sponsored united front with the Communists with a bloody purge. Song Qingling sided with the left, briefly seeking refuge in Moscow and Europe before settling back in Shanghai in 1931 as a determined critic of Chiang's Nationalist regime. She was protected from intense Nationalist persecution of Communists and the leftwing between 1927 and 1936 by her family connections: not only by being Sun Yat-sen's widow but also, perhaps just as importantly, the beloved older sister of Chiang Kai-shek's wife, Song Meiling. After returning to China, Song Qingling helped the Communist underground operation (for example, by liaising with the CCP, Soviet Union and Comintern in Shanghai, hosting meetings for those with CCP connections, finding sympathetic foreigners to mediate contact between Shanghai and the CCP Central Committee deep in rural China and even personally funding Mao's revolutionary base in the north-west of China).[55]

Municipal Shanghai farm work committee and the rural work committee of the Shanghai municipal people's committee report on the visits of foreign guests).

[54] SMA A-47–1–154 (1). See also SMA A-72–2–3.

[55] For more details, see Jay Taylor, *The Generalissimo* (Cambridge, MA, 2009), 96, 122, 135; Israel Epstein, *Woman in World History: Soong Ching Ling* (Beijing, 1993); Chen Guanren, *Song Qingling dazhuan* (Biography of Song Qingling) (Beijing, 2003).

Snow was one of several sympathetic, useful foreigners whom Song Qingling guided towards the CCP in the 1930s. He was a well-disposed but non-communist American with excellent media connections. Mao Zedong, Liu Shaoqi and Zhou Enlai invited him, through an underground network, to spend weeks visiting their beleaguered state in north-west China, which was under military threat from the Nationalists.[56] According to Jung Chang and Jon Halliday (who, in their biography of Mao, write scathingly of Snow's gullibility in the face of a CCP charm offensive), before Snow's arrival at Communist headquarters, Mao gave four instructions for the visit: 'Security, secrecy, warmth and red carpet.'[57] Mao and his confreres had chosen and primed their man well. The following year, Snow wrote up his impressions and interviews of the Communist base area in the north-west (heavily censored by Mao and Zhou) into the global bestseller *Red Star over China*. The book turned Mao into an international political personality, portraying him as a disarmingly laidback, affable patriot.[58]

Red Star was an important public relations success when the CCP was on the point of annihilation by Chiang Kai-shek's Nationalist government. Snow's 1961 book, *The Other Side of the River: Red China Today*, spoke out for Communist China at another crisis point: at the height of the post-Great Leap Forward famine, in which tens of millions died of starvation or the effects of malnutrition largely caused by state economic mismanagement.[59] Though not entirely without its criticisms of China, the book found in favour of the Communist regime under Mao. In his introduction, Snow insisted that he had been given perfect access during a six-month visit in 1960 (his first return to the country since the founding of the People's Republic in 1949): 'I cannot complain about lack of opportunity to see China. I was to travel, if anything, too extensively in the time I had available . . . I think I know more about all these people than I could possibly have understood had I never returned to China.'[60] Throughout, Snow described how, in his tour of the country, he caught up with old friends, both foreign and Chinese (and including Mao and Zhou), and was cheerily received by countless citizens of New China.

---

[56] For more detail, see S. Bernard Thomas, *Season of High Adventure: Edgar Snow in China* (Berkeley, 1996), 131; John Maxwell Hamilton, *Edgar Snow: A Biography* (Bloomington, 1988), 67–9.

[57] Jung Chang and Jon Halliday, *Mao: The Unknown Story* (2005), 199.

[58] Edgar Snow, *Red Star over China* (1937). See Thomas, *Season of High Adventure*, 169–89; Hamilton, *Edgar Snow*, 84–96; and Robert M. Farnsworth, *From Vagabond to Journalist: Edgar Snow in Asia, 1928–1941* (Missouri, 1996), 310–17, for details about the book's reception. Thomas, *Season of High Adventure*, 165, has details of CCP editing of the book.

[59] For two recent accounts of the famine based on extensive archival research, see Frank Dikötter, *Mao's Great Famine: The History of China's Greatest Catastrophe* (2010), and Yang Jisheng, *Tombstone: The Untold Story of Mao's Great Famine*, trans. Guo Jian and Stacy Mosher (2012).

[60] Edgar Snow, *The Other Side of the River: Red China Today* (1963), 21–2.

There was nothing to imply reserve, control or manipulation in his write-ups of these genial, comradely encounters. Most crucially perhaps, from a PRC propaganda perspective, the book denied famine and starvation several times:

> I diligently searched, without success, for starving people or beggars to photograph . . . I must assert that I saw no starving people in China, nothing that looked like old-time famine . . . that I do not believe there is famine in China at this writing . . . One of the few things I can say with certainty is that mass starvation such as China knew almost annually under former regimes no longer occurs.[61]

Files on preparations for Snow's visit in Beijing archives tell a different story. A top-secret planning document from 1960 dissected Snow's character and situation with clinical chilliness, with a view to exploiting his weaknesses for the PRC's benefit.

Snow's writing, the report observes, 'has [in the past] served a beneficial propaganda purpose for us. But he himself is not a progressive individual . . . we guess that he has some link with the State Department . . . In recent years he has suffered repeated professional frustrations and setbacks . . . big newspapers refuse his articles.' (By 1960, McCarthyism had driven Snow and his family into Swiss exile.) The report goes on:

> We suppose that Snow has two aims in coming to China: first, to win fame and fortune by writing a book; second, to carry out strategic espionage . . . In hosting him, we should be superficially friendly . . . On the surface we should seem relaxed; inside, we must be tense, to increase our vigilance. We should intensify our control of his activities . . . As regards his interview and writing requests, we should satisfy them according to our needs: we will let him see some of the things that we allow him to see, to bring him to understand a few things that we have prepared for him to understand . . . We must propagandise to him the dazzling achievements of socialist construction in every area, and the great victory of the general line, the Great Leap Forward and the People's Communes . . . We will make him see the unanimous unity of every nationality, the correctness of the CCP leadership, the absolute unity inside the party, and that the unity between China and the USSR can never be destroyed.[62]

To his diary, Snow confided his suspicions that all was not as it seemed:

> I realised what it is that is strange about these meetings and interviews thus far. I am cordially received and given every co-operation technically correct. But no intimacy is

---

[61] *Ibid.*, 619, 172.
[62] BMA 102-001-00118 (1960), 'Waijiaobu jiedai de Minzhu Deguo zhengfu daibiaotuan, Chaoxian zhengfu jingji daibiaotuan, Gangguo dangzheng daibiaotuan, Aerbaniya Zhongguo youhao xiehui daibiaotuan, Yingguo Menggemali yuanshuai, Yingguo zuojia Sinuo zaijing canguan huodong (The Foreign Ministry reception of a delegation from the German Democratic Republic, of an economic delegation from the government of North Korea, of a delegation from the Congolese party and government administration, of a delegation from the Albania–China Friendship Association, and on the activities of the English Field-Marshal Montgomery and the English [*sic*] writer Snow while visiting Beijing).

established no spark of human warmth established. It is as if you knew that you were never going to see a person again and it cannot be the beginning of a friendship . . . I wanted to combine renewal of friendship with interviews and business but Rewi Alley said that's the last thing to ask for. They'll do everything to avoid that.[63]

Indeed, Foreign Ministry archives on Snow's visit contain informants' reports on private conversations provided by old, non-Chinese 'friends' (and loyal servants of the Communist government) whom Snow described so warmly in his book: Israel Epstein and George Hatem.[64]

Yet in writing up *The Other Side of the River*, Snow kept his misgivings to himself. Once more, Mao and Zhou had chosen their man well: Snow had financial reasons for siding with China. He owed too much of his journalistic reputation to his writing on China through the 1930s and 1940s; he had a wife and two young children to support. He needed access to write a successful book on China; and he needed to write favourably enough about China to maintain future access.

Bill Jenner, now a retired professor of Chinese history, has spoken of the book's impact on him as a young doctoral student in 1962, just before he decided to travel to Maoist China himself to work for two years as a translator in Beijing's Foreign Languages Press, the government organisation that published China's so-called 'external propaganda' for foreign readers. He bought a copy of the book using prize money he had won at graduation.

There just wasn't much to read on contemporary China at the time, and the book's overwhelmingly positive image impressed me a lot . . . I think it's a far more pernicious book than *Red Star* because it was researched during the famine. He should have known better. However closely he was being watched by his minders, he should have seen through things. He ought to have known what he wasn't seeing. He'd been in China before.[65]

Communist hospitality also scored successes with hard-power implications: in 1962, the Communist leadership selected Jan Myrdal, a struggling Swedish leftwing novelist, to be invited on an all-expenses paid trip to China, including a month in a model village in the north-west. The paean to the Chinese rural revolution that resulted, Myrdal's 1963 book *Report from a Chinese Village*, became an international bestseller (thereby securing Myrdal's livelihood) and a rallying text for the radical leftwing and student rebels in 1960s Sweden.[66] As the founding member of a Swedish Maoist grouping formed in the 1960s, Myrdal subsequently

[63] Brady, *Making the Foreign Serve China*, 121–2.

[64] See, for example, ACFM 116–00189–06(1) (10 July 1960), 'Meiguo zuojia Sinuo qingkuang fanying' (Reports on the situation of the American writer Snow); ACFM 116–00265–03(1) (2 Sept. – 24 Nov. 1960), 'Guanyu Meiguo zuojia Sinuo de qingkuang' (Concerning the situation of the American writer Snow).

[65] Bill Jenner, interview by author, Cambridge, 29 Nov. 2013.

[66] Jan Myrdal, *Rapport från Kinesisk By* (Report from a Chinese Village) (Stockholm, 1963).

led protests against the Vietnam War; this spike in radicalism worried Sweden's ruling political party enough for it to take a neutral stance on American intervention in Indochina, thereby weakening international support for US policy.[67]

Thanks in part to Zhou Enlai's careful hosting of Prince Sihanouk of Cambodia through the 1950s and 1960s, the prince took refuge in China after he was ousted by a military coup in 1970. There, across the ensuing five years, the Chinese brokered an alliance between Sihanouk and Pol Pot's Khmer Rouge, one that dramatically boosted the Cambodian Communists' international and national respectability, and furthered Maoist China's aim of spreading communism through Southeast Asia.[68]

Skilful Chinese hospitality may also have helped export the Maoist revolution to Indonesia, with appalling consequences. The chairman of the Indonesian Communist Party, Aidit, a great admirer of Mao and his revolution, visited the same model commune twice, in 1959 and 1961, and was given the full propaganda treatment. Having emphasised that entry to the commune was entirely voluntary, his hosts in 1961 explained all the great transformations that had taken place in the preceding two years, and flatteringly presented him with a book that had reprinted an inscription that he had left in 1959. Aidit's Chinese minders in 1959 and 1961 deftly concealed the true nature of the Commune system – terror, starvation, cannibalism – and reinforced Aidit's respect for the Maoist experiment. The report on his visit commented that 'Aidit was very satisfied. He said: 'You can see that the changes here [over the past two years] are huge . . . I am delighted . . . I wish you ever greater success in the future.' Four years later, in 1965, directly encouraged and (some historians argue) funded by Mao and his lieutenants, Aidit helped launch a coup against the Indonesian army, expecting triumph for his Communist Party. Instead, the armed forces under General Suharto reasserted control and launched a purge that killed some 500,000 suspected communists, many of them ethnic Chinese.[69]

---

[67] See discussion in Perry Johansson, 'Mao and the Swedish United Front against USA', in *The Cold War in Asia*, ed. Zheng Yangwen et al., 217–40.

[68] For a discussion of the role played by the CCP in brokering the alliance between Sihanouk and the Khmer Rouge, see for example Philip Short, *Pol Pot: The History of a Nightmare* (2005). On the economic relations between mainland China and Democratic Kampuchea, see Andrew Mertha, *Brothers in Arms: Chinese Aid to the Khmer Rouge, 1975–1979* (Ithaca, 2014), and Ben Kiernan, *The Pol Pot Regime: Race, Power and Genocide in Cambodia under the Khmer Rouge, 1975–79* (New Haven, 2008).

[69] BMA 102–001–00190 (1961), 'Zhongdian waibin zaijing canguan' (The visits of VIP foreign guests to Beijing). For a discussion of the Indonesian coup of Sept. 1965 and the anti-communist, anti-Chinese purge that followed it, see John Roosa, *Pretext for Mass Murder: The September 30th Movement and Suharto's Coup d'État in Indonesia* (Madison, 2006).

Despite the fastidiousness of preparations, the archives also expose weaknesses in China's international hospitality machine. In 1953, at least, it seems clear that the smooth operation described by Robert Loh was not yet in place: foreign guests complained about getting earache from the constant comparisons of China's glorious present with its dreadful past; that a trip to China was a 'journalist's punishment'; that minders accompanied guests through meals to spy on them; that the Chinese were trying to buy their guests through farewell gifts of clothes and cash.[70] In a serious gaffe, one foreign affairs cadre revealed to one of the guests that every delegate had been extensively researched in advance.[71] A 1950 Foreign Ministry directive about how to receive foreign guests gives a flavour of how much the Ministry felt its employees had to learn in terms of international polish. It contained plenty of useful, factual guidance about the difference between a sit-down dinner and a buffet; about how to behave in the face of a bread roll (namely, you should break off a piece and butter it). But there was also a substantial amount of hectoring about more basic issues: reminding diplomats, when leaving the toilet, to check that their flies were done up; not to yawn openly in front of interlocutors, not to pick nose or ears.[72] Reports of visits by foreign guests well into the 1950s were studded with complaints that cadres were snapping at each other through stress and over-work;[73] or that they were ill-prepared, or wooden; or drunk.[74]

Sometimes, foreign guests seriously imperiled international camaraderie. Consider the following, slightly cryptic report: 'Recently, some foreign guests have engaged upon discourteous behavior towards female attendants, which has gone beyond the bounds of friendly unity with international friends... From now on, only male attendants will

[70] ACFM 113–00180–01 (8 Dec. 1953), 'Guanyu 1950–1953 nian zibenzhuyi tixi guojia laiHua waibin fanying de zonghe baogao ji qingkuang jibiao' (A summarising report on the responses of foreign guests visiting China from capitalist countries between 1950 and 1953); see also ACFM 117–00473–07 (1 Sept. 1955), 'Guanyu waibin yingsong, yanhui, songli ji jiaotong gongju zanxing guiding' (On provisional regulations for the reception and seeing off, banqueting and gifting of foreign guests, and for their means of transport).

[71] ACFM 113–00180–01.

[72] ACFM 117–00110–07 (1) (2 Jan. 1951), 'Duiwai jiaoji huodong zhong fasheng de wenti ji "dui waibin jiaoji xuzhi"' (Problems that have occurred in contact with foreigners and 'Essential information for contact with foreign guests').

[73] ACFM 117–00102–01 (19 Sept. 1951), 'Guoqingjie teyao waibin zhaodai weiyuanhui gongzuo zongjie' (Summary of work for committee in charge of receiving specially invited foreign guests).

[74] BMA 088–001–00404 (2 July – 26 Dec. 1963), 'Zongshe, shishe guanyu waibin canguan de qingkuang huibao deng' (Reports by the main and municipal offices on visits by foreign guests).

service the rooms of male guests.'[75] The sheer numbers of foreign travellers to Maoist China would suggest, moreover, that it was not logistically possible for every visit to be perfectly monitored and choreographed.[76]

The Chinese masses could prove unruly, also, and impervious to efforts to deploy them in the service of 'international friendship'. The archives are scattered with embarrassed reports of rude receptions: of Chinese children and adults gathering around African visitors to a Beijing hutong, pointing and laughing that 'their skin is like tree bark . . . their heads look like pigs';[77] of workers ignoring friendly Albanians, or gathering around the back of one Polish visitor, pointing at his neck (the work summary explained that it was very thick and red).[78] Despite the exhaustive, and exhausting, preparations for Kim Il-sung's visit described above, the commanding cadres still found fault with the performance of the masses. The team of welcoming students at East China Chemistry Institute, they specified, were extremely ill-disciplined: they did not shout slogans or sing songs, they messed about throwing flowers and strips of paper at each other, 'creating a very bad influence'.[79]

The thinness of the façade could be exposed with alarming ease. A report from a model commune near Shanghai, which from 10 to 14 October 1959 alone received at least two delegations of foreign visitors a day, suggests that the hosts at one point let slip the staged, Potemkin nature of what was on display.

> The people hosting one delegation to the new village took it upon themselves to ask if the foreign guests would like to visit some peasants. The foreign guests agreed but when they got there, every single house was shut up; there wasn't a single peasant to be found. It was the same when the foreign guests visited the commune hospital and reading room . . . the officials . . . had gone out for lunch.[80]

[75] ACFM 117–00189–01 (20 May 1952), 'Zhongyang guanyu Wuyijie waibin jiedai de zhishi ji gedi jihua he youguan qingkuang deng' (Central directives on the reception of foreign guests during Labour Day and relevant matters concerning the plans for all localities).

[76] Matthew Rothwell, for example, describes how, in later memoirs and interviews, several Latin American visitors of the 1950s and 1960s felt that it was possible to escape their hosts and have unscripted encounters in Chinese cities. Personal communication and *Transpacific Revolutionaries: The Chinese Revolution in Latin America* (Abingdon, 2013).

[77] ACFM 117–01299–01 (12 May 1961), 'Guanyu xiang qunzhong jinxing zhengque dui hei Feizhou waibin de jiaoyu tongzhi' (Notice about correctly educating the masses about receiving black African foreign guests).

[78] SMA B123–6–163 (1964), '1964 nian guowuyuan, Shanghaishi renwei waijingmaoban, shiwei waishi xiaozu ji Shanghaishi diyi shangyeju guanyu waishi gongzuo you guan wenjian' (1964 documents relevant to foreign affairs work from the State Council, the Shanghai People's Committee Foreign Trade Office, the Foreign Affairs Sub-Committee of the Municipal Party Committee and Number One Municipal Trade Bureau).

[79] SMA A-72–2–4.

[80] SMA A-72–2–3.

The experience suggests that even slightly spontaneous arrangements were fraught with risk.

Despite the research undertaken in advance by Chinese hosts, they could still misread their guests. After Mrs Pandit's minders in 1952 took her to call on Song Qingling, they observed that Mrs Pandit viewed Song as 'half-woman, half-goddess'.[81] Outside China, Mrs Pandit seemed less worshipful: in a debriefing conversation with the American ambassador in Delhi following her trip to China, she remarked that Song was 'closely confined' in Shanghai. 'She seemed bitter at world generally and had little to say.' Mrs Pandit's report to the Americans contradicted in other places the responses recorded by her Chinese minders. According to the Chinese report, the Indian delegations gasped with admiration at the socialist construction that they saw: on being shown a swimming pool, for example, they remarked that in India, building even a tap with running water would be a major event. To the US ambassador, Mrs Pandit said: 'Chi[nese] health conditions remain serious even worse than in India.' Mrs Pandit's Chinese handlers were confident that they had been warmly welcoming, stressing the Chinese people's love of peace. This is what she reported back to the Americans: 'The effort being made [to] educate people and particularly children is frightening in its thoroughness and doctrinaire qualities. From kindergarten up, every stage of education ruthlessly controlled.'[82]

The writer Frank Tuohy, on a visit to Nanjing in 1966, asked to see a children's drawing class, after visiting a classroom adorned only with pictures of Chairman Mao. The following day, his request was granted and he observed a primary school class copying 'clippings of girl guerrillas shooting down planes with rifles; paper tigers being throttled by the Viet Cong; three Americans – a bishop, a professor and a doctor – standing arm-in-arm over a pile of corpses; GIs with the features of President Johnson being bayonetted up the rear . . . The guide', he noted, 'seemed offended by our lack of enthusiasm.'[83]

A long and intricate paper-trail remains to be traced out, before the true impact of China's hosting work can be fully understood: we need to explore the post-China writings and public engagements of those carefully courted, and to work out who read and who listened to them. To gain a preliminary sense of this, we could return to the example of Edgar Snow. In Chinese, German and Italian translations, his writing on Chinese

---

[81] SMA A-47–1–154 (1).

[82] 793.00/7–752, 'Telegram: the Ambassador in India (Bowles) to the Department of State', 7 July 1952, Document 36, *Foreign Relations of the United States, 1952–1954, Volume* XIV, *Part 1, China and Japan*, at https://history.state.gov/historicaldocuments/frus1952–54v14p1/d36 (accessed 12 Jan. 2015).

[83] Frank Tuohy, 'From a China Diary', *Encounter* (Dec. 1966), 8–9.

communism was eagerly consumed by Chinese and Southeast Asian revolutionaries, and by European radicals between the 1940s and 1970s.[84] The careful suppression of the extent and causes of political cataclysms such as the famine of the 1960s – to which Snow contributed – made it possible for young sinologists of the late Maoist era to write influential academic articles and books that validated Mao and his revolution both before and after Mao's death in 1976.[85]

Maoist China's hosting programme, moreover, had a domestic as well as an international focus. Foreigners were the official target, but the government also used the spectacle to underscore at home the triumph of the revolution. A 1953 report observed that

> the masses at the sites visited by the foreign guests were all educated by the experience. One worker said that New China's international status must have improved... in the past, Chinese people went abroad. After the victory of the revolution, everyone comes to China... After multiple visits by foreign guests, workers at one nursery no longer felt that their work was trivial; they felt that they had done glorious, important international propaganda work.[86]

A Shanghai worker visited by a West German in 1957 drew similar, grateful conclusions: 'Before Liberation', she told the cadres who had trained her for the visit, 'who would have visited a worker like me? But now that we have "turned over" [*fanshen*, the Chinese communist term for having undergone revolutionary transformation], we are the masters/hosts... and foreign guests visit us: this is an unprecedented honour for my family.' The worker's family 'diligently prepared for the visit, wanting to show the foreign guest how well workers lived after the revolution'.[87]

---

[84] For indications of the international influence of Snow's writing, see the interview cited above with Bill Jenner and interview with Mark Selden, 29 May 2013; Niccolai, *Quando la Cina era vicina*; Kühn, *Stalins Enkel, Maos Söhne*; Thomas, *Season of High Adventure*; C. C. Chin and Karl Hack, eds., *Dialogues with Chin Peng: New Light on the Malayan Communist Party* (Singapore, 2005).

[85] Consider, for example, Mark Selden, *The Yanan Way in Revolutionary China* (Cambridge, MA, 1971); Jonathan Mirsky, 'China after Nixon', in *The Annals of the American Academy of Political and Social Science*, 402 (July 1972), 83–96; Committee of Concerned Asian Scholars, *China! Inside the People's Republic* (New York, 1972); Edward Friedman, 'The Innovator', in *Mao Tse-tung in the Scales of History*, ed. Dick Wilson (Cambridge, 1977), 300–21. Friedman, Mirsky and Selden all later underwent significant, even dramatic, changes in their assessment of Mao-era China (in particular, of the Great Leap Forward and the Cultural Revolution) when access to China increased somewhat after Mao's death. Examples of their later, far more critical, judgements can be found in Jonathan Mirsky's post-Mao journalism for publications including the *Times*, the *Spectator*, the *New York Review of Books* and in Edward Friedman, Paul Pickowicz and Mark Selden, *Chinese Village, Socialist State* (New Haven, 1991).

[86] SMA A-47-1-154 (1).

[87] BMA 101-001-00632 (13 Nov. 1957), 'Benhui, benbu youguan jiedai chuxi gonghui "Bada", "Wuyi" waibin ji riben Chuanqishi yihui, Riben gonghui liang daibiaotuan deng guoji gongzuo de jihua, zongjie, huanyingci, hepian mingdan deng youguan wenjian'

To Communist officials, preparing ordinary people to put on a show for foreign guests was part of a much bigger political project: mobilising the enthusiasm and energy of the masses for party political aims.[88] For this, and many other reasons, there is a certain melancholy to reading the archives on China's hosting machine: a sense of Maoist China being one vast stage-set – the Chinese playing to the foreigners, the foreigners playing back to the Chinese, and back and forth it goes.

(Relevant documents, including plans, summaries, welcome speeches, name lists for greetings cards, for international work receiving foreign guests and Kawasaki municipal parliament and Japanese trade union delegations for the Eighth Congress and Labour Day). See also SMA A-72–2–4, describing mass mobilisation in advance of Kim Il-sung's visit.

[88]See Chen, *Mao's China and the Cold War* for a discussion of the ways in which Mao used foreign policy to achieve domestic objectives, especially mass mobilisation.

Transactions of the RHS 25 (2015), pp. 159–185 © Royal Historical Society 2015
doi:10.1017/S0080440115000080

'CRAMPED AND RESTRICTED AT HOME'?
SCOTTISH SEPARATISM AT EMPIRE'S END*
The Berry Prize Essay

By Jimmi Østergaard Nielsen and Stuart Ward

ABSTRACT. The emergence of Scottish separatism as a viable political force in the 1960s is often seen as a reflection of Britain's wider political fortunes in a post-imperial world. It is indeed the case that the Scottish National Party emerged from electoral obscurity to become a credible political alternative in the 1960s, culminating in Winifred Ewing's by-election victory in Hamilton in November 1967. That this occurred in the wake of Britain's retreat from empire fuelled speculation that separatist momentum in Scotland represented an inward manifestation of the same pressures that had torn the empire asunder. This paper draws on sources from local politics to make two key arguments: first, that post-imperial influences were neither as pervasive nor even particularly prominent in the local politics of devolution as may be assumed. Equally, however, global processes of decolonisation contributed to the separatist agenda in ways more subtle than has hitherto been acknowledged. Indeed, there are several striking similarities between the gathering political momentum of the SNP and the sweep of 'new nationalisms' through the remnants of the British world in the 1960s, particularly in the former British Dominions of Australia, Canada and New Zealand. Thus, the relative absence of decolonising discourse in the local electoral source material does not necessarily rule out these global undercurrents, although the exact nature of their influence needs to be more carefully evaluated.

The idea that the eclipse of the British Empire brought direct and inherently corrosive consequences for the United Kingdom is as old as decolonisation itself, and has been reiterated by historians and commentators for decades. In particular, the emergence of Scottish separatism as a viable political force since the 1960s is commonly regarded as one of the most tangible and lasting domestic repercussions of imperial decline. With this paper, we wish to subject these assertions

* This research was supported by a Velux Foundation research grant to the 'Embers of Empire' project at the University of Copenhagen. We thank our colleagues Peter Harder, Ezekiel Mercau, Christian Damm Pedersen and Astrid Rasch for detailed comments on an earlier version of the paper, and John MacKenzie for his advice and encouragement. We also thank Maria Castrillo, Manuscripts Curator at the National Library of Scotland, for locating several sources referred to in the paper. For valuable feedback on the work presented during a University of Copenhagen workshop in 2013 we thank Jamie Belich, Liz Buettner, Stephen Howe, Joanna Lewis and Bill Schwarz.

to long-overdue empirical scrutiny, by investigating the ways in which the imperial–domestic link emerged as a topic of discussion in the Scottish nationalist debate. Our focus is the 1960s, the decade when the Scottish National Party (SNP) first saw substantial electoral success. We first present the underlying premises of the claim that there is a causal connection between imperial decline and centrifugal pressures on the British state, exploring the work of historians who have figured prominently on this theme. We then move on to examine the evidence for a post-imperial impetus behind SNP electoral gains. In particular, we turn our attention to the Hamilton by-election of 1967, universally recognised as a landmark event in Scottish nationalist history with the unexpected win by SNP candidate Winifred Ewing. On the basis of this material, we argue that certain variants of the end of empire thesis need to be discarded due to a sheer lack of empirical validation. Yet having done so, the remainder of the paper seeks alternative connections between imperial and domestic contexts. While explicit references to empire's end in the SNP success story are few and far between, global processes of decolonisation may well have contributed to the separatist agenda in ways more subtle than has hitherto been acknowledged. We shall point to striking similarities between the gathering political momentum of the SNP in the 1960s and the 'new nationalism' among the former British Dominions in the same decade, arguing that there were good reasons why the end of empire was never foregrounded in SNP rhetoric. We conclude that the relative scarcity of overtly 'imperial' commentary in the source material does not, in itself, dismiss the pervasive influence of decolonising pressures, although the exact nature of this influence has yet to be properly understood.[1]

The evolution of an argument

The connection between the end of empire and the strength of political separatism in Scotland has been the source of speculation among

[1] The preparation of this paper entailed extensive research using materials stored in various collections, among these: The National Library of Scotland (P.la.5746 PER, 'Scottish National Party Press Releases 1966–1968'; P.la.7030, 'Miscellaneous Pamphlets and Leaflets of the Scottish National Party 1957–1993'; Acc. 13099, 'Political Correspondence of Dr Gordon Wilson, Secretary of the SNP'; Acc. 10090/113, 'General Correspondence (1967–1968) of Dr Robert Douglas McIntyre, President of the SNP'; Acc. 10090/116, 'Misc. Party Leaflets 1962–1969'). University of Edinburgh Centre for Research Collections (Gen. 890–2, 909–10, 'Collection of Material relating to the Scottish National Party'). The National Archives of Scotland (SOE9/136 and SOE9/139, 'Materials relating to the 1976 Devolution Debate, and Statements and Papers by Political Parties and Other Organizations'). The Library of the SNP Headquarters in Edinburgh (various materials relating to the 1967 Hamilton by-election).

historians since the 1930s,[2] and cursory references to such a relationship were expressed as early as the late nineteenth century.[3] But it was only with the relatively sudden electoral successes of the SNP and Plaid Cymru in the mid-1960s that the idea of a direct causal relationship took hold. H. J. Hanham's classic 1969 formulation is worth quoting at length:

> At the height of its popularity the Union was inspired by a sense of purpose. Scots felt that they were sharing in a great imperial venture and took pride in the achievements of Scots all over the world. Now that the Empire is dead, many Scots feel cramped and restricted at home... To give themselves an opening to a wider world the Scots need some sort of outlet, and the choice appears at the moment to be between emigration and re-creating the Scottish nation at home.[4]

This view gathered momentum into the 1970s, popularised by James Morris's memorable turn of phrase: 'Who gets satisfaction from the present state of the Union? Who is really content with this grubby wreck of old glories?'[5] But it was only with the publication of Tom Nairn's 1977 *The Break-Up of Britain* that it appeared as a fully elaborated argument. In Nairn's view, the British state was decidedly geared towards running an empire. Its success in this regard rested on the uniquely successful large-scale agrarian and then industrial revolutions, developments that turned Britain into the world's first modern nation. This enormous initial success both at home and particularly overseas had immense consequences for the development of the British state itself.[6] To Nairn, it was above all Britain's 'external relations'[7] – of which the existence of a vast empire was the most important feature – which stood in the way of such important advances as constitutional reform, devolution, an abandonment of the hereditary parliamentary principle and a move away from an anachronistic class society. In Nairn's interpretation, the inevitable result of Britain's imperial ambition and success was a 'backward' state configuration and society: a society in which 'bourgeois radicalism and popular mobilisation were eschewed for the sake of conservative stability', and where 'stability had become paralytic over-stability'.[8] The Scottish elite, whose counterparts were responsible for mobilising successful nationalist movements on the European continent, readily sacrificed the Scottish cause for the lucrative business of empire: 'During the prolonged era of Anglo-Scots imperialist expansion, the Scottish ruling order found that it had given up statehood

---

[2] T. M. Devine, 'The Break-Up of Britain? Scotland and the End of Empire', *Transactions of the Royal Historical Society*, 16 (2006), 163–80.

[3] Tom Nairn, *The Break-Up of Britain: Crisis and Neo-Nationalism* (1977).

[4] H. J. Hanham, *Scottish Nationalism* (1969), 212.

[5] Quoted in Keith Robbins, '"This Grubby Wreck of Old Glories": The United Kingdom and the End of the British Empire', *Journal of Contemporary History*, 15.1 (1980), 83.

[6] Nairn, *The Break-Up of Britain: Crisis and Neo-Nationalism*, 21.

[7] *Ibid.*, 22.

[8] *Ibid.*, 22, 23, 42.

for a hugely profitable junior partnership in the New Rome.'[9] It was only with the demise of empire that the Scottish question became relevant to them, and therefore, 'it was the extraordinary external success of the transitional English state that permitted it [i.e. the unitary state] to survive so long'.[10] While the empire persisted, it is understood, the potential leaders of a Scottish nationalist movement were busy elsewhere, harvesting the fruits of imperial success. But with the end of empire, the British state's survival was predicted by Nairn to be shortlived, and, by allusion to other metropoles which had suffered significant loss of power or prestige, he considered it inevitable that Britain would also undergo a 'strong reaction'.[11] Nairn perceived the surge of Scottish nationalism in the 1960s and 1970s to be only preliminary, with much yet to come.

Subsequent accounts have likewise emphasised the empire's role as a vital (though less repressive) device through which UK unity could be maintained, and many historians have argued that Scottish nationalism was always bound to be emboldened by the demise of empire. The key to understanding this is to appreciate the very significant extent of Scottish involvement in the imperial adventure, explored at great length in Linda Colley's 1992 *Britons*. The Scottish made a 'disproportionate contribution to the Great Game [that] persisted throughout the nineteenth century and on until the end of the Empire',[12] and settling in the colonies, Colley argued, gave the Scots an opportunity to 'feel themselves peers of the English in a way still denied them in an island kingdom',[13] profoundly influencing their perception of themselves. It was thus largely the empire that made the Union between Scotland and England real, giving the Scots and the English 'a powerful distraction and cause in common'.[14] To Colley, this deep Scottish involvement in the empire naturally resulted in a profound reaction to its loss. In fact, Colley explicitly links the new lack of commercial opportunities caused by the end of empire to the popular late twentieth-century demand for Scottish independence: 'The Scots . . . who became British in 1707 in part because it paid such enormous commercial and imperial dividends, are now increasingly inclined to see partial or complete independence plus membership in a federal Europe as the most profitable strategy for the future.'[15] But to Colley, it was not merely relevant that the empire's demise changed the economic conditions and opportunities for the British people. An equally

[9] *Ibid.*, 129.

[10] *Ibid.*, 20.

[11] *Ibid.*, 80.

[12] *Ibid.*, 139.

[13] *Ibid.*, 137.

[14] Linda Colley, 'Britishness and Otherness: An Argument', *Journal of British Studies*, 31 (1992), 325.

[15] Linda Colley, *Britons* (orig. edn New York, 1992; London, 1996), 395–6.

if not more important change took place in the minds of Britons, who had long defined themselves against a range of external groups of 'others', including the subject peoples of the empire. The end of empire effectively closed off this key source of 'otherness', rendering the self somehow less cohesive and distinct. Or to use Colley's formulation, when the other 'is no longer available', the result is a 'renewed sensitivity to internal differences'[16] – a process which manifested itself in a revival of regional nationalisms and support for devolution.[17]

These claims often form an integral part of the narrative of the disintegration of the Union that is said to have taken place since the 1960s. Krishan Kumar, for example, sees the empire as having had an absolutely crucial role in the development of national British cohesion, providing 'the integument that . . . tightly meshed the parts of Britain together',[18] and 'containing'[19] regional nationalisms while it existed. Michael Gardiner, in *The Cultural Roots of British Devolution* (2004), similarly views the imperial context as the crucial adhesive, referring repeatedly to Britain as a nation that has 'become unsustainable without empire'.[20] This is often couched in terms of the empire as a common endeavour, which for centuries enabled the English, Scots and others to sink their differences in a shared bounty. Thus, for Andrew Gamble, 'the end of empire meant the disappearance of the project which for so long had defined Britishness and British institutions'.[21] Taken to the extreme, as in David Marquand's account, the very idea of 'Britain' is quite simply not amenable to 'reinvention', having lost its vital ingredient: 'Shorn of empire, "Britain" ha[s] no meaning . . . it is by definition impossible for Britain as such to be post-imperial.'[22] To Marquand, the end of empire is a process which must necessarily have dire consequences for the British state, and one that profoundly influences Britons' view of themselves.

[16] Colley, 'Britishness and Otherness: An Argument', 328. See also Stuart Ward, 'The End of Empire and the Fate of Britishness', in *History, Nationhood and the Question of Britain*, ed. Helen Brocklehurst and Robert Phillips (Houndmills, 2004).

[17] Colley has more recently distanced herself from an overreliance on the importance of the fall of empire in this respect, stating that 'claims that the end of Empire *must* also and desirably result in the disintegration of the UK, are driven at once by selective history and teleology'. See Linda Colley, 'Does Britishness Still Matter in the Twenty-First Century – and How Much and How Well Do the Politicians Care', *Political Quarterly*, 78 (2007), 28.

[18] Krishan Kumar, *The Making of English National Identity* (Cambridge, 2003), 172.

[19] Krishan Kumar, 'English and British National Identity', *History Compass*, 4 (2006), 434.

[20] Michael Gardiner, *The Cultural Roots of British Devolution* (Edinburgh, 2004), 163.

[21] Andrew Gamble, 'A Union of Historic Compromise', in *Imagined Nation: England after Britain*, ed. Mark Perryman (2008), 38.

[22] David Marquand, 'How United Is the Modern United Kingdom?', in *Uniting the Kingdom? The Making of British History*, ed. Alexander Grant and Keith J. Stringer (1995), 288.

Perhaps the best gauge of the pervasive influence of this view is the vehemence of its detractors. Keith Webb launched the first salvo in the counter-offensive in his 1977 *The Growth of Nationalism in Scotland* where he identified three main flaws in what he termed the 'decline of empire thesis'. First, there was precious little evidence to support the idea of Scottish nationalism as a reaction to the loss of long-standing economic benefits of empire; secondly, the new generation of nationalist leaders hardly matched the stereotype of frustrated would-be proconsuls, chafing at the closing-off of an imperial 'outlet'; and thirdly, the idea that Scottish identity had suddenly emerged to supplant the waning appeal of Britishness overlooked the delicate balance that had long existed between the two.[23] Keith Robbins echoed Webb's scepticism, pointing out that the first generation of home rulers in Scotland used the empire as an argument *in favour* of devolved constitutional powers in the late nineteenth century. Thus, to posit empire and devolution as polar opposites was a false dichotomy.[24] More recently, John M. MacKenzie has argued that the imperial experience actually may have reinforced the several nationalities of the United Kingdom, and that it therefore cannot be readily assumed that its demise was inherently conducive to a separatist agenda.[25] And T. M. Devine has found little merit in linking the end of empire to Scottish political nationalism, on the grounds that 'imperial decline failed to produce much political concern in Scotland'. He locates the root causes of devolution in the failure of Westminster to deliver prosperity north of the border, concluding that 'Mrs Thatcher has an infinitely greater claim to be the midwife of Scottish devolution than the factor of imperial decline.'[26]

Yet neither side of the debate has succeeded in closing the argument in their favour, mainly because none of the major protagonists – somewhat remarkably – has ever sought to subject the end of empire thesis to any detailed empirical scrutiny. Nairn's initial foray was almost wholly theory-driven, while Linda Colley's verdict was more concerned with providing some contemporary perspective on an argument about the eighteenth-century origins of Britishness. Nor does T. M. Devine's corrective provide sufficient insight into the local political context of post-imperial Scotland, relying instead on an argument about events in the 1920s and 1950s that 'conspired to corrode Scotland's emotional attachment to empire'.[27] The 1960s remain remarkably untilled ground as far as the lingering presence

---

[23] Keith Webb, *The Growth of Nationalism in Scotland* (Glasgow, 1977), 87.
[24] Robbins, '"This Grubby Wreck of Old Glories": The United Kingdom and the End of the British Empire'.
[25] John M. MacKenzie, 'Empire and National Identities: The Case of Scotland', *Transactions of the Royal Historical Society*, 8 (1998), 215–31.
[26] Devine, 'The Break-Up of Britain?', 163, 166.
[27] *Ibid.*, 174.

of empire in Scottish politics and society is concerned. We therefore now turn our attention to the very context that originally inspired the idea of a causal connection between imperial decline and Scottish nationalism – the remarkable electoral successes of the SNP throughout the decade. We begin by surveying the contemporary evidence for a decolonising discourse in the party's early political resurgence, before turning to a detailed analysis of the crowning SNP achievement of the decade: Winifred Ewing's victory at the Hamilton by-election in November 1967.

Scotland's wind of change?

It is by no means difficult to mount a case in support of the idea that Scottish separatism experienced an unprecedented electoral boost in the 1960s due to the wave of post-colonial independence struggles worldwide. The circumstantial evidence, in itself, is difficult to overlook. In the 1950s, the SNP was a fringe political organisation with no parliamentary presence in Westminster and few obvious prospects to improve their electoral appeal, polling no more than 1.3 per cent of the Scottish vote between 1945 and 1959.[28] Yet the 1960s witnessed a series of electoral milestones, beginning with the Bridgeton by-election in November 1961 when Ayrshire farmer Ian Macdonald polled an impressive 18 per cent. The following year in June, Billy Wolfe secured a surprise second place in the West Lothian by-election, winning nearly a quarter of the vote. Throughout the decade, SNP Party membership increased sixty-fold (from 2,000 members in 1962 to 120,000 in 1968), branch organisations increased from 21 to 472 and the party's share of the popular vote surged to the point where it was able to win its first seat in Westminster in a generation.[29] The party was reorganised along more professional lines, acquiring a full-time party organiser, propaganda unit, research department, communications office and a more efficient fund-raising machine. By the time of the October 1974 general election, it had secured 30.4 per cent of the vote and eleven seats across Scotland.[30] There is a broad consensus that the early breakthroughs of the 1960s heralded the emergence of the SNP as a credible force in British politics, marking the beginnings of 'devolution' as a byword for the slow dissolution of the Union. These developments followed a trajectory that coincided remarkably with the rapid unravelling of the British Empire, from the time of Harold Macmillan's 'Wind of Change' speech in February 1960, culminating in the Wilson government's decision to withdraw from 'East

[28] Robbins, '"This Grubby Wreck of Old Glories": The United Kingdom and the End of the British Empire', 92.

[29] Webb, *The Growth of Nationalism in Scotland*, 204.

[30] Robbins, '"This Grubby Wreck of Old Glories": The United Kingdom and the End of the British Empire', 92.

of Suez' in January 1968. This final act of imperial retreat had been forced by the devaluation of sterling two months earlier in November 1967 – the very month of the SNP's historic victory at the Hamilton by-election – amid widespread talk of national disorientation and inward decay.[31]

Contemporaries began to notice this conspicuous overlap from the mid-1960s, and drew what seemed to be obvious conclusions. The SNP-aligned weekly, the *Scots Independent*, surveyed the declining fortunes of the 'Empire states' of Europe in 1965, noting the inward strain this inevitably placed on national institutions: 'This is now happening to the Scottish people . . . The wind of change just doesn't blow suddenly as some English politicians would have us believe and then subside.'[32] The following year, these sentiments were echoed in a piece by Kenneth Tucker:

> The fundamental reason for the creation of the British state, world empire is a thing of the past and one cannot see circumstances in which it is ever likely to rise again, so the state apparatus is redundant and has already been discarded as a conception by the Irish, Scots and Welsh.[33]

By 1968, H. J. Hanham could observe that 'it has become fashionable in the press to refer to the sudden surge of nationalism as if it were somehow to be entirely explained by the loss of empire'.[34] The converse of this was to attribute the survival of unionism to a residual 'internal colonialism'.[35] This diagnosis appeared in the rhetoric of leading SNP figures of the day. For example, Billy Wolfe's Party Conference speech of October 1970 dwelt on the theme of Scotland 'stagnating and drifting backwards, held down by the burden of London's continuing imperial paternalism and pretensions'.[36] Indeed, the description of the Anglo-Scottish relationship as a 'colonial one' was not an uncommon motif in Scottish nationalist discourse of the decade. Here, it needs to be borne in mind that imperial and Commonwealth affairs were closely monitored in the Scottish press, and given widespread daily coverage. One might expect, then, that the achievement of independence throughout Asia and Africa would have provided an obvious context for understanding the contemporaneous

---

[31] David Blaazer, '"Devalued and Dejected Britons": The Pound in Public Discourse in the Mid 1960s', *History Workshop Journal*, 47 (1999), 121–40; Dominic Sandbrook, *White Heat* (2009), ch. 28.

[32] *Scots Independent*, 'Where Are the Empire States?', 20 Febr. 1965.

[33] *Scots Independent*, 'State or Nation?', 29 Oct. 1966; see also *Scots Independent*, 'The British Crisis: Scotland Must Act Herself', 3 Sept. 1966: 'Where can Britain really go? Time is long past when Britain sat smugly on her islands and the world came to her door.'

[34] H. J. Hanham, 'The Scottish Nation Faces the Post-Imperial World', *International Journal*, 23 (1968), 584.

[35] The phrase is Michael Hechter's, although this was not his view of the dynamic between separatism and unionism in the 1960s. See ch. 9 of *Internal Colonialism: The Celtic Fringe in British National Development, 1536–1966* (1975).

[36] Quoted in Billy Wolfe, *Scotland Lives* (Edinburgh, 1973), 148.

stirrings of Scottish political separatism. And occasionally, direct parallels were indeed drawn, such as the *Scotsman*'s 1962 verdict on Nyasaland's demands for succession from the Central African Federation: 'Presumably the answer of the Nyasaland leaders will be that of the Scots long ago. "It is not for glory, riches or honours that we fight: it is for liberty alone."'[37]

Further evidence supporting a link between the end of empire and the changing fortunes of the SNP can be found in the manuscript collections and memoirs of leading party figures. Billy Wolfe recounted his slow path of conversion to political nationalism, joining the SNP as late as 1959. Far from exhibiting a life-long commitment to the nationalist political cause, he was only belatedly 'convinced by the facts of Scotland's decline in the 1950s and by the logic of the double contention that if there is a nation of Scots it is entitled to self-government'.[38] By mid-1962, he had become 'moved to indignation and frustration' because he 'realized anew that the essence of Scotland was being so diluted and destroyed... It was a kindly English imperialism that was destroying them.'[39] At the October 1964 general election, Wolfe's first political advertisement read: 'Nyasaland now has independence – what about Scotland – but of course Scotland is a profitable colony. So long as we are a nation of labourers in our own land we will remain England's last satellite.'[40] Another pamphlet produced during the 1964 campaign surveyed 'recent events... taking place in the world', proclaiming:

> Proud imperial powers no longer steer their own course regardless of the rest of humanity. Least of all can Great Britain afford to ignore the rights of small nations. Her military policy and strategy have undergone a complete revolution, she is desperately seeking means of redressing her balance of payments, and she is trying to adjust herself to the implications of the European Common Market. Does it not seem odd to you that, despite these tremendous changes in the outside world, no thought is given in London to the need for an equally thorough-going reorganization within the British Isles?... Surely, you think, when the British Government can confer full nationhood so freely on former colonial peoples in Africa and Asia, the least that ancient Scotland can expect is federal self-government within a customs union.[41]

By early 1968, with the devaluation of sterling, Winifred Ewing's spectacular win at Hamilton and the winding back of Britain's military presence in the Far East, support for the SNP had reached an all-time high. The verdict of Scotland's leading newspapers was that Britain had reached an impasse. 'Yesterday was a great day for Little England',

[37] *Scotsman*, 'Composite Approach', 1 June 1962.

[38] Wolfe, *Scotland Lives*, 27.

[39] *Ibid.*, 10.

[40] Quoted in *ibid.*, 53.

[41] Neil Douglas, *How London Spends your Money* (Edinburgh), undated, but most likely 1964 judging from its general context and file placement in the Arthur Donaldson Papers, National Library of Scotland, Acc. 6038/2, 'Correspondence of and to Arthur Donaldson', Folder 2.

intoned the *Scotsman* following the East of Suez announcement, while the *Glasgow Herald* declared: 'Two centuries as a world Power, and of a military influence in the Far East that started with Clive in India, have been brought to a shabby end.'[42] The satirical 'Scotsman's log' appealed to readers to 'be calm – and if it's not too big a laugh these days – be British. Grab your life jacket . . . the old ship of state is sinking by the head.'[43] SNP chairman Arthur Donaldson reached for the exact same metaphor: 'We are on a sinking ship. We have left it rather late to take the necessary steps. But Scotland must get a boat of her own.'[44]

These events unfolded in tandem with burgeoning SNP electoral support, forcing the major political parties to pay greater attention to the nationalist agenda. A BBC *Checkpoint* programme in January 1968 surveyed seventy-one Scottish MPs and found that more than half – forty-three – were in favour of some sort of devolved assembly for Scotland. Only sixteen were opposed. The *Glasgow Herald* raised eyebrows at the opportunism behind this sudden conversion, but the fact remained: 'For so many Scottish MPs to make an admission which would have been unthinkable for all except the Liberals a short time ago is something of a landmark.'[45] Within a matter of months, opposition leader Edward Heath was publicly airing the possibility of a devolved Scottish regional assembly, while the Labour government established a Royal Commission to consider the matter. The unexpected windfall by way of increased subscriptions enabled a makeover of the *Scots Independent*, with a revamped design and more professional management. The new-look magazine (sporting the SNP political logo) featured a front-page editorial on its first issue in January 1968:

> From the start England has been determined that Great Britain should be merely a normal pseudonym to cloak her desperate ambitions. The same is even more true today with the Empire gone and world influence rapidly declining. Yet, despite devaluation, continuing economic chaos and a pathetic switch to the right by a Labour Party . . . England is still determined to cannibalize the Scots.[46]

Clearly, the fate of the British Empire had the capacity to shape contemporary perceptions of the growing separatist tendencies in Scottish politics in the 1960s, and even to serve as the root cause in some accounts. Even allowing for the fact that separatism was a minority issue, far from representative of the vast majority of the Scottish population, it remains

---

[42] *Scotsman*, 'A Paltry Package', 17 Jan. 1968; *Glasgow Herald*, 'Small World', 17 Jan. 1968; see also *Scotsman*, 'Prime Minister's Axe Ends an Era for Britain', 17 Jan. 1968.

[43] *Scotsman*, 'A Scotsman's Log: The Ship in a Terrible State', 18 Jan. 1968.

[44] *Scots Independent*, Arthur Donaldson's Diary 'The True Significance of Devaluation', 25 Nov. 1967.

[45] *Glasgow Herald*, 'Scottish Surprise', 13 Jan. 1968.

[46] *Scots Independent*, 'History's Next Big Date', 13 Jan. 1968.

possible to identify clear traces of a post-imperial context to the early success story of the SNP during that decade.

But does it necessarily follow that the end of empire was the fundamental cause of these developments? That imperial decline wove its way into the fabric of Scottish political culture, representing a domestic 'impact factor' of events and processes that had their origins in the decolonisation movements in Asia and Africa? It is here that we need to exercise caution, not least because the pursuit of empirical evidence linking the end of empire to the SNP only gets us so far. Bernard Porter has raised methodological objections to the practice of establishing the ever-presence of imperial influence in metropolitan culture through the cumulative piling up of evidence drawn from any number of sources and contexts. These concerns might equally apply to our presentation of the material assembled above. In reexamining the evidence *in situ* (Porter's prescription), we find that its pervasiveness and impact is far from self-evident.[47]

This applies particularly to the day-to-day activities of the SNP in the aftermath of its encouraging result at West Lothian in 1962. Billy Wolfe's startling electoral boost was given extensive coverage in the Scottish press, with any number of underlying causes posited by the pundits of the day. Yet not a single account of the 1962 campaign, before or since, sought to place it in the context of the liberation movements sweeping through colonial Africa.[48] Nor did Wolfe himself see any connection in the memoir he composed a decade later. The records of the SNP and the manuscript collections and correspondence of its leading figures bear witness to a very different – and avowedly local – set of preoccupations and concerns. Here, we find sustained attention to the minutiae of party organisation, campaign strategy, internal political jostling, branch management, finance, publicity and the meticulously recorded minutes of various sub-committees. References to wider issues affecting Britain's place in the world in general, or the empire in particular, are exceedingly rare, suggesting that these considerations were at best remote from the concerns of party activists. Nor did the end of empire feature prominently in campaign material. Despite the occasional examples cited above, the overwhelming and enduring political message of the SNP in the 1960s was Westminster's remoteness from Scotland's material concerns.

Only rarely did this persistent focus on Westminster's dominance draw upon any overseas example or inspiration. A draft constitution for an independent Scotland prepared in May 1963 made no reference

---

[47] Bernard Porter, *The Absent-Minded Imperialists: Empire, Society, and Culture in Britain* (Oxford, 2004), xiii; see also Andrew Thompson, *The Empire Strikes Back?* (Harlow, 2005).

[48] See for example *Scotsman*, 'By-election Frolics', 18 June 1962; *Glasgow Herald*, 'Protest Vote', 16 June 1962.

to the many new constitutions that had recently been enacted by new Commonwealth nations throughout Asia, Africa and the Caribbean (although some references to the older constitutions of Australia and Canada appeared).[49] The 1966 Party Manifesto, *Put Scotland First*, was virtually silent on international and Commonwealth issues, referring only to the question of membership of the European Economic Community.[50] And even a context where one might have expected a wider frame of reference – a memorandum sent by the SNP to twenty-seven European governments in May 1967 – confined its grievances to the centralisation of government in London and the deprivation of legislative and fiscal power to the Scots.[51] Indeed, to the extent that the SNP drew on any international role model to illuminate its aspirations, it was not to Ghana, Kenya or Malaysia that it turned, but to the decidedly un-imperial example of Denmark, Norway and Sweden – states with a broadly similar geography, population and resource base – to demonstrate how small nations could bring greater welfare returns to their citizens.[52]

Hamilton, 1967

In short, the periodic rhetorical flourishes that framed the political breakthrough of Scottish separatism in terms of the world-wide eclipse of empire are not borne out by closer attention to detail. A more thorough examination of the records, papers and activities of the SNP presents a cumulative picture of a highly *provincial* organisation, rather than a major conduit of global currents penetrating deep into Scottish political culture. This can be more vividly illustrated by focusing on Winifred Ewing's landmark victory at the Hamilton by-election of 1967, in which Ewing won 46 per cent of the vote, turning a Labour majority of more than 16,000 into a small SNP majority of 1,779. This event not only provided the SNP with crucial political momentum, but also placed Scottish separatism on the agenda in Westminster in unprecedented ways.

SNP press releases, pamphlets and other material published in connection with the Hamilton by-election, which have been preserved in various collections, indicate that the loss of empire was quite irrelevant to the election campaign. The most significant SNP publication produced during the campaign was the pamphlet *Hamilton Herald*,

---

[49] Arthur Donaldson Papers, National Library of Scotland, Acc. 6038/2, 'Correspondence of and to Arthur Donaldson', Folder 1, 'Sixth Revised Draft of Proposed Articles of a Provisional Constitution for Scotland', 16 May 1963.

[50] National Archives of Scotland, SOE 12/239, 'Putting Scotland First', 130–41.

[51] Arthur Donaldson Papers, National Library of Scotland, Acc. 6038/6, Folder 1, 'Memorandum to European Governments', 31 May 1967.

[52] E.g. National Library of Scotland, Acc. 11987/110, 'SNP Research Department Interim Report', 14 Mar. 1969.

which imitated a newspaper complete with vox pops and an election-related horoscope.[53] The one theme that pervaded the publication was the London government's failure to address the issues of particular importance to Scotland. Recent Labour and Tory governments were described as a 'proven disaster', to whom Scotland had been nothing but a 'region': 'a troublesome region occasionally but of no real importance'. This treatment was seen as a predictable result of the uneven geographical distribution of the British population: 'More than half of the people who live in the United Kingdom stay and work within 125 miles of London', an affluent region 'viciously protected by its M.P.s and the country's top civil servants'. The 'big unit' of the UK, rather than offering any benefits of large-scale operations, was perceived to have led to a neglect of Scotland, and the lack of necessary decentralisation threatened to turn Scotland into 'the 47th English county'. This consistent neglect of Scotland had, according to the *Hamilton Herald*, had disastrous consequences for the country, which at the time of the by-election experienced its highest unemployment rate since 1940, a stalling productivity and a downright 'brain drain' in the form of emigration because of a lack of opportunities at home. All of these issues figured prominently, as did the generally regrettable living conditions of the Scottish people, whose most basic requirements, such as housing and full-time education for children, were not seen to be adequately met. In the face of these exigencies, the SNP was said to offer the only viable alternative to the Conservatives and Labour, parties whose front figures were portrayed as 'virtually indistinguishable' from each other.[54] The SNP had an advantage over the two UK parties in that its policies were 'based on knowledge of the facts of the Scottish situation as they now are', and in her column in the *Hamilton Herald*, Winifred Ewing predicted that the 'first shackle of London-based control is going to be broken right here in Hamilton'.[55]

This summarises the general line in SNP material released in connection with the by-election, and it demonstrates that the specific British post-imperial context was not given any prominence. However, international developments in general were. The *Hamilton Herald* shows clearly that the SNP did invoke other nationalist movements in its struggle for an independent Scotland. Reference was made to the 'more than 60 nations – many smaller and most poorer than Scotland – [which] have gained freedom and a seat at the United Nations'[56] since the end of the Second World War. One SNP voter, participating in what was set up to look like a vox pop, contended that 'commonwealth countries have

---

[53] National Library of Scotland, P.1a.7030, *Hamilton Herald*.
[54] *Ibid.*
[55] *Ibid.*
[56] *Ibid.*

flourished on becoming independent of Westminster rule'. And the back page of the *Hamilton Herald* included a section giving details of recent Plaid Cymru electoral successes at Carmarthen and Rhondda. A reference was also made to the 1967 referendum in Gibraltar, in which a large majority of Gibraltarians voted to remain under British, rather than Spanish, sovereignty – intriguingly, this lone reference to a Commonwealth case was to one which did *not* further diminish Britain's role in the world.

When reference was made to nationalist activities elsewhere, no specific analogy was drawn between the case of Scotland and that of other countries. Most crucially, no reference at all was made to Britain's new role in a post-imperial world, or to imperial developments in general. The remnants of empire seem conspicuously absent from this as well as other publications prepared by the SNP for the by-election, among which we have been unable to locate a single comment linking Scottish nationalism to imperial decline. There is also a remarkable shortage of references to foreign policy more generally, except from a considerable number of statements concerning the feasibility of entry into the European Economic Community.

The fact that the eclipse of the British Empire was apparently not crucial to the SNP at the time of the by-election does not necessarily mean that it was insignificant to the Hamilton electorate. Newspaper coverage of the election may give an impression of why the SNP polled as well as it did, and in the following we turn our attention to newspaper articles, editorials and letters to the editor written in connection with the Hamilton by-election. We begin at the local level in the pages of the weekly *Hamilton Advertiser,* before moving to the Scottish focus of the *Glasgow Herald* and the *Scotsman,* and then, finally, the British perspective through the lens of articles and editorials appearing in the *Guardian* and the *Times.*

The local weekly newspaper the *Hamilton Advertiser* included extensive coverage of the by-election, but failed to predict an SNP win. As late as a week before the election, the *Advertiser* contended that 'it is hard to believe there can be other than a Labour victory'.[57] Not surprisingly, the paper had an avowedly local focus and was concerned with very concrete political issues of relevance to its readers. However, in an editorial describing the political climate surrounding the by-election published a week before the event, the perceived general 'apathy' of the Hamilton electorate was explained by reference to structural, non-local conditions:

There are no fiercely-held convictions to be debated, no furiously fought engagement in which to strike blows for great causes... It is this loss of the sense of reality which has taken the heart out of our political life. Britain has lost its vocation, its sense of destiny as a nation. Having handed over an empire, we are left without a role – our

[57] *Hamilton Advertiser,* 'Which?', 27 Oct. 1967.

occupation is gone . . . we cannot make our national will felt over a quarter of a million white Rhodesians; and we have forfeited the respect of peoples whom once we proudly ruled.[58]

Here we find a direct commentary on the fall from imperial grandeur and the suggestion that this had fundamentally influenced the way Britons perceived themselves at the local level. Yet for all the underlying sense of impotence and disorientation, the source does not link imperial decline directly to the electoral success of the SNP, or in any way view Celtic nationalisms as the answer to Britain's or indeed Scotland's predicament. On the contrary, the SNP is said to represent 'small-minded provincialism'. Nationalism, then, is neither seen as a natural response to – nor a logical consequence of – imperial decline. Crucially, the *Hamilton Advertiser* never returned to this theme in order to explain Ewing's success in the aftermath of the election. This is perhaps surprising, given this pre-election diagnosis; yet the connection was not made, even with the benefit of hindsight.

Instead, the paper made much of Ewing's personal appeal. Her candidacy was described as a 'kiss of life to a public that was suffocating from lack of interest'.[59] Furthermore, the SNP had, according to the newspaper, the distinct advantage that 'the election came for them at a moment when the major parties were in a state of disarray'.[60] Faced with a weak Labour electoral campaign, 'a classic instance of masterly inactivity',[61] the SNP emerged as the only alternative to Labour, which had held the constituency for the previous fifty years. The campaign was won at the local level, and lost in London by a party that 'suffered locally from the well-earned unpopularity of the Government at Westminster'.[62] In summary, the paper's coverage gives the impression that, while Ewing had a strong appeal to many voters, her success could more plausibly be interpreted as a vote against the current political establishment.

The theme of the protest vote, prominent in the *Advertiser*, was also taken up by the Scotland-wide newspaper the *Scotsman*, which interpreted the Hamilton result as 'a blow at the whole Labour Government, their policies and performance. It was an indication of resentment against Whitehall and Downing Street.'[63] Although the election was largely interpreted as a reaction *against* the government, the *Scotsman* emphasised that the Hamilton outcome could not be understood as 'a freak result'.[64]

---

[58] *Ibid.*
[59] *Hamilton Advertiser,* '"Scots wha hinnae" won for Winnie', 10 Nov. 1967.
[60] *Hamilton Advertiser,* 'After the Ball', 10 Nov. 1967.
[61] *Ibid.*
[62] *Ibid.*
[63] *Scotsman,* 'Vote Rebuff Turns Spotlight on Mr Ross', 4 Nov. 1967.
[64] *Scotsman,* 'By-election Aftermath', 4 Nov. 1967.

An editorial published on 4 November explicitly linked the by-election result to a perceived rise in *cultural* nationalism and warned the political establishment against underestimating 'the intellectual strength of the self-government movement'.[65] This is interesting, because the other newspapers analysed here did not make much of the relevance of Scottish cultural nationalism to the election result. That the *Scotsman* should choose to comment on the issue, however, suggests a deeper rift in a shared British cultural identity than the 'protest vote' argument would indicate.

In its first editorial commenting on the election, the *Glasgow Herald* identified as the most important reason for SNP success 'the widespread disillusionment with the Government's handling of Scottish affairs'.[66] This analysis was further developed in an editorial published a few days later, in which the sentiment of discontent in Scotland was related to a perceived UK-wide feeling of frustration with a government that was seen as running the country from a distant centre: 'A widespread feeling of remoteness from government is not confined to Scotland and Wales. It is a nationwide problem associated with the increasing power exercised by the central government, not least in local authority matters.'[67] This interpretation assumes the election result to be a consequence not of a crisis of national identity, but as a direct result of very concrete political decisions that had resulted in further concentration of political power in London. But it was after the fact, in what can reasonably be characterised as a U-turn, that both the *Scotsman* and the *Glasgow Herald* decided to interpret the SNP victory as a natural response to a distant London government whose political agenda insufficiently acknowledged Scotland's exigencies. And even with the benefit of hindsight, the two papers failed to identify the post-imperial dimension as having any immediate relevance.

Turning to the UK-wide press, the coverage in the *Times* clearly invoked a sense of national crisis, although, perhaps surprisingly, the SNP victory was described as an outcome which could alleviate rather than exacerbate the prevailing tensions. An editorial published the day following the election referred to the outcome as 'an excellent result, better in the jolt it will give Scotland's political future than either a Labour or a Conservative victory would have been'.[68] Ewing's triumph was declared a much-needed wake-up call to the other parties, which had for too long neglected Scotland's needs: 'The merit of Mrs Ewing's victory is that it forces British political parties to think in a fundamentally new

---

[65] *Ibid.*
[66] *Glasgow Herald*, 'Aftermath', 4 Nov. 1967.
[67] *Glasgow Herald*, 'Back Home', 6 Nov. 1967.
[68] *Times*, 'A Scottish Victory', 4 Nov. 1967.

way about Celtic nationalisms before it is too late.'[69] In other words, the Scots were seen to be choosing the only option available to them in the face of a government which had proven unable to deliver, and two major parties 'refusing over the years to apply more than palliative measures to the national claims of Scotland and Wales'.[70] The paper also saw the resentment in Scotland as based upon very real material issues, such as the 'comparative poverty'[71] of the country in comparison with England, and 'unemployment rates which are consistently higher and earnings which are lower than the English'.[72] In line with the Scottish newspapers, the *Times* refused to write off the Hamilton result as a mere aberration, emphasising that if this Labour stronghold could fall, so could many others.[73] The paper considered the vote of no confidence which the Hamilton election constituted to be based on purely economic factors.[74] In this newspaper, too, the imperial aspect was conspicuously absent from the election coverage, and cultural and historical factors were not considered particularly important to explaining the result.

The *Guardian*'s coverage differed significantly in that it placed considerable emphasis on the emotional and cultural aspect of the SNP's appeal to voters. To the *Guardian*, the Hamilton result and the Plaid Cymru victory at Carmarthen the previous year constituted a warning to the London-based parties that Scotland and Wales were 'increasingly impatient about Westminster's total failure to solve their special problems'.[75] Celtic periphery voters' dissatisfaction with the present state of affairs was specifically linked to Britain's new, less significant, world role:

> Large groups of voters are in a highly emotional mood, which has been caused by the shock of discovering Britain's reduced status in the world, and the pain of economic adjustments. Could not the Welsh or the Scots manage their own affairs better? The economic prod seems to be the sharpest goad towards nationalism, but once the question is asked in economic terms, cultural and historical prods are driven in.[76]

Nationalism, according to the *Guardian*, had achieved its present popularity not least because it was an 'untried means of escape from what seems to be a stagnation that has persisted';[77] it provided a 'third way', giving parties with a nationalist agenda a special appeal to voters: 'At present the Nationalists, alone among political parties, have a magic

[69] *Ibid.*
[70] *Ibid.*
[71] *Ibid.*
[72] *Ibid.*
[73] *Ibid.*
[74] *Ibid.*
[75] *Guardian*, '"History Made" in Scotland', 3 Nov. 1967.
[76] *Guardian*, 'Don't Laugh at the Threat, it Has Promise', 17 Nov. 1967.
[77] *Ibid.*

about them – can **generate** an emotional appeal before which logical calculations tend to crumble.'[78] Thus, the nationalist movement, far from being a movement with only a temporary appeal, was seen as having a deeper *raison d'être*, being based on more than just the major parties' inadequacies. The *Guardian* was the only newspaper to comment explicitly on the state of 'Britishness', portraying the election result as a symptom of a profounder rift between the Scottish and the English: 'There is also the English ascendancy, the vague but consistent English indifference to Scottish existence that has suddenly been seen in Scotland as part of the problem of being British. The Scots are expected to be British while the British remain English.'[79]

This 'sudden' realisation that the Anglo-Scottish relationship was a fundamentally unequal one may be suggestive of the kind of renewed sensitivity to internal differences which some historians have described as a predictable outcome of the disappearance of the imperial 'cement' of Union. But we are reading between the lines here. While the sources indicate that reasons for SNP success at Hamilton were many and profound – with well-grounded resentment towards successive Westminster governments and the 'relative deprivation' of Scotland within the UK being the primary ones – the end of empire was at best a remote context in the landmark events of October–November 1967. Our extensive trawl through SNP internal correspondence, campaign material and speeches bears little evidence of a sustained preoccupation with (or even awareness of) the electoral opportunities presented by Britain's declining fortunes abroad. A wider survey of press coverage reveals some residual commentary on the global situation, but this is far outweighed by local material grievances and public disaffection with the two major parties. The most that might be said is that the cumulative successes of the SNP played into a more general crisis of national purpose and cohesion, with the political situation in Hamilton repeatedly described as one of 'apathy', 'stagnation' and 'remoteness from government'. Conversely, Ewing's victory in 1967 brought scenes of hope, even euphoria, in nationalist circles that might seem vaguely analogous to the independence celebrations that characterised the decade the world over. But remarkably few contemporary sources made that connection explicitly.

A hypothesis too good to be false?

It seems tempting to conclude that H. J. Hanham's 'cramped and restricted' verdict about the post-imperial provenance of 1960s Scottish

---

[78] *Guardian*, 'Seeds of Defeat?', 5 Dec. 1967, emphasis in original.
[79] *Guardian*, 'After Hamilton, what now for Nationalists?', 4 Nov. 1967.

separatism is simply false; a classic case of *post hoc ergo propter hoc*, mistaking an alluring historical coincidence for a fundamental causal relationship. To the extent that we can find evidence of contemporaries drawing such connections, these too could be dismissed as the mistaken diagnosis of journalists and intellectuals, scrambling for plausible explanations for unprecedented political developments that eluded their grasp. Post-colonial nationalism only rarely presented any serviceable framework for packaging and pedalling the political message of the SNP. To the extent that the wind of change blew through Scotland, it was arguably a northerly, with little or no relationship to the southern gusts that swept aside the last remnants of empire in Africa.

Yet this somehow fails to capture the full complexity of the issue, and it is therefore worth considering whether there are alternative readings or perspectives that might help to make sense of the recurring shards of evidence that do place Scottish separatism in a wider, global context. As we have already noted, the circumstantial evidence tying Scottish separatism into contemporaneous liberationist discourses in other parts of the globe seems difficult to dismiss as a mere coincidence. Whether we consider the rapid pace of African decolonisation, the civil rights movement in the US, the 'Quiet Revolution' in Quebec, the indigenous rights movement in Australia and New Zealand, the eruption of the 'Troubles' in Northern Ireland or even the secession of Jamaica from the West Indian Federation in 1962, powerful philosophical currents in the 1960s fostered a favourable climate for national separatism and self-determination. Can we reasonably conclude that Scotland was *sui generis*, peculiarly impervious to the outside world?

Here, we need to bear in mind that there were two very good reasons why the SNP might have actively distanced itself from any philosophical alignment with post-colonial struggles elsewhere. The first goes to the very heart of nationalism as an organising principle, namely that while the nation is an inherently modern phenomenon (at least, in its overt political claims), a principal component of its social appeal relies on establishing its pre-modern or even primordial credentials.[80] Thus, it hardly served the philosophical inclinations or political purposes of Scottish nationalists in the 1960s to present the SNP's successes as a sudden windfall, drawing opportunistically on contingencies external to Scotland. It was emotionally more satisfying to claim a deeper mantle, with the SNP reaping the rewards of generations of nationalist endeavour. This explains, for example, the time and energy invested by the SNP in refurbishing Bannockburn Day as a more visible, popularly observed

---

[80] This is the standard modernist interpretation, as articulated in e.g. Ernest Gellner, *Nations and Nationalism* (Oxford, 1983); Benedict Anderson, *Imagined Communities* (1983); Ruth Wodak *et al.*, *The Discursive Construction of National Identity* (Edinburgh, 2009).

totem of nationalist teleology.[81] At Winifred Ewing's first Bannockburn rally following her 1967 victory, she openly challenged the 'propagandists' and 'political myth-makers' who would explain away the political advances made by her and her party. In her speech, she highlighted specifically (among other fallacies) 'The legend of our rise is due to the British Empire's fall'; a rare SNP invocation of the imperial decline thesis, yet deployed here for the purposes of refuting its explanatory power.[82] It is hard to imagine a more explicit disavowal of the central premise we have set out to test, yet we need to be wary of its implications. It obviously and emphatically did not suit the needs of the SNP to depict Scottish separatism as a belated reaction to the sudden disappearance of the fringe benefits of being British.

The other reason why the SNP might have sought to distance itself – consciously or otherwise – from post-colonial nationalism elsewhere is related to the key challenge the party faced into the 1970s: to convince the electorate that Scotland could encompass the material, natural and human resources to constitute a viable nation-state. The idea that Scotland was either too small, too poor or too isolated to make its way in the world as an independent nation was (and remains) the constant companion of SNP candidates, and the task of refuting it was its number one imperative. To this end, aligning Scotland's cause with ailing states such as Nigeria, Ghana or the Congo, all of which had experienced political violence, civil disorder and economic mismanagement, was hardly going to sway the argument. This also explains why the relatively sedate cities of Oslo, Copenhagen and Stockholm appear more readily in the SNP records and public rhetoric than Salisbury, Nairobi or Lusaka. The immediate purposes of garnering electoral support militated against any direct, self-conscious alignment of the SNP cause with a global liberationist ethos.

Therefore, the relative absence of any direct, self-conscious anchoring of Scottish separatist discourse in the global eclipse of empire does not necessarily decide the matter. But it does allow us to rule out certain variants of the imperial decline thesis. First, the notion that the momentum for Scottish independence somehow had its material or spiritual origins in the colonial world, only belatedly making its presence felt in the metropole once the empire had been rent asunder, can be safely discarded. There can be no simple recourse to a decolonising 'impact factor', with events on the colonial periphery rebounding inwards on the

---

[81] National Library of Scotland, Acc. 6038/6, Folder 4, Memorandum by Dr Andrew W. Lees on Bannockburn Day, 7 Jan. 1968. See also papers relating to the enhanced status of Bannockburn Day in *ibid.*, Folder 8.
[82] *Ibid.*

imperial state.[83] Secondly, there is every reason to doubt the economic argument, eloquently summarised by Michael Fry, 'that Scots exchanged national independence for imperial profit 300 years ago and now, seeing no more profit in prospect, promptly reverse their loyalties'.[84] Although material imperatives were at the forefront of the SNP agenda, these were never framed in terms of lost earnings from imperial adventures. Nor is there any obvious correlation between the SNP's uneven electoral appeal and specific regions economically affected by imperial retreat.[85] The 'cramped and restricted' metaphor is not at all borne out by emigration figures, which held firm throughout the decades of decolonisation – there was no simple 'closing off' of opportunities in this sphere as a consequence of imperial decline.[86] And, finally, the more generalised notion that the collapse of empire removed from the equation an entire spectrum of 'others', which had hitherto lent meaning and purpose to a common Britishness, makes little sense in empirical terms. If anything, the 'othering' of Commonwealth British subjects was at its most intense in the 1960s, with a series of highly public debates about curbing Commonwealth immigration, the plight of Kenyan/Ugandan Asians, and impending 'rivers of blood'.[87]

There remains, however, one potential framework that might encompass the post-imperial dimensions of Scotland's separatist surge in the 1960s – one that has never been seriously invoked despite decades of historical debate. But it is not to be found in the 'grubby wreck of old glories' in Asia and Africa. Rather, the fate of imperial civic culture in the once self-styled 'British' Dominions offers some compelling parallels that deserve closer attention. In 2008, A. G. Hopkins called for a root

---

[83] On the 'impact' paradigm, see Stuart Ward, 'The MacKenziean Moment in Retrospect', in Andrew Thompson, *Writing Imperial Histories* (Manchester, 2013).

[84] Fry himself dismissed this as a 'cynical view' in *The Scottish Empire* (Edinburgh, 2001), 498.

[85] Economic historians have in fact emphasised the surprising resilience of the British economy during the decades of decolonisation, which saw unprecedented levels of sustained growth. See for example Charles H. Feinstein, 'The End of Empire and the Golden Age', in *Understanding Decline: Perceptions and Realities of British Economic Performance*, ed. Peter Clarke and Clive Trebilcock (Cambridge, 1997); Jim Tomlinson, 'The Decline of the Empire and the Economic "Decline" of Britain', *Twentieth Century British History*, 14.3 (2003), 201–21. Although some of the SNP's early successes were in areas particularly affected by industrial decline (Hamilton 1967, Glasgow-Govan 1973), this was not the case with Donald Stewart's win in the Western Isles at the 1970 general election.

[86] Scottish emigration to Australia in the three decades after 1945, for example, was nearly three times the level of the preceding three decades. See Malcolm Prentis, *The Scots in Australia* (Sydney, 2008), 77.

[87] Although the major studies pay virtually no attention to Scotland; see for example Kathleen Paul, *Whitewashing Britain: Race and Citizenship in the Post-War Era* (Ithaca, 1997); Randall Hansen, *Citizenship and Immigration in Post-War Britain: The Institutional Origins of a Multicultural Nation* (Oxford, 2000).

and branch 'rethink' of decolonisation, widening the concept to include the profound changes to settler colonial societies wrought by the end of the British Empire, and the corresponding corrosion of the idea of a 'British world'.[88] Although these communities – with the exception of the rebel regime in Rhodesia – did not actively struggle for liberation from imperial rule (having secured self-government generations earlier), they nonetheless exhibited profound nationalist tendencies that would transform their civic landscapes, erasing many of the older British rites, rituals and public symbols, and substituting them with local, home-grown alternatives.

In Canada, this was dubbed the 'nouvelle nationalisme' in 1964 by the editor of *Le Devoir*, Claude Ryan (referring explicitly to English Canada, not Quebec).[89] The same term was to appear four years later in Donald Horne's assessment of the 'new nationalism' in Australia, which he defined as an impulse to dispense with the language of loyalty and instigate a wholesale renovation of the national civic fabric.[90] Heated debates about the designs of new flags stripped of their Union Jacks, new national anthems in place of 'God Save the Queen', new oaths of allegiance, new national holidays, new royal styles and titles, and even new official names for the nation itself, became the order of the day. Progress was uneven, and in some instances remains incomplete – witness the ongoing flag debates in Australia and New Zealand – but the changes in attitudes and allegiances were nevertheless profound. And these inevitably found their political champions who to this day remain symbols of the new nationalism in their respective communities: Pearson and Trudeau in Canada, Gough Whitlam in Australia, Norman Kirk in New Zealand and, for a time, Southern Rhodesia's Ian Smith. Although representing widely differing political inclinations, they each proved adept at harnessing the mood for national renewal, drawing political momentum from their capacity to move the idea of the nation beyond the bounds of Britishness. New Zealand's Keith Sinclair captured the prevailing mood in 1963: 'For us to want to be British is a poor objective, like wanting to be an understudy or a caretaker – or an undertaker.' He spoke of the 'very many changes in New Zealand, of a kind which make me believe that a New Zealand civilization is not impossible'.[91]

---

[88] A. G. Hopkins, 'Rethinking Decolonization', *Past and Present*, 200.1 (2008), 211–47.

[89] 'Le dilemme du drapeau', *Le Devoir*, 15 Aug. 1964. Jack L. Granatstein saw fit to use a rhetorical question mark in his chapter: 'The New Nationalism? Symbol vs. Reality', in *Canada, 1957–1967: The Years of Uncertainty and Innovation* (Toronto, 1986).

[90] Donald Horne, 'The New Nationalism?', *Bulletin*, 5 Oct. 1968.

[91] Keith Sinclair, 'The Historian as Prophet', in *The Future of New Zealand*, ed. M. F. Lloyd Pritchard (Christchurch, 1964).

There now exist sufficient studies of the new nationalism to allow identification of its key characteristics.[92] First, it is clear that the common denominator was the dwindling purchase of a universal Britishness as a unifying principle. New nationalist rhetoric was invariably predicated on the substitution of older, more remote attachments and loyalties with something more immediate, and self-validating. Secondly, these new sensibilities emerged virtually in lockstep with the dwindling moral force of the British Empire as a credible framework to sustain the idea of a British world. Although the specific issues that animated public awareness varied widely from one context to the next, a broader chronology beginning around the time of the Suez crisis and culminating in British entry into the EEC in 1973 is now well established. Thirdly, the driving impulses behind these developments were, more often than not, material and political grievances associated with Britain's inability to provide the economic, military or moral leadership of an imperial metropole – far more so than innate cultural forces, welling up to overwhelm the popular resonances of Britishness. Fourthly, this meant, in turn, that the new nationalism proved to be neither uniform nor universal in its appeal, and struck deep pockets of popular resistance to relinquishing the British ties. Thus, the refitting of the national firmament was invariably characterised by often bitter public quarrels, rooted in an absence of popular consensus over the appropriate scope and emphasis of the new-look nation. The Canadian flag debate of 1964 and the Australian national anthem contest in 1973 were among the most visible of these protracted controversies.[93] And lastly, and perhaps most intriguingly in relation to the Scottish dilemma, in only rare instances did the new nationalism register any awareness of the global currents that had lent it shape and conviction. Australians might cast an occasional envious glance at Canada's Maple Leaf Flag, but by and large no attention was paid to parallel developments elsewhere. The new nationalists were content to view their project as the long-delayed arrival of subterranean rumblings in the native soil. Indeed, finding a self-sufficient, home-grown sense of the people was the very object of the exercise.

---

[92] See Stuart Ward, 'The "New Nationalism" in Australia, Canada and New Zealand: Civic Culture in the Wake of the British World', in *Britishness Abroad: Transnational Movements and Imperial Cultures*, ed. Kate Darian-Smith, Stuart MacIntyre and Patricia Grimshaw (Melbourne, 2007), 231–63. On Canada, see José Eduardo Igartua, *The Other Quiet Revolution: National Identities in English Canada, 1945–71* (Vancouver, 2006); C. P. Champion, *The Strange Demise of British Canada: The Liberals and Canadian Nationalism, 1964–68* (Montreal, 2010); for Australia, James Curran and Stuart Ward, *The Unknown Nation: Australia after Empire* (Melbourne, 2010); on Rhodesia, Peter Godwin and Ian Hancock, *Rhodesians Never Die: The Impact of War and Political Change on White Rhodesia 1970–1980* (Oxford, 1993).

[93] See Ward in Thompson, *Writing Imperial Histories*.

What has all this to do with political nationalism in Scotland? Here we need to be clear about two things. Scotland was no Dominion, and despite an older tradition of Home Rulers in Scotland and Ireland aspiring to something akin to Dominion status, there is no mistaking the very peculiar constitutional context that gave rise to new nationalist currents in the old Commonwealth. And there can be no suggestion that these currents somehow provided the underlying inspiration or impulse behind separatist politics in Scotland. Australasia and Canada (still less southern Africa) were self-evidently not the fundamental cause of devolutionary pressures in the UK. But their example does provide an entirely new way of understanding the momentum behind Scottish separatism in a post-imperial context. Virtually all of the five characteristics outlined above – the diminished resonance of Britishness, the chronological overlap with imperial decline, the importance of material and political divergence from the metropole, the lack of popular consensus and the blinkered national optics – can be identified to a greater or lesser extent in the SNP's electoral progress through the 1960s and into the 1970s.

A further comment is warranted here about the decisive role of material grievances. Keith Webb pointed out in the 1970s that the dilemma in accounting for the SNP's sudden emergence into the political spotlight lies not in explaining the existence of national feeling, which had long been 'a permanent feature of Scottish culture'. 'What is needed', he argued, 'is an explanation for why nationalist feelings already held by many Scots became politicised when they did.'[94] The Hamilton sources clearly demonstrate that the breakdown of an Anglo-Scottish community of culture was rather less important than the collapse of a shared community of interest; the economic disparities between north and south weighed far more heavily than issues relating to cultural self-determination. The chief adversary was invariably Westminster and the governing elite, not the English people framed in terms of a cultural 'other'.[95] Webb and others tended to view this as conclusive proof of the absence of any significant interface with the demise of empire, but this is based on a narrow reading of the handover of constitutional power in Asia and Africa. The striking parallels with the diverging material interests that underpinned the 'new nationalism' in the old Commonwealth have never been seriously considered. Winifred Ewing's February 1968 lament that 'this Government cares more about dead birds on English beaches than about living men in Glasgow' had echoes throughout the British world

---

[94] Webb, *The Growth of Nationalism in Scotland*, 74.

[95] This reluctance to campaign on Scotland's cultural distinctiveness was remarked upon as early as the mid-1970s, with Michael Hechter going so far as to conclude that 'the SNP tacitly admits the cultural indistinguishability of Scotland from England by resorting to [the economic] justification for national independence'. In *Internal Colonialism*, 308.

in the years of decolonisation.[96] Indeed, only a month prior to this statement, the New Zealand *Dominion* editorialised against the Wilson government's defence cuts, urging: 'Can we trust Britain again? The British Government's duplicity compels us to ask the question. How much reliance can we put on Britain's word?'[97] Little wonder that Rhodesia's rebel regime blithely assumed that it would find a kindred spirit in Mrs Ewing. The government's minister for agriculture, Lord Graham of Montrose (himself a Scot), wrote to her in the most affectionate terms, recording his conviction 'that the battle for Scottish independence is against the same enemy as we are battling'.[98]

This confluence of opinion about London's inability (or unwillingness) to sacrifice its own interests for the greater British good was invariably coupled with talk of Britain as a spent force in the world – a perception that was directly informed by the political and material realities of imperial decline. In 1973, J. G. A. Pocock reflected on the deeper currents that had produced these centrifugal pressures towards greater civic autonomy throughout the British world. Speaking from his native Christchurch, he concluded:

> The British cultural star-cluster is at present in a highly dispersed condition, various parts of it feeling the attraction of adjacent galaxies; the central giant has cooled, shrunk and moved away, and the inhabitants of its crust seem more than ever disposed to deny that the rest of us ever existed. Since it no longer emits those radiations we felt bound to convert into paradigms, we are free and indeed necessitated to construct cosmologies of our own.[99]

In much the same way, the 'shrinking' and 'cooling' of Britain's imperial reach occasionally registered in Scottish separatist discourse, but not as a direct, self-conscious guide to action, emulating the independence upheavals in Asia and Africa. Rather, it provided a key formative context, subtly linking Britain's declining fortunes in the world with the weakening capacity of the metropole to serve the interests of the periphery – and hence the imperative of taking independent action to find a new way forward.

In the light of this deeper subtext, it seems less surprising that the end of empire did not feature prominently and regularly in the internal workings of the SNP, or the daily grind of the Hamilton by-election – or that it only broke the surface of public awareness occasionally, and only in certain contexts. It is not necessary to locate copious references

---

[96] Quoted in the *Observer*, 'Celtic Threat', 18 Feb. 1968.

[97] *Dominion*, 'The Day Britain Let Us Down', 18 Jan. 1968.

[98] National Library of Scotland, Acc. 10090/113, Montrose to Ewing, 8 Dec. 1967. Ewing's side of the correspondence is not preserved in the archive, but there are clear indications in Lord Montrose's letter that her replies were decidedly cooler in tone.

[99] J. G. A. Pocock, 'British History: A Plea for a New Subject', *Journal of Modern History*, 47 (1975), 21.

to Canada, Australasia or other settler societies in Scottish sources to see these wider commonalities at work. It is far more profitable to observe how these ideas circulated, chiming in with a transnational perception of an empire that was no longer able to deliver, but a perception that resonated in highly specific, localised ways in the many contexts where it mattered. In Scotland, it was not until the second half of the 1960s that it made its presence felt, in the wake of the Rhodesian crisis, the defence cuts of 1967/8, the devaluation of sterling and the perception that the Commonwealth had run its course as a vehicle of British influence (derided by the *Scots Independent* in 1966 as 'no more than an integrated club whose black members even talk of throwing Britain out').[100] These ingredients were by no means a constant presence, but they did tend to appear at times of deeper reflection about the changes affecting Scotland's place in the Union. One final, telling example is Ludovic Kennedy's meditation on 'the Disunited Kingdom', broadcast on the BBC in June 1968:

> Now, there can be no denying that this union brought to Scotland a stability in her affairs which she had never before had. And there can be equally no denying that we on our part greatly helped you, first by force of arms, to establish and then to administer, the biggest and richest empire there has ever been. Well, that empire is now dead. It didn't, as empire's [*sic*] go, last long... And it may seem to you – as it does to many of us – that it was the empire above all, that made and kept us British. Today it is mainly you – the English – who think of yourselves as British. Most of us up here think of ourselves as Scots.[101]

The point is not that Kennedy accurately conveyed the views of 'most of us up here', or indeed that he got the imperial dynamics of Scotland's deliverance from Britishness right. The significance lies in how the cold facts of an empire 'now dead' lent shape and meaning to the contemporary relevance and utility of being British – a process that was duplicated in myriad ways throughout the British world.

A. G. Hopkins has termed these subtle interconnections 'post-colonial globalization' – connections that were by no means confined to the new nationalisms of the settler-colonial world.[102] But these parallels are particularly useful as they offer a coherent, empirically verifiable and hitherto unexplored way of understanding the inner workings of imperial decline in the emergence of the new political nationalisms of the 1960s, not least in Scotland. At the very least, they offer a more productive way forward than to dismiss the imperial context out of hand as a complete irrelevance. To be sure, more work is needed to establish and elaborate the

---

[100] *Scots Independent*, 'The British Crisis: Scotland Must Act Herself', 3 Sept. 1966.

[101] National Library of Scotland, Acc. 10090/113. Ludovic Kennedy, 'The Disunited Kingdom', transcript of BBC broadcast, 12 June 1968.

[102] Hopkins, 'Rethinking Decolonization', 246–7.

interconnections between the new nationalisms of the former Dominions and the contemporaneous surge in national separatism in Scotland – not to mention Wales and England – in the 1960s and 1970s. But we would do well to recall the rarely cited subtitle of Tom Nairn's 1977 classic that triggered so much debate: 'Crisis and *Neo-Nationalism*'.

Transactions of the RHS 25 (2015), pp. 187–214 © Royal Historical Society 2015
doi:10.1017/S0080440115000092

'BEAMED DIRECTLY TO THE CHILDREN':
SCHOOL BROADCASTING AND SEX EDUCATION
IN BRITAIN IN THE 1960s AND 1970s
The Rees Davies Prize Essay

By Mara Gregory

ABSTRACT. This paper presents findings from a larger research project that addresses the production, content and reception of sex education broadcasts produced by the British Broadcasting Corporation and Independent Television in the 1960s and 1970s. More than educational aids, these programmes were vehicles of communication with explicit and implicit messages regarding sexual morality and the nature of childhood. With a focus on the broadcast media and their modes of address to children, this paper connects sex education *content* with classroom *practice* and broadly questions how broadcasts portrayed and authorised certain images, types of knowledge and methods for teaching children about sex.

Introduction

In the autumn of 1969, the British Broadcasting Corporation's School Broadcasting Council announced its intention to air sex education programmes for primary school audiences.[1] Controversy immediately ensued, with a storm of emphatic press headlines proclaiming, 'Sex Education on Television at Last' or, 'Sex Lessons from Auntie BBC? – Oh Please, NO'.[2] While proponents praised the broadcasts for providing candid answers to children's questions, many opponents felt that televised sex education threatened to usurp the rights of parents or other responsible adults to control the sexual knowledge of children. The significance of television as a medium was highlighted by many observers; as the archbishop of Cardiff argued in a letter to *The Times*, these programmes were dangerous because they were 'beamed directly to the

---

[1] School Broadcasting Council for the United Kingdom (SBC), *School Broadcasting and Sex Education in the Primary School* (1971), 3.

[2] Wellcome Collection, London, Family Planning Association Archives and Manuscripts (FPA), SA/FPA/A17/123, 'Sex Education on Television at Last', *FPA News* (Nov. 1969); Sandra Bisp, 'Sex Lessons from Auntie BBC? – Oh Please, NO', *South Wales Echo*, 30 Oct. 1969.

children'.[3] The controversy surrounding the primary school programmes thus drew together significant contemporary debates regarding sexual morality and the media, the nature of childhood and the roles and responsibilities of adults in providing sex education to children.

This paper presents findings from a larger research project that addresses the production, content and reception of the primary school programmes and other sex education school broadcasts by the British Broadcasting Corporation (BBC) and Independent Television (ITV) in the 1960s and 1970s.[4] Throughout this project, I contend that broadcasts functioned as more than educational aids; they were vehicles of communication with explicit and implicit messages regarding sexual morality, gender, the nature of childhood and the practice of education. Correspondingly, educators and public commentators supported or contested these understandings. By focusing on the communicative elements of these programmes – the broadcast media and their modes of address to children – I question not only what messages were conveyed, but also how they were transmitted and why they became controversial. As Alison Bashford and Carolyn Strange argue in a study of mid-twentieth-century Australian radio, there is a significant historiographical gap regarding the *media* of sex education.[5] By examining how the visual and broadcast nature of programming shaped the tone, extent and practice of sex education, this paper employs a methodology that can address this gap.

After an overview of the historiography, this paper provides a detailed examination of the media and content of key sex education broadcasts from the 1960s and 1970s. First, I discuss how supporters and opponents of the programmes drew attention to broadcasting as a welcome solution or dangerous contribution, respectively, to the problem of sex education in the 1960s and 1970s. I then examine the form and content of the programmes, noting ways in which they emulated older conventions in audio-visual sex education while also incorporating modes of address specific to school broadcasting. Throughout this analysis, I pay specific attention to the visualities and vocabularies used to teach children of different ages about sex. Following Robert Eberwein's assertion that sex education films often 'narrativi[se] the

[3] John A. Murphy, 'Sex Education Broadcasts: The Duty of Parents', *Times*, 7 Nov. 1969, 11.

[4] Mara Gregory, 'Beamed Directly to the Children: School Broadcasting and Sex Education in Britain in the 1960s and 1970s' (M.A. dissertation, University of Warwick, 2013).

[5] Alison Bashford and Carolyn Strange, 'Public Pedagogy: Sex Education and Mass Communication in the Mid-Twentieth Century', *Journal of the History of Sexuality*, 13.1 (2004), 71–99.

educational process',[6] I also describe ways in which the broadcasts modelled teaching methods, thereby promoting particular educational theories and classroom practices.

As David Buckingham and Sara Bragg argue in a recent study of sex in the media, both sides in adult debates 'invoke ideas about the "natural" form of sexuality, and about children's inherent needs or interests... While they may purport to speak on behalf of children, they also construct "the child" in ways that can be seen to reflect broader social and political considerations.'[7] This paper thus focuses primarily on adult understandings of childhood as revealed through the media of sex education broadcasts. At the same time, however, I acknowledge that the programmes had an uneven impact on the practice of sex education and the responses of individual children. Accordingly, following Harry Hendrick's contention that historians must distinguish between *childhood* (a concept) and *children* (historical people),[8] I also examine the sources for glimpses of children's experiences as audience members. Through the lens of the media, therefore, this paper connects sex education *content* with classroom *practice* and broadly questions how broadcasts portrayed and authorised certain images, types of knowledge and methods for teaching children about sex.

Historiography

The history of sex education is a quickly growing field within the broader historiography of sex and sexuality.[9] Until recently, much of the scholarly work on sex education and its history came from the disciplines of sociology, psychology and education.[10] However, Michel Foucault's theories on the discursive production of sexuality and feminist critiques

---

[6] Robert Eberwein, *Sex Ed: Film, Video, and the Framework of Desire* (New Brunswick, 1999), 117.

[7] David Buckingham and Sara Bragg, *Young People, Sex and the Media: The Facts of Life?* (Basingstoke and New York, 2004), 4.

[8] Harry Hendrick, 'The Child as a Social Actor in Historical Sources: Problems of Identification and Interpretation', in *Research with Children: Perspectives and Practices*, ed. Pia Christensen and Allison James (2nd edn, London and New York, 2008), 40–1.

[9] Recent edited volumes on the history of sex education, with chapters on Britain, include *Shaping Sexual Knowledge: A Cultural History of Sex Education in Twentieth Century Europe*, ed. Lutz D. H. Sauerteig and Roger Davidson (London and New York, 2009); *Sexual Pedagogies: Sex Education in Britain, Australia, and America, 1879–2000*, ed. Claudia Nelson and Michelle H. Martin (New York and Basingstoke, 2004).

[10] For contributions from the fields of social science and policy, see Christine Farrell with Leonie Kellaher, *My Mother Said... :The Way Young People Learned about Sex and Birth Control* (1978); Isobel Allen, *Education in Sex and Personal Relationships* (1987); Philip Meredith, *Sex Education: Political Issues in Britain and Europe* (London and New York, 1989); for the field of psychology, see *Sex Education: Rationale and Reaction*, ed. Rex S. Rogers (1974); for the field of education, see Dorothy M. Dallas, *Sex Education in School and Society* (Windsor, 1972).

of sex education as a form of social control have each contributed to growing historical interest in sex education.[11] As Lutz Sauerteig and Roger Davidson point out, much of this recent historiography focuses on official educational policies.[12] Similarly, many historians have examined the place of sex education within broader social climates and debates. Lesley Hall, for example, provides an overview of sex education in Britain from the nineteenth to the twenty-first centuries and argues that it has reflected changing social concerns regarding national health, morality, sexuality and childhood.[13] With regard to the period under question in this paper, James Hampshire and Jane Lewis examine how sex education was drawn into debates about sexual mores and 'permissiveness'.[14] While such works provide useful insight into the broad contours of public debates, they generally neglect *specific* concerns raised about different forms of sex education and their roles in the classroom.

Indeed, British sex education films and visual sources have received limited treatment, and broadcasts appear only in scattered references

[11] For Foucault's influence, see Lutz D. H. Sauerteig and Roger Davidson, 'Shaping the Sexual Knowledge of the Young: Introduction', in *Shaping Sexual Knowledge*, ed. Sauerteig and Davidson, 1; Roy Porter and Lesley Hall, *The Facts of Life: The Creation of Sexual Knowledge in Britain, 1650–1950* (New Haven and London, 1995), 8–9. For feminist critiques of sex education see, e.g., AnnMarie Wolpe, 'Sex in Schools: Back to the Future', *Feminist Review*, 27 (1987), 37–47; Nicky Thorogood, 'Sex Education as Social Control', *Critical Public Health*, 3.2 (1992), 43–50.

[12] Sauerteig and Davidson, 'Introduction', 5. See, e.g., Roger Davidson, 'Purity and Pedagogy: The Alliance-Scottish Council and School Sex Education in Scotland, 1955–67', in *Shaping Sexual Knowledge*, ed. Sauerteig and Davidson, 91–107; Jane Pilcher, 'School Sex Education: Policy and Practice in England 1870 to 2000', *Sex Education*, 5:2 (2005), 153–70; Jane Pilcher, 'Sex in Health Education: Official Guidance for Schools in England, 1928– 1977', *Journal of Historical Sociology*, 17.2/3 (2004), 185–208; James Hampshire, 'The Politics of School Sex Education Policy in England and Wales from the 1940s to the 1960s', *Social History of Medicine*, 18.1 (2005), 87–105; James Hampshire, 'Sex Education: Politics and Policy in England and Wales', *Education and Health*, 21.2 (2003), 29–34.

[13] Lesley A. Hall, 'Birds, Bees and General Embarrassment: Sex Education in Britain, from Social Purity to Section 28', in *Public or Private Education? Lessons from History*, ed. Richard Aldrich (London and Portland, OR, 2004), 93–112. For an analysis of early twentieth-century sex education and its links with 'medico-moral discourse', see Frank Mort, *Dangerous Sexualities: Medico-Moral Politics in England since 1830* (2nd edn, London and New York, 2000), 123–69.

[14] James Hampshire and Jane Lewis, '"The Ravages of Permissiveness": Sex Education and the Permissive Society', *Twentieth Century British History*, 15.3 (2004), 290–312. See also the work of David Limond on controversial sex education materials from this period: David Limond, 'The UK Edition of The Little Red Schoolbook: A Paper Tiger Reflects', *Sex Education*, 12.5 (2012), 523–34; David Limond, '"I Hope Someone Castrates You, You Perverted Bastard": Martin Cole's Sex Education Film, Growing Up', *Sex Education*, 9.4 (2009), 409–19; David Limond, '"I Never Imagined that the Time Would Come": Martin Cole, the Growing Up Controversy and the Limits of School Sex Education in 1970s England', *History of Education*, 37.3 (2008), 409–29.

throughout the secondary literature.[15] A detailed content analysis of British sex education broadcasts has not previously been attempted.[16] However, this paper draws on a rich theoretical and historiographical corpus from the fields of visual culture and film studies. Gillian Rose contends that the visual is 'bound into social power relations' that produce certain types of images and ways of seeing.[17] Indeed, historians of science and medicine have increasingly employed visual sources to question how scientific and medical power, operating through visual media, has produced knowledge about life and bodies.[18] Timothy Boon, for example, examines the role of science films and television as 'vehicles of scientific communication' between scientists, filmmakers and the public.[19] These films employed certain genre conventions and 'modes of address' in order to construct 'particular relationships . . . between the authority they represented and their audiences'.[20] Thus, the form and content of health education films could assert medical expertise in order to prompt certain responses and behaviours in the viewing public.

Historians of sex education have similarly used images and films to examine the operation of medical power through visual culture. In an analysis of twentieth-century German sex education literature, for example, Sauerteig considers how visual materials defined or attempted

[15] The controversies surrounding BBC sex education broadcasts in the early 1970s are mentioned briefly in Hall, 'Sex Education in Britain', 104; and Hampshire and Lewis, 'Ravages of Permissiveness', 303–4. Neither provides a description or analysis of content.

[16] Indeed, within the historiography of broadcasting in Britain, school broadcasting in general has received scant attention. David Crook provides a brief but informative 'exploratory history' of school broadcasting in Britain; see David Crook, 'School Broadcasting in the United Kingdom: An Exploratory History', *Journal of Educational Administration and History*, 39.3 (2007). The most comprehensive histories have been written by broadcasters themselves. See, e.g., Kenneth Fawdry, *Everything but Alf Garnett: A Personal View of BBC School Broadcasting* (1974); *Teaching and Television: ETV Explained*, ed. Guthrie Moir (Oxford, 1967).

[17] Gillian Rose, *Visual Methodologies* (2001), 9–15.

[18] These studies incorporate Foucauldian conceptions of power as inseparable from and productive of knowledge. See Michel Foucault, 'Body/Power', in *Power/Knowledge: Selected Interviews and Other Writings 1972–1977*, ed. Colin Gordon, trans. Colin Gordon, Leo Marshall, John Mepham and Kate Soper (New York, 1980), 59. For further discussion of Foucault's influence on the visual turn in the history of science and medicine, see Roger Cooter and Claudia Stein, 'Coming into Focus: Posters, Power, and Visual Culture in the History of Medicine', *Medizinhistorisches Journal*, 42 (2007), 180–209; Lisa Cartwright, *Screening the Body: Tracing Medicine's Visual Culture* (Minneapolis and London, 1995), xi–xv; Ludmilla Jordanova, *Sexual Visions: Images of Gender in Science and Medicine between the Eighteenth and Twentieth Centuries* (New York, 1989), 5–6.

[19] Timothy Boon, *Films of Fact: A History of Science in Documentary Films and Television* (London and New York, 2008), 5–6, 107.

[20] Timothy Boon, 'Health Education Films in Britain, 1919–1939: Production, Genres and Audiences', in *Signs of Life: Cinema and Medicine*, ed. Graeme Harper and Andrew Moor (London and New York, 2005), 54. See also Boon, *Films of Fact*, 142–5.

to naturalise heterosexual identities and activities.[21] In addition to medical expertise, however, sex education materials also drew on *pedagogical* authority. In his comprehensive analysis of American sex education films, Eberwein finds that films for schools presented 'accurate but incomplete' information, carefully legitimised for classroom viewings.[22] Significantly, these films often employed 'mise-en-abyme' depictions: a class might view a sex education film portraying yet another sex education class.[23] In addition to providing information about sex, then, films also promoted particular educational methods and defined appropriate roles for teachers and pupils in sex education.

Although visual and cinematographic sources can provide rich historical material, it is important to note the limitations of these sources. As Kelly Loughlin points out, strict access requirements and lack of preservation often restrict the sources available to historians.[24] In the content analysis below, I refer to broadcasts viewed at the British Film Institute National Archive and Library as well as written descriptions found in production files and reports by the BBC and ITV companies.[25] I have also utilised information contained in pupils' pamphlets and teachers' notes published by the BBC to accompany broadcasts. In addition to television broadcasts, this paper will refer frequently to radiovision, or radio broadcasts that schools could record and use with accompanying filmstrips. In selecting these programmes, I have attempted to represent a range of genres and intended audience ages, while also focusing on programmes for which the most comprehensive contextual and descriptive data are available.

The educational problem of sex

Martin Lawn and Ian Grosvenor argue that an educational technology, such as school broadcasting, is 'sold as a solution to an educational

---

[21] Lutz D. H. Sauerteig, 'Representations of Pregnancy and Childbirth in (West) German Sex Education Books, 1900s–1970s', in *Shaping Sexual Knowledge*, ed. Sauerteig and Davidson, 129–60. For a similar assessment of medicine's power to define and represent reproductive and sexual bodies through sex education, see Uta Schwarz, '*Helga* (1967): West German Sex Education and the Cinema in the 1960s', in *Shaping Sexual Knowledge*, ed. Sauerteig and Davidson, 197–213.

[22] Eberwein, *Sex Ed*, 2–6.

[23] *Ibid.*, 4–5.

[24] Kelly Loughlin, 'The History of Health and Medicine in Contemporary Britain: Reflections on the Role of Audio-Visual Sources', *Social History of Medicine*, 13.1 (2000), 142–5. Unfortunately, many sex education broadcasts from the 1960s and 1970s are not publicly accessible or do not survive in full.

[25] BBC production files were accessed at the BBC Written Archives Centre in Reading. ITV archives are much more difficult to access due to individual company policies. Therefore, this paper draws from published reports on ITV programmes. Due to copyright restrictions, I am not able to reproduce here any still images from BBC or ITV broadcasts.

problem'.[26] In the case of sex education, such 'problems' were manifold. In 1964, the British Medical Association's (BMA) report on *Venereal Disease and Young People* influentially concluded that sexually transmitted diseases had risen markedly among young people.[27] The BMA report argued that this trend, along with rising illegitimacy and teenage pregnancy rates, resulted from liberalised sexual mores and promiscuous behaviour.[28] Among its recommendations, the BMA suggested that better training and materials for sex education should be made available to teachers and parents. In another influential study of the 'sexual attitudes and behaviour of young people', Michael Schofield questioned the idea of youth permissiveness and concluded that promiscuity was 'not a prominent feature of teenage sexual behaviour'.[29] Nevertheless, Schofield maintained that sexual activity occurred often enough among teenagers to warrant better sex education, especially with regard to contraception and sexually transmitted diseases.[30] The Department of Education and Science (DES), however, took what Hampshire calls a stance of 'non-decision-making' regarding sex education throughout the 1960s and 1970s.[31] Preferring to leave choices regarding this sensitive matter to the local level, the Department provided periodic guidelines that were suggestive rather than authoritative.[32] Teachers, moreover, often lacked resources or were simply too embarrassed to broach the subject of sex education.[33]

To producers and supporters of school broadcasting, the broadcast media held the potential to address this gap in education by reaching large numbers of pupils and providing professional, state-of-the-art aids to teachers. Following contemporary trends in education, broadcasters drew upon 'child-centred' theories to design programmes that could

[26]Martin Lawn and Ian Grosvenor, '"When in Doubt, Preserve": Exploring the Traces of Teaching and Material Culture in English Schools', *History of Education*, 30.2 (2001), 120.

[27]British Medical Association, *Report of Venereal Disease and Young People* (1964), quoted in Michael Schofield, *The Sexual Behaviour of Young People* (1965; repr. 1967), 6.

[28]'Venereal Disease and Young People', *British Medical Journal*, 1.5383 (1964), 576.

[29]Schofield, *Sexual Behaviour*, 253.

[30]*Ibid.*, 247–9, 253–4.

[31]Hampshire, 'Politics', 99.

[32]This 'official guidance' is well covered by the historiography. See, e.g., Pilcher, 'Sex in Health Education', 185–208; Pilcher, 'School Sex Education', 153–70; Hampshire, 'Sex Education', 31; Hampshire and Lewis, 'Ravages of Permissiveness', 290–312.

[33]See Hera Cook, 'Getting "Foolishly Hot and Bothered"? Parents and Teachers and Sex Education in the 1940s', *Sex Education*, 12.5 (2012), 557–64; Hall, 'Sex Education in Britain', 107–8. For an oral history recounting reticence, embarrassment and lack of knowledge about sex during this period, see Angela Davis, '"Oh No, Nothing, We Didn't Learn Anything": Sex Education and the Preparation of Girls for Motherhood, c. 1930–1970', *History of Education*, 37.5 (2008), 661–77.

foster children's imaginations and curiosity.[34] Although child-centred approaches had been slowly gaining credence throughout the early twentieth century, they achieved particular prominence with the 1967 Plowden Report on primary schools. The report, prepared by the Central Advisory Council for Education, suggested that children's questions should be answered 'plainly and truthfully', but also with due regard to age appropriateness.[35] Child-centredness therefore promoted the expertise of certain adults (educationists or psychologists), who understood the stages of childhood development.

In line with such theories, broadcasters collaborated with experts in child development and education to produce programming for both BBC and ITV school broadcasts.[36] BBC school radio and television services were overseen by the School Broadcasting Council for the United Kingdom (SBC), an independent body representing education ministers, local education authorities and teachers.[37] Although ITV's entrance to the field of school television in 1957 prompted concerns from educationists and BBC officials alike about commercial motivations, ITV's companies also worked within a complex structure of liaison with the educational community.[38] By the mid-1970s, the efforts of broadcasters to collaborate with schools and teachers had indeed paid off; the 1977 Annan Report on the Future of Broadcasting estimated that 90 per cent of British schools used radio and 82 per cent used television.[39]

---

[34] Harry Hendrick describes child-centred doctrine as 'emphasis on creative effort, self-regulated learning and a variety of informal techniques'. Harry Hendrick, *Children, Childhood and English Society, 1880–1990* (Cambridge, 1997), 77.

[35] Central Advisory Council for Education (England), *The Plowden Report: Children and their Primary Schools* (2 vols., 1967), I, 259, available online at Education in England, www.educationengland.org.uk/documents/plowden/ (11 Jan. 2015).

[36] The production of school sex education broadcasts is discussed in detail in Gregory, 'School Broadcasting', 21–48.

[37] The National Archives, Kew, Records of the Department of Education and Science and of Related Bodies (TNA, ED), 147/559, 'Committee on Broadcasting: Memorandum of Evidence by the School Broadcasting Council for the United Kingdom' (1960), 3.

[38] TNA, ED 147/557, Ministry of Education Minute Sheet, 'I.T.V. Programmes for Schools' (24 Jan. 1957). Initially, the Children's Advisory Committee, made up of experts in education and child development, provided advice to the Independent Television Authority. Following the Television Act of 1963, this structure was replaced with the Educational Advisory Council and a subsidiary Schools Committee. Programme proposals from the school broadcasting departments of ITV companies needed approval from company educational advisory bodies as well as the overarching ITA Schools Committee. Bernard Sendall, *Independent Television in Britain*, II: *Expansion and Change, 1958–68* (London and Basingstoke, 1983), 274, 285–7.

[39] Committee on the Future of Broadcasting, *The Annan Report* (1977), 304.

Although the BBC had produced school radio programmes addressing aspects of human reproduction since the 1940s,[40] several changes in the provision of sex education broadcasting in the late 1960s and early 1970s brought increased public attention to these programmes. The first school television series on sex education, *Understanding*, was broadcast by the ITV company Granada in 1966.[41] In 1970, the BBC broke new ground by creating television and radiovision sex education programmes for primary school audiences as young as eight or nine. In defending their decision to target this young age group, producers attested to exhaustive collaboration with experts. The medical consultant for the programmes, a Health Education Department employee at the DES, noted that the primary school broadcasts addressed children in the 'latency period', in which they were curious about sex but not yet 'emotionally involved in their own sexuality'.[42] While the programmes encouraged responsible behaviour, they did not stress issues of morality, love or marriage. Producers felt these were topics better reserved for older pupils who, moving beyond the phase of detached curiosity, began to have emotional concerns about sexuality.[43] In this way, producers used medical expertise and a framework of normal sexual development to authorise their programmes for different target age groups.

Public commentators, in turn, often confirmed or contested the ways that broadcasters defined and reached their child audience.[44] Indeed, these pioneering broadcasts came at a time when sex education was already gaining publicity as a heated topic of debate. As Hampshire and Lewis argue, opponents of sex education during this period drew on broader concerns about the 'permissive society' and argued that sex education was dangerous to the young – promoting, rather than preventing, social problems.[45] Although some detractors questioned the suitability of *any* sex education, many commentators raised concerns

[40] FPA, CB/13/4, Kenneth Fawdry, 'Sex Education: An Approach through Broadcasting', in *Sex Education of Schoolchildren*, ed. James Hemming, Maud P. Menzies, Marjorie Proops and Kenneth Fawdry (1971), 32.

[41] Granada Television, 'A Report on "Understanding"', in *Sex Education*, ed. Rogers, 197–216.

[42] BBC Written Archives Centre, Reading (WAC), T69/58/1, 'Consultants Views on Nudity in Relation to Merry-Go-Round' (undated), 2. The idea of the 'latency period' comes from Freud's theory of psychosexual development. See Diederik F. Janssen, 'Picturing Sex Education: Notes on the Politics of Visual Stratification', *Discourse: Studies in the Cultural Politics of Education*, 27.4 (2006), 497.

[43] T. J. Lambert, 'The Contribution of BBC School Broadcasts to Sex Education for Primary Schools', in *Sex Education in Schools*, ed. Isam R. Nazer (Carthage, 1976), 74, 82.

[44] For a detailed discussion of the public reception of sex education broadcasts, see Gregory, 'School Broadcasting', 88–97.

[45] Hampshire and Lewis, 'Ravages of Permissiveness', 163–7, 292, 298–9. 'Permissiveness', a term employed predominantly by moral conservatives, characterised perceived changes in society related to issues such as rising rates of illegitimacy and venereal disease, sexual

about the media employed. Significantly, mass communications blurred the boundaries between public and private by presenting the intimate subject of sex through the forums of the mass media.[46]

Broadcasting intended for schools transcended another boundary: that between the home and the classroom. As David Limond argues, ideas about what constituted 'explicit' material depended not only on content but also on the physical location and makeup of the audience.[47] A 1972 report published by the Longford Committee Investigating Pornography, for example, cited concern regarding the viewership of the sex education broadcasts. Although careful to note that the BBC programmes should not be considered 'pornographic' as such, the report nevertheless maintained that sex education should be a 'private affair', tailored to individual children's needs.[48] Broadcast sex education, troublingly, transmitted the same message to all children who viewed it. Thus, in order to understand the contested nature of sex education broadcasts in the 1960s and 1970s, it is important to acknowledge the ways in which these programmes challenged moral boundaries in terms of medium and mode of address. The content analysis below, therefore, highlights the visual and broadcast nature of the programmes and the communicative methods they used to speak to children in schools.

Audio-visual genres in sex education

Although the sex education television broadcasts of the 1960s and 1970s were the first of their kind, they existed within a broader context and longer history of sex education films. Loughlin argues that content analyses of audio-visual sources should maintain 'an awareness of particular forms or formats – the way they develop over time, [and] their association with and/or distinction from other modes of representation'.[49]

content in the media, the growing pornographic industry and legislation that increased availability of the contraceptive pill and abortion. See Jeffrey Weeks, *Sex, Politics and Society: The Regulation of Sexuality since 1800* (3rd edn, Harlow, 2012), 322–5; Lesley A. Hall, *Sex, Gender and Social Change in Britain since 1880* (2nd edn, Basingstoke, 2013), 148–64.

[46] Bashford and Strange, 'Public Pedagogy', 73–5. Trends in the 1960s towards decensorship were accompanied by growing numbers of complaints about explicitness in the media. In 1964, notably, Mary Whitehouse founded the Clean Up TV Campaign (later the National Viewers' and Listeners' Association), which became a prominent lobby for morality in the media. See Weeks, *Sex, Politics and Society*, 368; David Hendy, 'Bad Language and BBC Radio Four in the 1960s and 1970s', *Twentieth Century British History*, 17.1 (2006), 74.

[47] Limond, 'Martin Cole's Sex Education Film', 415. David Hendy pursues a similar argument in his discussion of controversies surrounding bad language on BBC Radio Four; he notes that 'different standards existed for different audiences in different places'. Hendy, 'BBC Radio Four', 76.

[48] Longford Committee Investigating Pornography, *Pornography: The Longford Report* (1972), 345, 352–3.

[49] Loughlin, 'Audio-Visual Sources', 134–5.

However, the task of comparing broadcasts with other forms of sex education used throughout the 1960s and 1970s is complicated by the fact that classroom practices varied greatly. Hall notes that individual teachers, health education officers, visiting doctors, clergy and even hygiene product manufacturers often undertook sex education programmes with varying materials and methods.[50]

Some insight into the use of sex education materials, however, can be gained from a 1967 Birmingham Education Committee report, which analysed sex education provision and included an extensive list of available textbooks, pamphlets, novels, visual aids and audio-visual resources.[51] Visual aids included graphs, diagrams and wall-charts covering topics such as reproductive anatomy, birth and human development. The report also listed eighteen filmstrips and thirty-one films, produced between the 1930s and the 1960s, that addressed topics ranging from animal and human reproduction, to growth and development, menstruation, venereal disease, dating and parenting. The Central Council for Health Education, British independent film companies and charities produced the majority of the films, although the list also included several American films.[52]

Thus, by the late 1960s, broadcasters could emulate or modify conventions from a wide range of audio-visual sex education materials. Barbara Crowther points out that many of the earliest educational films displayed a notable *absence* of sexual information, thereby restricting sexual knowledge of the young in line with a 'broader culture of opaqueness and evasion'.[53] Resources often literally took a 'birds and bees' approach by describing reproductive processes in plants or animals and referring euphemistically to human behaviour.[54] Filmmakers employed this 'nature-analogy' formula in *The Mystery of Marriage* (1932), in which images of animal 'marriage' rituals are intercut with scenes of human courtship.[55] Such films fall into a category that Eberwein

---

[50] Hall, 'Sex Education in Britain', 102–5.

[51] TNA, ED 50/862, Sir Lionel Russell, *Sex Education in Schools* (1967), 43–9.

[52] It is worth noting that British educationists were often wary of American films. Minutes from a meeting between the DES and the Ministry of Health, for example, note that officials felt American films on venereal disease were 'not entirely suitable for British teenagers'. TNA, ED 50/862, 'Notes of a Meeting Held in the Ministry of Health on V.D. Health Education' (23 May 1966).

[53] Barbara Crowther, 'The Partial Picture: Framing the Discourse of Sex in British Educative Films of the Early 1930s', in *Shaping Sexual Knowledge*, ed. Sauerteig and Davidson, 176–96.

[54] Hall, 'Sex Education in Britain', 94–5.

[55] Crowther, 'Partial Picture', 188–92. *The Mystery of Marriage* is also available in a British Film Institute compilation of sex education films, covering the period between 1917 and 1973. *The Mystery of Marriage*, dir. Mary Field (British Instructional Films Ltd, 1932), in *The Joy of Sex Education*, prod. Katy McGahan (British Film Institute, 2009) (on DVD). It is

calls 'informational' sex education, which makes use of documentary-style techniques such as voice-over narration and animated diagrams.[56] Notably, informational films could carry social as well as biological messages. In a later example of this genre, *Learning to Live* (1964), a male narrator's description of adolescent development is accompanied by anatomical diagrams and film sequences showing teenagers at home, in school and socialising at a dance hall.[57] Throughout this work, the importance of marriage and family is stressed; the narrator states that, with childbirth in wedlock, 'the sex act has reached its intended end'.

While some films opted for politeness and metaphor, sex education resources could also challenge the cultural boundaries of appropriateness. Another informational film, *Growing Up* (1971), attracted considerable controversy for its explicit visual depictions, which include close-up shots of human genitals and film sequences of male and female masturbation and sexual intercourse.[58] Although a number of historians have focused on the radical nature of these portrayals,[59] this film also contains content that reflects more conventional aspects of the informational genre. The film's creator, Dr Martin Cole, states in his narration that women tend to be 'maternal' while men are more 'inventive and creative'. Animated diagrams then portray hormonal pathways as Dr Cole explains that oestrogen is linked with 'femaleness' and testosterone with 'maleness'. The film thus employs scientific terminology to depict the source of sex traits and, at the same time, naturalises gender distinctions and heterosexuality.

Ideological messages are often even more pronounced in another sex education genre: the narrative or 'moral tale'.[60] Unlike films that focus on anatomical and mechanical aspects of reproduction, narratives use fictional formats to portray 'the manifestations and effects of sexuality'.[61]

---

important to note that *The Mystery of Marriage* was likely intended to be humorous as well as informational.

[56] Eberwein, *Sex Ed*, 106–13.

[57] *Learning to Live* was produced by Eothen Films for London Rubber Industries. *Learning to Live*, dir. Guy Fergusson and Phillip Sattin (Eothen Films, 1964), in *Joy of Sex Education*. Despite its conventional content, this film stirred controversy because it was produced by a condom manufacturing company, London Rubber Industries. The controversy is described in TNA, ED 50/862, DES Internal Memorandum (5 Aug. 1968).

[58] *Growing Up* was produced by Global Films in association with the Institute for Sex Education and Research. *Growing Up*, dir. Dr Martin Cole (Global Films, 1971), in *Joy of Sex Education*.

[59] Dominic Sandbrook, *State of Emergency: The Way We Were: Britain, 1970–1974* (Kindle E-book) (2010 [2011]), ch. 11; Limond, 'Martin Cole's Sex Education Film', 409–19; Limond, 'Growing Up Controversy', 409–29; Hampshire and Lewis, 'Ravages of Permissiveness', 303.

[60] Boon describes the use of 'moral tales' in interwar health education films. He defines these as 'fictional stories . . . using moral narratives . . . intended to convey a health implication'. Boon, 'Health Education Films', 47.

[61] Eberwein, *Sex Ed*, 134.

A classic example of this genre is the venereal disease narrative, which gained prominence during the interwar period. As Boon notes, venereal disease films often carry heavy moralistic tones regarding sexual behaviour and stress 'obedience to medical authority' – typically in the from of a stern but knowledgeable doctor doling out advice to nervous patients.[62] Narrative films for young people likewise deal with issues such as teenage relationships, the pressures to have sex and the potential consequences of intercourse.[63] In a strikingly conservative example from 1973, *Don't Be Like Brenda*, seventeen-year-old Brenda falls in love with Gary, becomes pregnant and is forced to place her baby for adoption after Gary marries another woman.[64] The calm and uncompromising male narrator then admonishes Brenda for 'spoil[ing] two lives – her own and her child's', and ruining her chances for marriage, 'everyone's dream'.

Filmmakers employed informational and narrative formats in films for both school and general audiences; however, Eberwein also identifies a uniquely 'schoolroom' genre.[65] This style typically depicts classroom lessons, activities or lectures, thereby 'narrativizing the educational process'.[66] Significantly, a number of these films portray groups of pupils discussing their concerns about adolescence and sexuality with an adult moderator. Such films thus evoke child-centred ideas of education based on participatory learning. However, it should be noted that the final film products were edited to reflect producers' intentions rather than children's unmediated voices.

In addition to film genres, school radio and television producers could also draw upon the stylistic conventions of broadcasting. Boon notes that television science programmes often rely on 'the personality factor' of an engaging presenter, who communicates in a more conversational manner than traditional film narrators.[67] Indeed, school broadcasting producers alleged that children responded to the familiarity of well-known presenters and enjoyed the 'intimate and personal' character of television as opposed to film.[68] In practice, however, the media of broadcasts and

---

[62] Boon, 'Health Education Films', 48–9. The common depiction of doctors seated authoritatively behind a desk and providing advice is also discussed in Crowther, 'Partial Picture', 183; and Eberwein, *Sex Ed*, 138.

[63] See examples in Eberwein, *Sex Ed*, 134–47; Jack Stevenson, 'When the Lights Go Down (in the Classroom)', in *Fleshpot: Cinema's Sexual Myth Makers and Taboo Breakers*, ed. Jack Stevenson (2nd edn, Manchester, 2002), 49–62.

[64] *Don't Be Like Brenda*, dir. Hugh Baddeley (Hugh Baddeley Productions, 1973) in *Joy of Sex Education*.

[65] Eberwein, *Sex Ed*, 113–33.

[66] *Ibid.*, 117.

[67] Boon, *Films of Fact*, 231.

[68] TNA, Records of the Home Office, 256/406, 'Report of an Enquiry into the Special Contribution which Television Might be Expected to Make' (1954), 4.

films overlapped, as television programmes were made available on film or were recorded by schools.[69] Furthermore, as will be discussed below, many broadcasts emulated or reworked the informational, narrative or schoolroom film genres.

Primary school programmes

The BBC's *Nature* radiovision programmes and *Merry-Go-Round* television programmes represented the main contributions to sex education broadcasting for primary schools in the 1970s. A close reading of their dialogue, visuals and accompanying materials can provide insight into the formal means by which producers advanced child-centred objectives and attempted to address the gap in sex education for young children. As indicated by the title of the first radiovision programme, 'Where Do Babies Come From?', these programmes responded to children's common questions about babies and growing up. However, as Sauerteig points out, sex education materials that purported to answer children's questions also carried ideological underpinnings; they 'directed children's attention to the relevance of a *specific* knowledge of reproduction'.[70] Accordingly, the BBC programmes portrayed particular answers and teaching methods as appropriate responses to primary school children's 'natural' curiosity.[71]

The BBC radiovision programmes consist of two filmstrips and corresponding radio broadcasts.[72] Each of the filmstrips contains a series of colour illustrations, presented in a fanciful style reminiscent of children's picture books. Warm hues and a decorative background were intended to 'soften the impact of reality' for child viewers.[73] The radio portion provides narration by a calm female voice. Eberwein argues that sex education narrators typically represent male authority, and that female narration indicates a progressive agenda;[74] however, the use of a motherly female narrator in this case may reflect producers' desire to foster a safe

[69] For the recording of broadcasts, see Fawdry, *Alf Garnett*, 189–93.

[70] Sauerteig, 'Pregnancy and Childbirth', 129 (emphasis added).

[71] The SBC contended that these programmes would assist teachers 'to give responsible answers to those questions about sex which the 8 year old naturally asks'. SBC, *School Broadcasting*, 1.

[72] Information on the content of these programmes is drawn from the teachers' notes, which contain images of the filmstrip frames and transcripts of the radio dialogue, available at the Institute of Education Library, University of London (IOE), BBC Broadcasts to Schools Collection, Vol. CXLVIX, Leaflets, Notes 175–6 (Spring 1970). The radiovision programme 'Growing Up' is also available as part of the BBC's adult education series, *Sex Education in Primary Schools*. During this television programme, the filmstrip images and accompanying radio narration are presented as they would be in schools. A viewing copy of this programme is available at the British Film Institute (BFI), London, Ref. 333711, 'Growing Up', *Sex Education in Primary Schools* (BBC, 20 Jan. 1970) (on VHS).

[73] SBC, *School Broadcasting*, 12.

[74] Eberwein, *Sex Ed*, 103.

atmosphere for the young audience. This impression is further enhanced by gentle guitar and harp music following the narration for each slide. In practice, the music cued teachers to change the slides, but also allowed children a moment to look at the illustrations without narration. The format of the programmes thereby evokes the pedagogical idea that young children respond more to visual images than words.[75]

The first programme, 'Where Do Babies Come From?', begins and ends with images of parents taking care of a young child. With the story thus framed in the context of family life, the programme addresses reproductive anatomy, conception, pregnancy and birth. The narrator's tone is direct and unemotional, and the vocabulary alternates between 'homely' and 'scientific'.[76] In answer to the title question, for example, the narrator states, 'from inside their mother's tummies, that's where babies come from'. The following slide, however, explains that the baby grows in the mother's 'womb', and emerges through the 'vagina'. Male anatomy and conception are similarly treated with a mixture of familiar and anatomical language. The narrator describes an image of a nude man and woman embracing, depicted from the waist up, as: 'the father lying very close to the mother, so that his penis can fit into her vagina'. Again, familial relationships ('father' and 'mother') are emphasised. Thus, explicitness is avoided in favour of simple language and stylised visuals that create a tone of domestic affection.

Despite this storybook quality, the programme also invokes medical authority through its reference to scientific ways of seeing and its depiction of birth. A slide that illustrates a foetus within the womb is accompanied by narration stating, 'If you had X-ray eyes, this is what you could see.' The programme thus provides a specific way for children to view a pregnant torso. In answer to the likely ensuing question, 'how does the baby get out?', the narrator explains, 'Well, it comes out quite naturally, usually with a little help from a doctor or a nurse.' The corresponding slide, from the viewpoint of someone standing at the mother's shoulder, depicts a women lying calmly in a hospital bed as a doctor assists with the birth.

Notably, the baby is the visual focal point of both the X-ray and birth slides. While emphasis on the family or medical expertise could serve to 'authorise' these images for use in schools,[77] the conceptual focus on babyhood also legitimises this programme for young audiences. Indeed, the SBC noted that children 'identified mostly with the baby'.[78]

---

[75] For children's interest in the visual, see TNA, ED 147/559, Allen, 'BBC School Television' (1960), 5, 7–8.

[76] SBC, *School Broadcasting*, 12.

[77] Eberwein argues that sex education materials utilised certain 'authorised' forms to both display and occlude sexual desire. Eberwein, *Sex Ed*, 2–3.

[78] SBC, *School Broadcasting*, 28.

Producers likewise used audience identification to justify the subject matter of the second *Nature* radiovision programme, 'Growing Up' (not to be confused with Dr Cole's controversial film, *Growing Up*), which was intended to address children's concerns about puberty.[79] The narration accompanying the first slide, depicting a newborn baby, associates the audience with the subject by means of a direct, second-person address: 'You probably looked like this when you were born.' The following slides illustrate male and female growth from childhood through puberty, and portray development as a natural but individually varied process: 'All girls have periods like this from about 10 or 11, but like growing breasts, everyone is different.' Intended for children of the age at which pubertal changes were just beginning, this programme thus legitimises its content by speaking to children's anxieties about their own bodies and growth.

Like the radiovision programmes, the BBC's *Merry-Go-Round* television series also presents content carefully tailored for a primary school audience. The sex education series consists of three broadcasts, 'Beginning', 'Birth' and 'Full Circle', initially transmitted in June 1970.[80] In a typical television format, animated diagrams and film footage are intercut with shots of a presenter in a studio. The male presenter was a 'regular and popular' persona from the *Merry-Go-Round* series and was chosen for his familiarity to children.[81] Following a 'birds and bees' sex education approach, each programme begins with images of animals and draws comparisons between humans and animals throughout. The accompanying teachers' notes likewise suggest that teachers supplement the programmes with biology lessons and by keeping classroom pets.[82] The programmes also include footage from classrooms, in which children demonstrate these potential follow-up activities. Reflecting the 'schoolroom' film genre, the *Merry-Go-Round* programmes therefore establish a particular *context* for sexual information to be provided to schoolchildren.

The first programme in the series, 'Beginning', addresses foetal development and pregnancy. Like the *Nature* programmes, 'Beginning'

---

[79] Descriptions of this programme are based on the images and script in IOE, BBC Broadcasts, Vol. CXLVIX, Leaflets, Note 176 (Spring 1970).

[80] SBC, *School Broadcasting*, 12–13. The first two programmes are available for viewing in full at the British Film Institute: BFI, Ref. 567975, 'Beginning', *Merry-Go-Round* (BBC, 1 June 1970) (on VHS); BFI, Ref. 568031, 'Birth', *Merry-Go-Round* (BBC, 8 June 1970) (on DVD). The last programme is not available to view in full, but a preview is included in the BBC's adult education series: BFI, Ref. 211028, 'Full Circle', *Sex Education in Primary Schools* (BBC, 10 Feb. 1970) (on VHS). Unless otherwise noted, descriptions of these programmes are based on personal viewings.

[81] *Merry-Go-Round* was a popular miscellany series that addressed a wide variety of topics in addition to sex education. The presenter was Richard Carpenter. SBC, *School Broadcasting*, 12.

[82] IOE, BBC Broadcasts, Vol. CXLXI, Leaflets, Note 4 (1970), 29, 34.

provides children with specific ways of seeing life and development. Unlike the imaginative invocation of 'X-ray eyes'; however, 'Beginning' notably focuses attention on scientific instruments themselves. In an introductory scene, the studio presenter sits next to a microscope and, as the camera zooms in to a close-up shot of the instrument, he explains that the audience will view a film depicting a rabbit egg through a microscope. The following footage uses microcinematography to display cells dividing, while a voice-over explains that 'this egg has been filmed in a special speeded-up way'. Lisa Cartwright argues that microscopic films represent 'a mechanism through which science reorganized its conception of the living body, ultimately rendering the physical body a more viewer-friendly site'.[83] In this case, the programme allows children a technical means of viewing embryonic growth while also describing it in a child-friendly manner.

A film sequence depicting pregnant women visiting their doctors further links foetal development with technology; one doctor uses a 'ducktone' to listen to the baby's heartbeat, and another helps a mother to listen with a stethoscope. While these scenes represent medical authority, they also serve a pedagogical purpose. In the following scene, children in a classroom are shown listening to their own heartbeats. Correspondingly, the teachers' notes suggest that pupils should learn about their bodies in order to foster feelings of 'kinship' with the foetus.[84] The format and presentational style of the programme similarly direct children towards particular enquiries. Throughout, the presenter poses questions followed by brief pauses, presumably allowing children time to think about the answers. In the final scene, he holds a chick and gives his audience a precise task: 'Where and how did he grow? *You* find out.'

Picking up where the first left off, the second television programme, 'Birth', begins with a chick emerging from an egg. The programme then addresses anatomical questions with a delicate 'birds and bees' approach. The presenter explains that other baby animals emerge from their mothers' bodies through a 'special opening'. A cat is shown giving birth, after which the presenter kneels next to a female dog in the studio and points out the dog's 'special opening'. In a close-up shot, he distinguishes this opening from the anus, described tactfully as 'where the dog goes to the lavatory'. This scene is necessary, according to the teachers' notes, to dispel the common childhood belief that babies emerge from the anus.[85]

Moving beyond animal birth, the programme utilises a series of increasingly explicit visual techniques to presage a film of a human birth. Following the 'informational' format, anatomical drawings and simple animation illustrate the birth process while the presenter provides

---

[83] Cartwright, *Screening the Body*, 82.
[84] IOE, BBC Broadcasts, Vol. CXLI, Leaflets, Note 4 (1970), 25.
[85] *Ibid.*, 27.

narration. The programme next cuts to a pregnant woman in a hospital bed, and the voice-over explains that doctors and nurses are there to assist her. Then, from the viewpoint of the doctor, the film depicts the last moments of the delivery as the baby fully emerges. The mother appears happy, and the scene closes with the father holding the baby and talking affectionately with the mother. Looking back on the production of this scene, a BBC representative recalled producers' struggles to depict human birth without frightening children or inciting public criticism.[86] This brief but visually explicit footage is thus framed with introductory depictions of animals and diagrams, and the actual birth takes place within an atmosphere of medical care and familial affection. The birth scene is further legitimised as a starting point for children's exploration of their own babyhood, as the following scene shows schoolchildren talking about their weights at birth and examining baby photographs.

The *Merry-Go-Round* series leaves the topic of conception – the 'most difficult concept' – until the last programme, 'Full Circle'.[87] Like human birth, however, this potentially controversial subject is addressed following a meticulous progression of information that begins in the animal world. After a series of images of newborn animals, the presenter explains that babies inherit characteristics from both mother and father. In this way, a discussion of babies and families provides the background for a description of the roles of sperm and egg, which are illustrated with microscopic film.

As with the birth scene, producers of 'Full Circle' attempted to present information about sexual development and intercourse in an appropriate context. The programme addresses sex differences through a series of films showing nudity in 'acceptable and natural' environments: babies in a bath, nine-year-old children in a pool and nude male and female models in a life-drawing class.[88] Sexual intercourse, on the other hand, is not depicted visually. Instead, the studio presenter explains, 'So the man lies close to the woman, and puts his penis into her vagina. This can give the man and the woman great pleasure, and is one of the ways in which they can show how much they love each other.' The programme concludes with films of young animals and a family on the beach. Thus, while the programme provides information about intercourse (and, interestingly, acknowledges pleasure), it does so in a carefully delineated manner. The programme describes but does *not* illustrate coitus and sets this subject within a framework of love, family and the natural world. The teachers'

[86]TNA, Records of the Ministry of Health and Related Bodies, 156/490, Felicity Kinross, 'Talk Given at the British Symposium on Population Education and Sex' (2 July 1974), 3.

[87]IOE, BBC Broadcasts, Vol. CXLI, Leaflets, Note 4 (1970), 26.

[88]*Ibid.*, 31.

notes further suggest that, in follow-up, 'the ideal of the family must be stated'.[89]

Although the primary school radiovision and television sex education programmes differed in style, they provided similarly circumscribed information to children. In each case, content was legitimised through references to medical and pedagogical authority and focus on babies, childhood and family life. By thus associating educative material with children's experiences of growing up, producers reflected and endorsed a child-centred focus on children's developmental needs.

Secondary school programmes

In secondary schools, where sex education was more likely to be an established and accepted aspect of the curriculum,[90] broadcasts were numerous and took highly varied approaches to the subject. Emulating the 'informational' film style, several programmes from the 1960s and 1970s situated sex education within the subject of biology. In line with a 'teenage-centred' approach, other programmes emphasised young people's feelings and the social aspects of sex. However, as will be discussed below, these two general approaches often overlapped, and both contributed to an expert-authorised pedagogy that defined appropriate topics and teaching methods for adolescent sex education.

One of the earliest examples of televised sex education, Grampian Television's *Living and Growing* series (1968), serves as an example of the biological approach.[91] The series was intended for the early secondary school years and therefore is similar in content to the primary school programmes discussed above. Producers designed the series, consisting of eight programmes, to 'give the facts of human reproduction'.[92] Its creators avoided addressing moral or social issues because these were considered 'inappropriate in a television series for this age'.[93] Like the primary school programmes, then, *Living and Growing* provides information tailored to a specific age group and stage of development. The programmes describe animal and human life cycles, provide a 'basic vocabulary of the sex organs' and present diagrams of human pubertal

[89] *Ibid.*, 33.

[90] Differences between provision in primary and secondary schools are discussed in the 1967 Birmingham study on sex education. The survey found that junior schools rarely covered sex education, but that the majority of secondary schools showed concern with addressing the physical and emotional aspects of sex. TNA, ED 50/862, Sir Lionel Russell, *Sex Education in Schools* (1967), 16–20.

[91] Programmes from this series are described in a report produced by Grampian Television. Grampian Television, 'A Report on "Living and Growing"', in *Sex Education*, ed. Rogers, 227–38.

[92] *Ibid.*, 227.

[93] *Ibid.*, 227.

development, fertilisation, foetal growth and birth.[94] Despite producers' claims that social issues would be avoided, the programmes emphasise the importance of family throughout. Fertilisation, for example, is described as the result of 'affection between parents', and human birth is called 'the culmination of the act of love 38 weeks earlier'.[95] The seventh programme of the series depicts a group of children asking questions about topics from the previous programmes; thus, *Living and Growing* models appropriate pupil responses to its own subject matter.

The BBC employed a similar biology-lesson approach in its programmes designed for young secondary school pupils. First broadcast in 1966, the BBC school radio programme, *Reproduction and Growth* (for ages eleven to thirteen), introduces human reproduction alongside information about cell division, fertilisation and growth in plants and animals.[96] Although the pupils' pamphlet includes a diagram of human male and female reproductive organs, the text describes mammalian (rather than specifically human) reproduction. This programme's approach therefore corresponds with the idea, expounded by the Board of Education in 1943 and prominent throughout the 1950s and 1960s, that sex education should be incorporated into biology curricula so as to avoid 'undue emphasis' on the subject.[97]

In 1972, the BBC replaced *Reproduction and Growth* with a new series, *Life Cycle*, which demonstrated a shift away from the strictly biological approach. According to a BBC press release, the series was intended to 'put the Science of human physiology where it belongs, against the background of human experience'.[98] Its eight programmes employ an 'imaginative and sometimes fantasy approach', including a plot line in which the 'Incredible Shrinking Man' takes a cellular voyage into the human body.[99] The series also includes a radiovision programme, 'Into the Wide World', which specifically addresses sex education. This programme follows a typical informational format, with photographs and diagrams depicting development from conception through puberty.[100] In keeping with a teenage-centred approach, producers also attempted to 'reassure all children about adolescence'.[101] Correspondingly, the pupils'

[94] *Ibid.*, 227–8.

[95] *Ibid.*, 228.

[96] IOE, BBC Broadcasts, Vol. CXLX, Pamphlet 84 (Summer 1970).

[97] Board of Education, *Educational Pamphlet No. 119: Sex Education in Schools and Youth Organisations* (1943), 9. Provision of sex education as part of the biology curriculum is also discussed by Pilcher, 'School Sex Education', 157–8; and Hall, 'Sex Education in Britain', 98–9.

[98] WAC, R165/77/1, BBC Press Service, 'BBC School Radio: *Life Cycle*' (Summer 1972).

[99] *Ibid.*

[100] WAC, R165/77/1, 'Into the Wide World' Script and Outline (1971).

[101] WAC, R165/77/1, Arthur Vialls, 'Life Cycle: The Saga of the Incredible Shrinking Man', *Health Education Journal* (Autumn 1974), 111.

pamphlet mixes information about hormonal changes with discussion of dating and falling in love. Pupils are also directly identified with the subject matter; the pamphlet states, 'You're growing up now. You're at the stage of your life called *adolescence* or *puberty*. And you can fall in love at any time after adolescence. So look out!'[102] Alongside its teenage-centred material, however, other elements of the programme maintained a more conservative emphasis on reproduction within the context of marriage. The pupils' pamphlet, for instance, alleges that matrimony is the starting point for a couple to live 'happily ever after'.[103]

It is notable that all the programmes discussed thus far, for primary and early secondary school pupils, reassuringly depict human reproduction and growth in terms of normality. However, a number of programmes for older adolescents approach the potential *negative* consequences of sexual behaviour. Granada's 1973 'Love Now Pay Later', part of *The Facts Are These* series for thirteen- to sixteen-year-old pupils, uses an informational format to address the topic of venereal disease (VD).[104] The programme begins with a physician sitting at his desk and discussing possible causes, symptoms and treatments for VD. Calmly and authoritatively, he explains that VD may be caused by 'promiscuity' or 'ignorance'. A medical-scientific viewpoint is emphasised, as extreme close-up shots of gonorrhoea and syphilis symptoms accompany his descriptions. Afterwards, the programme shifts to a dramatised scene in which a man attends a VD clinic, learns that he has gonorrhoea and receives advice from a doctor about treatment and contact tracing.

Although this programme is expository, it employs many conventions from venereal disease narrative films, such as an authoritative doctor 'breaking the bad news'.[105] Furthermore, in the final scenes, the doctor explains that 'if people stick to one sexual partner, whether married or not, there is little or no risk'. While the programme thus avoids moralising about marriage, it nevertheless emphasises the dangers of promiscuity. By directly addressing the audience about the risks of sexual behaviour, the doctor also plays a pedagogical role. Essentially, he enacts a televised version of the lectures commonly provided to schools by visiting medical officers.[106]

[102] WAC, R165/77/1, *Life Cycle* Pupil's Pamphlet (Summer 1972), 11.

[103] *Ibid.*, 13.

[104] Descriptions of this programme are based on a personal viewing at the British Film Institute Reuben Library: BFI, Ref. 16765, 'Love Now Pay Later', *The Facts Are These* (Granada Television, 22 Feb. 1973) (digitised).

[105] This stylistic convention is described in Eberwein, *Sex Ed*, 138–40.

[106] In a 1964 survey, the DES noted that health visitors, school medical officers, health education officers and general practitioners provided specialist lessons on venereal disease for many schools. TNA, ED 50/862, Minute Sheet, 'Notes on Sex Education in Schools' (25 Aug. 1964), 2.

Other programmes for older secondary school pupils, such as the long-running BBC series, *Scene*, take less didactic approaches.[107] Most *Scene* programmes are dramatic plays, often written by prominent playwrights. The plays typically feature 'ordinary young people' facing difficult decisions, and were intended to promote classroom discussion.[108] Several of the plays address issues of adolescent relationships and sexuality, such as the aptly named 'Consequences' (1977).[109] The director envisioned this programme as 'a realistic play about a real, believable love affair and what can happen to it'.[110] 'Consequences' thus explores common sex education topics, such as young love and the risks of sexual behaviour, through a wholly fictional and narrative format.

The protagonists of the play, Paul and Liza, are teenage school-goers who fall in love. Initially, sentimental montages portray their early courtship and a blissful camping trip. In an abrupt transition, however, the camping trip sequence is immediately followed by scenes in which Paul and Liza reveal to their parents that Liza is pregnant. Paul's father indignantly asks, in an interesting reference to the purpose of the play itself, 'Don't they teach you sex education at your school?'[111] Both sets of parents contemplate the possibilities of adoption or abortion, but Paul and Liza insist on keeping the baby and planning a life together. Their initial optimism quickly fades, though, as they face difficulties finding employment and a flat that accepts children. Unable to cope with the situation, Paul eventually leaves to attend university and Liza raises the baby herself.

Unlike the expository sex education broadcasts discussed above, 'Consequences' does not provide any direct instruction. The camping trip is the only clue as to how Liza became pregnant and, in contrast to other programmes' focus on children, Liza's baby appears only briefly in a montage. Instead, this programme concentrates on the impact of pregnancy on the young couple themselves. Although it does not fall into the category of 'informational' films, 'Consequences' nevertheless conveys a specific message: teenage pregnancy causes hardship and leads to difficult decisions for both parents. Significantly, by touching on issues such as sex education in schools, contraception and abortion,

---

[107] *Scene* ran from 1968 to 2007, with repeats until 2009. Ben Clarke, 'Scene', Broadcast for Schools, www.broadcastforschools.co.uk/site/Scene (16 July 2013).

[108] *Scene Scripts*, ed. Michael Marland (1972; repr. 1979), vii.

[109] The script of this programme, including stage directions, is published in a compilation of *Scene* scripts. Leonard Kingston, 'Consequences', in *Scene Scripts Three*, ed. Roy Blatchford (Burnt Mill, Harlow, 1982), 69–101.

[110] Leonard Kingston, 'Writing "Consequences"', in *Scene Scripts Three*, ed. Blatchford, ix–xvi.

[111] Kingston, 'Consequences', 82.

the programme also pinpoints topics for classroom discussion following the broadcast.

While *Scene* uses drama to foster dialogue, other programmes, reflecting the 'schoolroom' film genre, depict actual discussions among adolescents. Granada's *Understanding*, first broadcast in 1966, consists of a series of six programmes in which boys and girls between the ages of fifteen and sixteen discuss topics raised by their own questions.[112] Issues covered include puberty, childbirth, unmarried mothers, venereal disease, the sexual behaviour of young people and the family and marriage. Producers noted that neither abortion nor homosexuality was discussed because 'the children themselves did not raise them'.[113] In this way, the programmes convey a teenage-centred focus on adolescents' own interests and apprehensions about sex.

Although the discussions in *Understanding* are unscripted, a Granada interviewer and a doctor or specialist moderates each programme. In addition to spotlighting young people's concerns, therefore, the series also incorporates elements of a more traditional sex education approach in which teachers or medical authorities provide, moderate and authorise information. Furthermore, by depicting a select group of teenagers discussing a particular range of topics, the programmes exhibit appropriate content and methods of sex education. Indeed, producers hoped the programmes would provide a model for schools to emulate: 'We felt that by ... showing children talking freely and responsibly to adults, the same atmosphere might be carried into classroom discussions.'[114] Like other sex education broadcasts, then, teenage-centred discussion programmes invoked the authority of medical, educational and broadcasting expertise in order to promote certain sex education practices for the classroom.

Technology and practice

Despite many variations in approach, the sex education broadcasts examined in this paper all convey messages about *how* children should be taught about sex. As discussed above, these messages are inscribed in programme content through particular vocabularies, visual styles and depictions of educational processes. However, for the teachers who used the broadcasts, classroom practice was also affected by the material nature of the media. Lawn and Grosvenor observe that, as new classroom technologies were introduced, they 'intervened in, complicated and yet

---

[112] The children in the series were five boys and five girls from a range of geographic locations and types of school (independent, grammar and secondary modern). Granada, 'Understanding', 197–216.

[113] *Ibid.*, 200.

[114] *Ibid.*, 198.

became essential to the daily work of the teacher'.[115] Indeed, in the late 1960s and early 1970s, a number of technological developments changed the nature of broadcasts in schools. The introduction of radiovision, in 1964, required the use of audiotape recorders and filmstrip projectors. Furthermore, although school television was more than a decade old by 1970, a report the following year found that many schools had only recently procured equipment and still struggled to find suitable ways to use this technology.[116] In the early 1970s, video-recording equipment – which allowed teachers greater flexibility in using broadcasts – was also increasingly used in schools.[117]

The introduction of such apparatus into the classroom materially altered the roles of teachers, who served as operators of these technologies. This was acknowledged in several publications that provided advice regarding the proper use of broadcasting equipment. A 1969 pamphlet distributed by the BBC acknowledged that teachers might be reluctant to use audiotape due to 'fears of technical problems'.[118] According to the pamphlet, female teachers were especially nervous about this technology; although, the text states reassuringly, 'the knowledge required is no more difficult than that required for using a kitchen food-mixer or a washing machine'.[119] Significantly, the use of broadcasts could also physically alter classroom layouts. For optimum viewing and listening conditions, teachers were advised to arrange desks at proper viewing angles, use curtains to avoid screen glare and ensure that sound was clear and audible.[120]

In addition to providing technical guidance, broadcasters also produced literature that recommended methods for integrating broadcast media into the wider curricula. Teachers' notes for the BBC primary school programmes, for example, contained numerous recommendations for creative and interactive projects following a child-centred model of education. As discussed above, the notes suggested that children could collect baby photographs, measure their own growth or raise animals. In its evaluation of the *Nature* and *Merry-Go-Round* programmes, the BBC indeed found that many teachers followed these suggestions and that collecting baby photographs was a particularly popular activity for engaging children with the subjects of birth and development.[121]

---

[115] Lawn and Grosvenor, 'Teaching and Material Culture', 120.
[116] TNA, ED 235/10, *Report by H. M. Inspectors on a Survey of the Use of Broadcasts* (1971), 6–7, 25.
[117] Fawdry, *Alf Garnett*, 39–41.
[118] IOE, BBC Broadcasts, Vol. CXLXII, Pamphlets, 'School Radio and the Tape Recorder' (1969), 7.
[119] *Ibid.*, 7.
[120] Enid Love, 'Television and the Teacher', in *Teaching and Television*, ed. Moir, 54.
[121] SBC, *School Broadcasting*, 27, 30, 35.

It is important to note, however, that technical and educational advice from broadcasters did not seamlessly translate into classroom practices. As Lawn and Grosvenor point out, teachers often develop their own methods for incorporating technology into the classroom.[122] In fact, the SBC reported that some teachers provided their own commentary to accompany *Nature* radiovision filmstrips, rather than using the radio broadcasts.[123] Moreover, communication regarding the use of school broadcasts was collaborative, as producers actively encouraged teachers to provide feedback on their experiences. Compared with the moral panic in the media, the reactions of teachers were notably mild and, often, unreported.[124] Indeed, nine years following the initial broadcasts of the *Merry-Go-Round* sex education programmes, a producer observed that 'in spite of the invitation in the teachers' notes, there have not been a great many reactions from schools and teachers'.[125] However, among those teachers who did respond to the BBC programming, feedback was generally favourable throughout the 1970s.[126]

Broadcasters were also concerned with reactions from pupils themselves. Children sometimes wrote to producers about their experiences with the programmes, and producers carried out detailed audience research.[127] It should be noted that, even where researchers quoted children's verbal or written reactions, these examples were selected and possibly edited by adults.[128] However, certain clues to how children felt as they watched these programmes can be glimpsed from the data. An unpublished report on the BBC's secondary school series, *Life Cycle*, for example, noted that audience attention tended to diminish throughout the programmes and that some children expressed unexpected questions and critiques.[129] Producers of the series had decided to stress the importance of marriage in response to complaints about sex education from the

---

[122] Lawn and Grosvenor, 'Teaching and Material Culture', 121–2.

[123] SBC, *School Broadcasting*, 27.

[124] Responses of teachers, parents and students are discussed in greater detail in Gregory, 'School Broadcasting', 97–106.

[125] WAC, T69/58/1, letter from Claire Chovil to a Student (28 June 1979).

[126] WAC, R43/4412/1, 'Merry Go Round: Sex Education', and T69/58/1, 'Merry Go Round: Sex Education Parts 1–3'.

[127] A number of these letters and producer responses related to the *Nature* series (though not the sex education programmes) survive in the BBC Written Archives Centre programme files. See, e.g., WAC, R16/1181/1 and R16/1175/1, Schools Programmes: Nature, Programme Correspondence (*c.* 1960s).

[128] This limitation regarding sources dealing with children is discussed in Russell Viner and Janet Golden, 'Children's Experiences of Illness', in *Medicine in the Twentieth Century*, ed. Roger Cooter and John Pickstone (Amsterdam, 2000), 578.

[129] WAC, R165/77/1, Education Officer's Notes, 'Life Cycle: End of Term Summary: Summer 1972' (Oct. 1972), 3–5.

moral right; however, several students raised queries about birth control, and one girl complained: 'You are always telling us how to get a baby, but what we want to know is how to stop one.'[130] As Hall notes, 'adolescents themselves . . . seldom get a chance to have any input into [sex education] programmes deployed for their supposed benefit'.[131] Such reactions therefore represent discrepancies between adult conceptions of child- or teenage-centred sex education and children's own interests and ideas about sex.

The primary school broadcasts also elicited unanticipated reactions from children. In a survey of responses to the *Merry-Go-Round* programmes, psychologist Rex S. Rogers found that between 85 and 88 per cent of children reported favourable immediate reactions.[132] The 'Birth' programme drew the most unfavourable responses and, contrary to adult expectations, pupils tended to dislike the kitten birth more than the human birth.[133] The SBC's education officers likewise noted that some pupils, especially boys, appeared bored by the 'Growing Up' filmstrip on puberty, and other children expressed embarrassment or nervousness.[134] In the case of the *Merry-Go-Round* programmes, images of breast-feeding, male nudity, birth and the newborn baby – which some children disliked due to its 'sliminess' – were the most common sources of distress.[135] Some children also critiqued the visual style of the programmes. The 'X-ray' view of a pregnant woman was confusing to several children, and others felt the 'imaginative' background of the radiovision slides was too unrealistic.[136] Indeed, several children complained that flowers (shown in the background of multiple slides on pregnancy) improbably 'stayed fresh for nine months!'.[137]

Despite such critiques, reports by social scientists and education officers overall tended to corroborate producers' understandings of their audience; children were frequently described as engaged and eager to discuss the information provided. However, it should be noted that the power relations of the classroom, in which pupil behaviour was highly regulated by adults, might have prevented children from acting out or voicing their full reactions. As a critic of the ITV series, *The Facts Are These*, argued, children viewed such programmes without

---

[130] *Ibid.*, 3.

[131] Hall, 'Sex Education in Britain', 107. Hall uses the term 'programme' in a general sense, denoting sex education curricula in schools rather than broadcast programmes.

[132] Rex S. Rogers, 'The Effects of Televised Sex Education at the Primary School Level', in *Sex Education*, ed. Rogers, 256.

[133] *Ibid.*, 262–3.

[134] SBC, *School Broadcasting*, 28–9, 33–5.

[135] *Ibid.*, 33.

[136] *Ibid.*, 29.

[137] *Ibid.*, 29.

choice and were prevented from criticising them due to 'the formal group situation' in which they watched.[138] Furthermore, instances where children sniggered, paid little attention or critiqued the broadcasts suggest that producers could never completely understand or anticipate the child audience. As Buckingham *et al.* explain, children 'in different ways...are seen to resist and evade the definitions that are imposed upon them' by the adults who attempted to construct their nature as an audience.[139]

Conclusion

Through a close examination of the media and content of these programmes, I have taken the approach that sex education broadcasts must be understood as complex exchanges between educationists, producers, members of the public, teachers and pupils. Producers, educationists and public commentators attempted in different ways to define the needs of the child audience; at the same time, teachers and pupils responded to producers regarding their experiences. Thus, the communications involved in sex education were multi-directional, and reflected both support for and resistance to the aims of school broadcasting.

By focusing on the communicative elements of these programmes – the media and modes of address – I have attempted to move beyond an analysis that views programme content as either strictly traditionalist or progressive, permissive or anti-permissive. Rather, a close reading reveals that most broadcasts incorporated traditional content and styles (often borrowed from older sex education film genres), with more progressive, child-centred elements. It follows that these programmes communicated on more than one level; they carried ideological messages regarding sex and morality, certainly, but they also expressed ideas about the needs and nature of childhood and appropriate pedagogical methods. Asserting medical, technological and pedagogical expertise, these programmes thus delineated appropriate vocabularies, visualities and practices of sex education.

While this paper addresses a significant gap in the historiography regarding school broadcasting in Britain, the methods employed may be useful in studies on the impact of other emerging media in the history of sex education. Indeed, a focus on the media can raise significant questions

---

[138] WAC, T69/58/1, Leila Berg, 'Birth with Violence', *Times Educational Supplement* (10 Feb. 1978). Leila Berg was a children's author who wrote favourably of other sex education broadcasts, such as the BBC *Merry-Go-Round* series. See T69/58/1, Leila Berg, 'Listening to Children' (14 Apr. 1978).

[139] David Buckingham, Hannah Davies, Ken Jones and Peter Kelley, *Children's Television in Britain: History, Discourse and Policy* (1999), 11.

about how sex education materials defined and addressed their audiences and how they affected educational settings and practices. Too often adult discussions of sex education – whether in academia or in public debates – take a generalised view that neglects the specific impact of different forms of sex education, actual classroom practices and real children's experiences.